When David W Marpole left school, he wanted to be a chemist but he had to start work at 16 and was unable to go to university to study. His best opportunity was to work as a junior assistant chemist at a large sewage treatment works where his employers expected and encouraged him to study part time. As a qualified professional, he subsequently made his career in water pollution control, largely in the field of wastewater management, working in UK plus seven foreign countries where he encountered many different attitudes to water pollution control.

I would like to dedicate this work to all my immediate family members, past and present, and to all my close friends.

To: My wonderful son Adrian

From: David W Marpole

David W Marpole

SHIT HAPPENS!

AUSTIN MACAULEY PUBLISHERS™

LONDON ∗ CAMBRIDGE ∗ NEW YORK ∗ SHARJAH

A CIP catalogue record for this title is available from the British Library.

ISBN 9781528989299 (Paperback)
ISBN 9781528989305 (ePub e-book)

www.austinmacauley.com

First Published 2022
Austin Macauley Publishers Ltd®
1 Canada Square
Canary Wharf
London
E14 5AA

Chapter 1
Childhood Memories

When I was a little boy, I had ambitions for my adult life. At first, I believed I would be a soldier and fight victoriously in terrible wars against fanatical foes. I would be a hero and receive medals and honours and be pursued by the prettiest girls. Other men would show me great respect and none would dare to incur my wrath. Even comic book heroes like Superman and Batman would be nobodies when compared to me.

Then, as I grew a little older and heard of the exploits of Neville Duke and others breaking the sound barrier in the latest jet aircraft, the idea of becoming a crack fighter pilot appealed to me most strongly. Flying a supersonic jet plane was more than just a dream; it would definitely happen when I grew up. I imagined getting the enemy in my sights and blazing away at him until his aeroplane exploded, whereupon I would perform a victory roll and fly through the bits.

Later on, my fantasy was to become an admiral in the navy and help to rule the seas for good old England. Maybe it would be the Fleet Air Arm and I would command a massive aircraft carrier and lead an armada of jet planes as well.

Always these childhood dreams would be realised when my call-up (conscription) came at the magic age of eighteen, so that by twenty-one or twenty-two I would be the feted veteran of a dozen campaigns, wealthy beyond words and generous enough to pay for small objects with gold coins and never expect any change. The prettiest girls would always be around and would be at my beck and call at all times.

Of course, everything changed a little later when I reached the age of eleven and then grew into my early teens, labouring through secondary education at the Latymer Grammar school in Edmonton, North London. All the pretty girls and, for that matter, most of the ugly ones too were scornful of my ordinary physique, my non-descript sporting capabilities and my average at best academic achievements. SHIT was already happening and my little boy dreams were well and truly shattered!

The one subject I enjoyed most at the grammar school was chemistry, which was skilfully forced into my skull by a very old-fashioned teacher named P. G. Blackwell. I was quite good at it too. The decision was therefore made and I would follow a career in chemistry, become a real scientist who would make wonderful discoveries and be feted and honoured in different ways from those of my childhood dreams. Conscription was scheduled to be finished by the time I was sixteen so I would miss the call-up anyway and my parents wouldn't allow me to join the armed services as a volunteer so I had to do something else!

To have one of their sons become a chemist would be perfect for Mum and Dad. The eldest of my two brothers was "at the meteorological office", a term difficult for my mother to say and therefore commanding interest and respect from the neighbours. My other brother was doing well in the army, also commanding interest and respect because most of the neighbouring men folk were ex-servicemen in those days. A chemist, like old Mr Gower, would be splendid indeed. Old Mr Gower was actually the proprietor of one of the local pharmacies, traditionally known as chemist shops in England, and was possibly, though not necessarily, a qualified pharmacist but definitely not a chemist. He sold proprietary pills and potions and many kinds of traditional cure-alls but also made up prescriptions written out by the local medical practices. Most people didn't understand what the doctor had written and therefore presumed it to be in Latin. Mr Gower, rightly or wrongly, was therefore accredited with being fluent in Latin and this was confirmed when the manufacturer's labels on the pillboxes or cough syrup bottles displaying mysterious words like Acetyl Salicylic Acid or Aqua Tussive were carefully covered with helpful labels saying "The Tablets" or "The Mixture" that ordinary non-Latin speakers could understand. Many people also seriously believed that chemists (i.e. pharmacists) were would-be doctors that had somehow just failed to make the grade as a General Practitioner. Thus a chemist in the family, like old Mr Gower, would justifiably command interest and respect from the neighbours. My parents had no idea that being a chemist is completely different from running a pharmacy shop or that it would require a good deal of tertiary education to qualify in a scientific profession.

So it was that at the age of sixteen I was obliged to leave school and admonished to seek a job as a chemist and my first step was a visit to the Youth Employment Office in Edmonton. After a discussion with Mr Holmes, a kind, fatherly gentleman, I was directed to two places for interviews. The first was at the EVEREADY battery factory in Pegamoid Road and the second at the East Middlesex Main Drainage Plant, otherwise known as Deephams Sewage Works.

The first interview was fruitless, largely because my interviewer was an ill-mannered bully who spoke to me as if I were a dog. I had difficulty understanding his questions and was unable to provide answers to most of them. He explained nothing about the work I would be doing and didn't even know what salary would be offered. The interview took place in a dark, filthy office adjacent to a dark, filthy laboratory with zombie-like people working in it and it was the last place on earth I wanted to be at the start of my career. When told by the bully I could start as a Laboratory Assistant the following Monday I summoned the courage to say, "No thanks, I want to be a chemist not a lackey in a dirty old factory!"

His response was immediate and very cutting. "What did you come 'ere for then boy? You'll never be a chemist as long as you've got an 'ole in yer arse!"

The second interview was much more productive. It took place in a neat, tidy little office, which was part of a converted bungalow or gatekeeper's house comprising two offices and a smart little two-roomed laboratory. My interviewer on this occasion was a pleasant Yorkshireman named Dr Roy Whitehead, a highly qualified chemist. He made me feel at ease and explained the work I would be doing in such a clever way that I was really excited at the prospect of being a Junior Assistant Chemist at this major sewage treatment works in North London. Furthermore, I would be expected to study part-time to obtain a professional qualification in chemistry. When subsequently offered the said position at the grand salary of £250 a year plus annual London weighting allowance of £25 I immediately accepted the job and started work a couple of weeks later on 24th August 1959.

My parents were pretty disappointed that I had accepted a job at the 'sewerage farm' and for the rest of their lives never understood why one of their sons worked at such a place. All my siblings, two older brothers and two older sisters taunted me for years about shit-shovelling at a turd-farm or packet-factory, even when it was no longer amusing to anybody. SHIT really had happened into my life in a big way and it was to remain there one way or another for the rest of my working career. I did, nevertheless, qualify as a professional chemist, not a pharmacist like old Mr Gower, becoming a Licentiate of the Royal Institute of Chemistry and did it through part-time study comprising one day and two evenings a week for several years without the privilege of a spell at university. Some years later I was elected and admitted on merit as a Fellow of The Royal Society of Chemistry and therefore a Chartered Chemist, a title finally commanding some respect from my siblings and one that would have made my parents probably feel quite proud had they lived to see it.

The book that follows is an account as far as I can recall of the noteworthy events of my career that I want to share with you, reader; amusing, hilarious, tragi-comic, some simply tragic, others almost unbelievable and pretty-well all of them involving SHIT.

*****

I fell into the Black Dye Ditch

At the time I decided to write this little book I was asked by a relative why I had followed a career in water pollution control. I considered it to have been due to the way I obtained my first job at Deephams Sewage Works but upon reflection, it may well have been due to something else. After all, I didn't have to stay in the dirty water business; there were plenty of other opportunities for trainee chemists in a variety of other industries. In fact, I was one of only four part-time students at college who worked in the industry and furthermore the other three were subsequently members of my staff when I became Manager at Deephams. All the other students worked in very different organisations; some in explosives-research, some in paint-manufacturing, some in rubber-goods manufacturing, fragrance and flavourings, brewing, pharmaceuticals etc., in fact a whole host of different industries, many of which often seemed to be more interesting than mine. One student was even employed in the research section of a company making plastic interlinings for shirt collars! He went on to obtain a PhD and subsequently had a very rewarding career.

I have concluded that the reason I stayed in the water pollution control industry was because I had a natural desire to see CLEAN water wherever and whenever I could. As a child in North London, the only really clean water I ever saw was what came out of the tap. The local canalised section of the River Lee was the place where most of us learned to swim but the water was never clear enough to see right down into it. Other, smaller, streams were sometimes heavily polluted too in those days, even the ones that trickled their way through parts of

Epping Forest, which was our ultimate playground. An occasional trip to the seaside was often spoilt by the colour of the water and frequently places like Southend or even Clacton in Essex were not at all inviting so far as a desire for swimming in the sea went.

My first memorable encounter with really polluted water occurred when I was nine or ten years old. Flowing alongside the railway at Ponders End, where I was born and raised, was a filthy little stream that everybody knew as The Black Dye Ditch, though whence came its name I have never been able to find out. Years later when I worked for the Lee Conservancy Catchment Board it was only referred to as The Ponders End Intercepting Drain but there was never any reference to what it intercepted. It flowed for two or three miles until its confluence with the Salmons Brook, not far from where Deephams Sewage Works was eventually built. On its left bank was a huge coal yard belonging to a company called H. C. Silk & Sons, a service road for a number of factories and a large timber yard. At least one of the factories had been served by a railway siding during World War 2, the lines of which still crossed the stream mounted on stout steel beams. This factory was known as the Warrior Works Tap and Die Manufacturers; it may have been the miss-spelt source of the Black Dye name for the watercourse. The road had been resurfaced at that point and the railway siding taken away but the stream-crossing remained as originally built. This gave the local urchins, of which I was one, a place to cross the stream and even, though we never really did it, gain access to the main London / East Anglia railway line.

The Black Dye Ditch was well known for being filthy, even though there were occasionally small fish and tadpoles to be seen in it but it was aptly named because the bottom of it was most certainly black, possibly having been used for the disposal of black dye in the distant past. It was also known for being contaminated with faecal waste, toilet paper and sheath contraceptives, which many years later I discovered came from a storm overflow on the grossly overloaded sewerage system of the area that was still awaiting final repairs after being seriously damaged by wartime bombing.

My mother had decided that I was now old enough to fend for myself for an hour or so each afternoon when I came home from school and she had found herself a new job at the Ediswan factory in Duck Lees Lane, about half a mile away from our house, and started one fine Monday in the late spring. My two older sisters would be getting home from school around 4.30 pm anyway so Mother could work until 5.30 pm without a problem. I remember that we had been to the Enfield Highway Co-operative Society store the previous Saturday to buy me a new blazer and a pair of short trousers, which I had worn to school for the first time that day.

After school, I went with a couple of my friends to do a bit of train spotting at Ponders End station but after a short time the 'named engines' had already passed hauling the expresses and there were only the boring, local N7 tank engines to be seen so we went street raking* alongside the Black Dye Ditch on Wharf Road.

When we reached the siding bridge, we started walking on the steel beams from one side to the other. This was easy because these 'I' beams were six inches wide at the top and bottom so my friend Richard suggested we all do it with our eyes shut. After a couple of tries this too became easy so I, trying to be a clever dick, suggested we should hang on the beams with our hands and cross the stream hand over hand. "All right then let's see you do it," said Donald, the other boy. Of course, I could do it, so carefully sat on the wall and let myself down until I was hanging on the beam, then hand over hand I crossed the stream. Easy! The other two boys didn't make the attempt so just to show-off even more, I decided to hang from the bottom of the 'I' beam, where only my fingers could take my weight. Needless to say, SHIT happened!

I knew I was going to fall in and I yelled for my friends to help me. They couldn't and indeed wouldn't because they would have fallen in too. I remember yelling, "Get a man quick! Get someone to pull me up!" but all to no avail. I fell into the stinking, faeces ridden, bog-paper littered, condom infested, Black Dye Ditch. I fell vertically for about a couple of yards and my shoes sank into at least a foot of stinking black silt. The foul water came up to my waist and soaked the bottom of my new blazer. Slowly I squelched my way out of the stream, up the steep bank next to the wall supporting the railway beams and then realised I was in REALLY DEEP SHIT! It served me right of course and I learnt a lesson about not being a clever dick show-off. My friends knew I was in trouble too and they accompanied me to my home but, no doubt fearing some retribution themselves, stood on the other side of the street as I knocked on the door of our house. I heard my mother's voice as she came to open the door. "Ah here comes David. I thought he would have been home by now. Hope everything's all right." Then as she opened the door and saw the state of my new clothes, "YOU LITTLE BLEEDER, YOU'VE BEEN DOWN THAT BLOODY RIVER AGAIN! I

TOLD YOU NOT TO GO THERE! LOOK AT YOUR BLOODY CLOTHES! WHERE'S ALL THAT BLACK MUCK FROM?"

At this point, one of my friends yelled, "He fell in the Black Dye Ditch Missus!" and they both fled. At this, my mother entered the paroxysm of fury, took off all my clothes on the doorstep and gave me a fairly sound thrashing, after which I was scrubbed quite violently and unnecessarily with a household scrubbing brush and a bar of household soap until Mother had calmed down.

The following day all the neighbours were obliged to hear about how I had fallen in the filthy Black Dye Ditch, which incidentally, my mother had probably never even looked upon, and how I was covered from head to foot in muck, how I had to be scrubbed and how all my clothes had to be burnt, which was all exaggerated nonsense. There was even a story told that I left black footprints all the way up the street, which was of course completely untrue but my eldest sister, who possibly wasn't even at home when I was being chastised, still trails out that tale after more than sixty years! My mother may well have dumped my socks, which would have been caked in muck and undoubtedly darned around the heels many times already, but the rest of my clothing was simply washed along with the rest of the family's laundry. It is possible that my new blazer might have been sent to the dry cleaners but I suspect it was simply dried and then brushed clean. The story of me falling into the Black Dye Ditch has become a family legend that will probably pass on down further generations!

For sure it is something I shall never forget and it may well have influenced me a great deal to stay in the water pollution control industry. There was no need for that little stream nor, for that matter, any other watercourse on this earth to be so badly polluted and some of us must take responsibility for preventing such things from happening. I can honestly say that years later I was largely responsible for stopping pollution of that watercourse, as well as many others, through my work with the Lee Conservancy Catchment Board. On one occasion, many years later, when I returned on leave from Egypt, I drove to Ponders End to have a nostalgic tour of my boyhood haunts, though unfortunately most of them had long since disappeared, and was proud to see that the offensive Black Dye Ditch, or Ponders End Intercepting Drain was a neat and tidy little stream with CLEAN water flowing through it!

*****

Chapter 2

Junior Assistant Chemist
at Deephams Sewage Works

<u>As a 16-year-old, I knew Whistling Rufus.</u>

Most of the men I was working alongside in those days had been in the services and many had fought in the 1939-1945 war. More than a few of them bore the scars of armed conflict and had artificial limbs or disfigurement from serious injuries or burns. Several had even served in World War 1 and often told me of their dreadful experiences on the Western front or at the Dardanelles, though much of it laced with a good deal of black humour. All these men were different characters but the one thing they all had in common was that death did not faze them, probably because they had all seen so much of it.

One of the older fellows, known as 'Whistling Rufus', because he was always whistling, used to walk past the laboratory windows every morning and every afternoon. Once as he passed, he stopped whistling and shouted, "Aw right boy? Still, buggerin' abaht wi' that chemistry set then? 'Aven't turned base metal inter gold yet 'ave yer?" With that, he hooted with laughter and began whistling again exactly where he had left off. I felt terribly embarrassed that Rufus had derided me in such a way.

An hour or so later, I was walking along the same path to collect samples when the store's van drove up rapidly behind me. I asked the store-man what was the rush and he said, "It's Rufus. He's snuffed it in the pumping station." I couldn't believe it. Rufus had been so full of life just a short time ago.

SHIT was happening all right but nobody could have guessed how much.

Bill the storekeeper and his mate picked up Rufus, laid him not too gently in the back of the van and then drove off with him. A while later they came back to the pumping station, took Rufus out again and laid him back down where they found him, just moments before an ambulance came onto the site. After a quick check for a pulse by the ambulance medic, Rufus was put gently onto a stretcher, covered completely with a red shroud and placed rather more carefully this time into the ambulance, which then drove off to the mortuary.

The story of what happened was repeated several times over the next few days and went something like this: Rufus had either a stroke or a heart attack and dropped down dead. He was found by fellow worker Bill Creaske, a veteran of the Western Front in World War 1, who recognised that the man was well and truly dead but not knowing what else to do summoned the Admin officer, a veteran of El Alamein in World War 2, who had lost a leg in the conflict. The Admin Officer asked Bill the storekeeper to get Rufus taken away so without further ado the body was put into the store's van and driven to the mortuary adjacent to the North Middlesex Hospital. The mortuary staff, however, refused to accept Rufus without proper documentation. "How much bloody documentation do you want?" asked the storekeeper. "Any silly bugger can see he's dead."

"You need a doctor's note, mate," came the reply, "you should have called an ambulance."

"Well I didn't and he's here now so just put him on the slab."

"Can't do that, mate, he can only come in here on a trolley from the hospital or on an ambulance from where he snuffed it and he must have the proper documentation. You'll have to take him back. If you're not careful they'll think you had something to do with it, mate so my advice is to take him back where you found him and call an ambulance."

"Can't you call one for us, mate there's no phones around here?"

"All right but look sharp and get going else they might get there before you do and then you'll really be in trouble."

And so it was that the ambulance arrived moments after Rufus had been brought back to the place where he died. It came rapidly onto the site with its bell ringing, in those days they didn't have sirens like they do today, but left again with noticeably less haste. For days everyone was laughing about the fiasco surrounding the death of Whistling Rufus but the final tribute to the man was made by Jim Maddock, the laboratory attendant and himself another veteran of the Flanders killing fields. "At least we don't have to listen to that bloody whistling anymore, thank Christ. It was always out of tune anyway!"

I couldn't forget Whistling Rufus but I never even knew his real name.

*****

<u>The senior engineer sat in sludge.</u>

When I first started work at Deephams there was no overall manager of the plant. Instead, for over three years, it was administered from Middlesex County Council's other huge treatment plant at Isleworth, known as Mogden Sewage Works, which had been completed in 1936. Dr Whitehead, my immediate senior, was the plant's Chief Chemist and another gentleman named Bill Gillies was the senior engineer. Between them, they shared responsibility for the operation and maintenance at Deephams, including the commissioning and start-up of newly constructed sections as they were completed by the main contractors. They each occupied one of the two offices in the laboratory building. At regular weekly intervals, each of these two individuals would be visited by their respective bosses who were chauffeur-driven from Mogden. Interestingly the visitors never travelled in the same car and rarely arrived on the same day and I never saw all four men sit down together for a general discussion on the performance or progress of construction of the new sewage treatment works. Management was different in those days!

As was to be expected there were frequent disagreements between Messrs. Whitehead and Gillies and sometimes, though fortunately very rarely, harsh words were spoken. On one such occasion reference was made to the quality of analysis being performed and I was obliged to join the conversation and sternly correct a very clear misinterpretation of my results by Mr Gillies. His response, however, was to apologise in the manner of the gentleman he was and the matter was dropped. Subsequently, he asked the laboratory attendant, Jim Maddock, for a cup of tea. Jim always made our morning tea as a part of his routine duties but he was about to drive around the site to deliver the next set of sample bottles so I agreed to make the tea for everyone. As I took the tray into his office, I jokingly told Mr Gillies, "The whiskey's at the bottom."

"More likely cyanide," was his mumbled reply.

"No, you've got it wrong," I said, "the cyanide's at the top so we can get the whiskey back later!"

"Okay, okay," was the response, "at least you didn't spit in it!" I then told him I had been taught never to admit spitting in someone's tea until AFTER they had drunk it!

"All right Davey boy, you'll do!" was his final comment, said with a smile.

Shortly after that incident, a further section of the activated sludge aeration system was put into operation. It had performed its aeration tests perfectly well using clean water in the tank but apparently, after filling it with the 'mixed liquor'* there was now some malfunction of the aeration diffusers within one section. The unit was drained down almost to the top of the diffusers so that Messrs Whitehead and Gillies could inspect them and determine the cause of the problem. Apparently, Dr Whitehead wanted the tank to be hosed out clean before climbing into it because they only had ordinary wellington boots and they were only just high enough to clear the surface of the activated sludge. Mr Gillies, however, thought it would be too time-consuming and the diffusers might function properly if they were hosed down, so insisted on them entering the tank without further ado. Down the ladder he went and stepped gingerly onto the concrete floor, just to be sure his boots were indeed long enough. Whether or not they were was completely academic because with his first step he slipped and fell, or rather sat, into over a foot of activated sludge. Being no spring chicken and rather portly too, Mr Gillies had some difficulty standing up and in consequence saturated every inch of his clothing with SHIT. Of course, he filled up his boots with it too! I didn't see him until he squelched his way back to his office to get his clothes changed before going home for a bath etc. but it was the funniest thing I had ever seen at that time. He reminded me of a somewhat slimmer version of 'Billy Bunter'* wearing a three-piece suit, complete with watch and chain in the waistcoat I recall, collar and tie plus a folded handkerchief in the breast pocket of his jacket. To go with that he had one black Wellington boot and one white one*. The whole package was dripping SHIT and I could not stop myself from howling with laughter. His words to me were rather curt but prophetic. "Go on, have a bloody good laugh but mark my words young David, it's going to happen to you too one day!" How right he was!

Dr Whitehead's description of the incident had most people in stitches later that day but he was especially critical of the fact that the tank hadn't been hosed out before entry. "The silly old fool wouldn't have had a problem if he'd listened to me!" was heard a number of times.

There was a further occasion when the hosing out of a tank could have averted a rather nasty problem. It was one of the storm sedimentation tanks, which in those early days were being used for primary settlement because construction of the new primary tanks was still ongoing. Apparently, the scraper's blade-lowering system had failed to operate correctly so sludge was not being properly scraped along the tank floor. The sewage level had been lowered sufficiently for the scraper blade to be seen and indeed inspected but there was still a layer of raw sludge on the tank floor that one would have to stand in to look at it closely. Once again Mr Gillies had decided to enter the tank, with other people, to help determine the cause of the problem but this time there was no three-piece suit or wellington boots. He was wearing a pair of thigh waders and a boiler-suit type overall; clearly, he didn't want to get himself coated in the filthy muck again. I actually saw him in the tank on this occasion as I walked past on my way to collect some samples and was moved to call down to him rather cheekily, "You just be careful now Mr Gillies! Don't you go falling in all that shit"! Several people sniggered but obviously, a comment like that coming from someone less than eighteen years old was unacceptable in those days. The reply I received was sobering enough.

"Just get on with your work and stop wasting time! This has nothing to do with you!" snapped Mr Gillies and I quickly left the scene.

SHIT did happen, however, and once again it was the senior engineer that collected it. I was told later that he slipped when about to climb the ladder out of the storm tank and once again finished up sitting in sludge. This was raw sludge, however, very thick, stale and extremely foul. I well remember Mr Gillies being escorted to the new, temporary shower facility to get cleaned up and change his clothes but decided never to mention it to him. It was the talk of Deephams, however, for a few days and I think secretly I was rather pleased after the way he had ticked me off. Nevertheless, I suspect I would have done the same thing had our roles been reversed.

*****

I was attacked by a hissing grey monster while walking home.

In the late autumn of 1962, the London area experienced the most dreadful fogs for several weeks. Because of the smoke from coal fires and the remaining steam railway engines of those days these fogs became smog and were so dense that it was often very difficult to see more than a yard or two ahead. I had found it almost impossible to drive my new motorbike to work because I literally could not properly see where I was going, so I decided to walk to and from work. It was, after all, only two and a half miles and I was well acquainted with the walk so it did me no harm and gave me a bit of added exercise as well.

One night at around 5.45 pm I was striding out across the works road towards the entrance gate. It was already dark and the streetlights afforded very little illumination because of the smog. I was obliged to wear a facemask to avoid inhaling the mucky atmosphere and also wore a pair of laboratory safety glasses to try to keep it out of my eyes. The glasses of course soon fogged up so my vision was significantly impaired.

Once I reached the middle of the works I began to feel cold and also rather lonely, even though I could hear the nearby throb of the power generating plant, but Deephams at that time had few people around after darkness had fallen and most of those were in the main building rather than on the site roads.

Imagine then my shock and hair-raising horror as a strange grey shape appeared in front of me, seemingly floating spectral-like and hissing in a rather malevolent way. I stopped and began to edge backwards away from the weird monstrosity, my heartbeat having multiplied two or threefold, but suddenly it surged forward and I was enveloped in its strange tentacles which were unbelievably cold, wet and sticky, not to mention rather odorous. I think I may well have screamed from fear as this awful SHIT happening occurred, for that was certainly what it was and I needed several seconds to realise precisely what had happened. It was ghastly!

At that time there were still hard detergents in use that were not readily biodegradable and an activated sludge plant like Deephams produced large quantities of foam on the aeration tanks, sometimes several feet deep. The foam was controlled by the drip-feeding of antifoaming oil on the tanks but presumably, this had been somewhat ineffective that day or may have run out and not been refilled. Clearly, a large mass of foam had risen from the tanks and drifted slowly with the smog across the works and in the murky atmosphere I could not tell what it was. Scared I certainly was for a few moments, even terrified as the evil presence enveloped me but when I realised what it was, I was more than furious. The foam carried all sorts of filth with it, sludge, slime, small bits of trash etc., etc., and it had liberally coated me with it. It was indeed a very personal SHIT happening on that occasion and I had to walk home in it. Furthermore, I had to remove most of my clothing before entering the house and my mother could not understand what on earth I was doing. My explanation of what had happened was completely lost on her and she undoubtedly thought I had fallen into a tank in the dark. Yet another reason for her to wonder what one of her sons was doing working at the 'sewerage farm'!

"Can't you find a better job than that David?" was a question I was asked over and over again. "We all thought you were going to be in a chemist shop like Gower's".

The reaction from my work colleagues on the following morning when, incidentally, the smog had more or less disappeared, was of course rather different. Most of them just split their sides with laughter and naturally I had to follow suit. Nevertheless, I was always extremely cautious when crossing the works in the dark after that incident, fog or no fog!

*****

I took a spare-time job as a barman at a pub.

In order to pay for my new motorbike and still be able to afford a few other minor luxuries, I decided to find a spare-time job. I was attending college for one day and two evenings a week and I needed at least one further evening and an afternoon every weekend to complete my homework so I had little spare time available for additional work. Nevertheless, I decided to try it and managed to get a job as a barman at a very nice pub in Edmonton, called The Stag and Hounds.

The elderly tenant licensee, named Charles, and his wife Daisy formally owned the business but the pub was really run by their son-in-law Ken and their daughter Daphne, all of them charming people. I actually worked there most Friday, Saturday and Sunday evenings plus Sunday lunchtimes and one other evening a week whenever time allowed. It was an ideal way for me to socialise and learn how to recognise the different characteristics of ordinary people. I thoroughly enjoyed it all.

There was, nevertheless, an occasional moment of strife and one that could only be described as a SHIT happening; an incident that I shall never forget if I live for a hundred years! It happened one evening just after I had arrived at the pub to start work, at around 6.30 pm.

The Stag and Hounds, like many nice pubs in those days, had three bars. A Public bar where mostly men would gather to have their pints of ale, play darts, play cards occasionally and games like 'shove-ha'penny'.* At weekends, there would be someone there to play the piano and occasionally there would be a bit of a sing-song. There was a Saloon bar, which was rather better decorated and with more comfortable seating and tables. It tended to attract more couples and there were no games played and no piano. Instead, there was quite refined background music from a tape player that encouraged people to relax and enjoy their evenings rather more quietly. These two bars were separated by a much smaller one known as the Private bar, where sometimes elderly ladies would meet with a friend to have a gossip over a glass of sherry or a Guinness.

It was to the Private bar that a large red-faced man would often come in the early evening to have a few shots of whiskey at the end of his working day. He was Irish and was a doctor with a local practice. Many people knew him well, probably because they were his patients, and he in turn, was always sociable and friendly. Everybody knew him as Doc Murphy.

On that fateful evening, there were three of the regular elderly ladies sitting in the Private bar, each of them nursing a glass of Guinness and whispering some sensitive gossip to each other, when in marched Doc Murphy, huffing and puffing and clearly very eager for a drink. There were only one or two other customers in the pub and I was standing behind the bar at the Saloon end where I could effectively see the three bars and attend to them all on my own during the quiet period.

"Hello, dere young fellow," called Doc Murphy, "Oi'd loike a laarge Jameson's please," in his strong Irish brogue. "Yes sir," I replied while moving quickly to the appropriate point behind the Private bar to serve his drink.

Having received the whiskey, he immediately gulped down half of it and then asked mc to get a Guinness for each of the three elderly ladies, all of whom he clearly knew very well. This duly done and the three drinks placed on the counter the doctor handed one to each of the old ladies, who thanked him courteously. His next action was to stagger slightly to the bar, quickly swill the remainder of his whiskey, burp quietly and then very politely ask for another large Jameson's.

I had to walk to the end of the saloon bar to get his second drink because the optic measure in the Private bar was only half full, indicating that the bottle was empty. It probably took me less than one minute to put the two shots in the glass and return to the Private bar, where there was now no sign of Doc Murphy and the three old ladies were staring open-mouthed at the spot he had so recently occupied. "Where's Doc Murphy gone?" I asked. "He's on the floor," came the

21

reply as one of the old ladies left her seat and walked to the spot. I peered over the counter and saw that big red-faced man lying on his back absolutely 'sparko'* and very obviously, to me, well and truly drunk! SHIT had certainly happened and had to be dealt with immediately.

Ken had just finished his evening meal when I entered the family's living room and told him that Doc Murphy was 'rat-arsed' * on the floor in the Private bar.

"Oh, Christ Almighty, he's such a bloody piss-head that bloke!" cried Ken. "OK, Dave give us a hand and let's get him out of there!"

Off we went to the Private bar where the three old ladies were now all standing around wringing their hands and muttering something about the poor fellow being overworked and being worn out.

"Right Dave," said Ken. "You get his feet while I get his arms and we'll take him into the gents to sober him up!"

"Is he all right do you think?" asked one of the ladies.

"Yes love," said Ken. "Just blind bloody drunk, that's all!"

"Ooh I say!" was her simple reply as she opened the door to the Public bar for us to carry the man to the toilets. As we laid him on the tiled floor, however, I began to have my doubts as to whether Doc Murphy was indeed all right.

"Ken," I said, "are you sure he's all right? He doesn't seem to be breathing!"

Ken, a veteran of the Battle of Arnhem in World War 2, had seen many men who were not breathing. He immediately felt the man's pulse, then put his ear to his chest to listen to his heart.

"Christ, Dave you're right, I think he's dead!" whereupon he started to pump his chest and listen again for a heartbeat but all to no avail.

"Quick Dave, go and phone for an ambulance! This bloke's definitely had it"!

As I ran to the living room to call 999, Daisy, Daphne and Charles were all in the bars attending to customers and Charles anxiously asked if everything was all right. I ignored him for a few moments until the call was made and of course everyone in the pub overheard my telephone conversation. Imagine then the topic of discussion that ensued for the rest of the evening and, for that matter, the rest of the week!

After a few minutes, the ambulance arrived and the unfortunate Doc Murphy was placed on a stretcher, shrouded completely and laid carefully in the vehicle before being taken to the North Middlesex Hospital's mortuary. A little later there was a visit from the local police who required a statement as to the circumstances of the man's death but this was quickly dealt with by Ken and required no corroboration from me. It transpired that Doc Murphy had died from a massive heart attack and his demise was considered by many people to be a very sad loss to the local community. Judging by what I was subsequently told by those that knew him well, his problem had more likely been caused by overwork rather than his love of Irish whiskey. I have often thought what a pity it was that the poor fellow 'popped his clogs'* just a few moments before he could have had the last taste of his favourite drink. I suppose his compensation might be that he never paid for the last one he did drink nor the Guinness for the three elderly ladies!

Some years later, when I was manager at Deephams, I went to The Stag and Hounds frequently, not as a barman but as a lunchtime customer. There were several occasions when I was asked if I remembered the evening Doc Murphy dropped dead in the bar. How could I ever forget such an event? It was only the second occasion in my youth that I had experienced the sudden death of someone I knew and the only difference was that this time I actually knew the fellow's real name!

*****

Chapter 3

Assistant Pollution Inspector with Lee Conservancy Catchment Board

After nearly five years working at Deephams as a Junior Assistant Chemist it was time to move on in my career in water pollution control. I therefore applied for and was appointed to one of three vacancies as Assistant Pollution Inspector with the Protection of Water Department of the local river-management organisation, known as the Lee Conservancy Catchment Board.

<u>Brusher</u>

The area I covered included a small sewage treatment plant at Hatfield Heath in Essex, which I visited weekly. It was a very old plant requiring a good deal of manual input to maintain it and most of this work was performed by a real salt of the earth, hard-working man in his sixties, known to everyone as Brusher.

Brusher was always pleased to see somebody come to the plant, probably because it was such a lonely place to be all day, so he loved to stop and chat for a while. Unfortunately, it was extremely difficult to understand whatever he said because poor Brusher had a serious speech defect caused by a cleft palate that must never have been surgically corrected when he was a child. To my ears most of his conversation consisted of "amuh anuh abuh mnuh" and similar unintelligible sounds so after a while I tried to avoid talking to him and restricted myself to a distant wave of the hand and such a call as, "Morning Brusher, how's it going mate, all OK?" whilst I hurried past to the effluent outfall to take samples. Brusher would sociably wave back from where he was working and utter his indecipherable greeting with a smile on his face so I assumed he was happy.

One day I went to Hatfield Heath STW with my senior colleague Bill, who was the Area Pollution Inspector. We went in Bill's car and drove to the centre of the plant. We looked around for Brusher and saw him waving from one of the primary tanks; he used to empty these every few days then climb into them by ladder and hose the sides clean of sludge. We could see the spray from the hose and just Brusher's head above the parapet of the tank so he was obviously standing on the ladder and cleaning away as usual. His words of greeting were of course lost on both of us.

Bill and I walked the quarter-mile to the outfall where we took samples of the effluent and also upstream and downstream of the receiving watercourse for a hundred metres or so. It was a lovely day so we took our time and didn't return to the car for well over an hour. Brusher was still, apparently, hosing out the tank so we waved again, loaded the samples into the car and prepared to drive off. Only then did we realise that Brusher was still calling to us and what's more his tone of voice had risen by a couple of octaves. Clearly, he needed to tell us something so Bill and I trudged up the slope to the primary tanks. We found SHIT had happened!

Poor Brusher was not standing on the ladder hosing down the empty primary tank. He had fallen headfirst into the full up tank next to it and couldn't climb out. He'd been holding onto the scum board for hours waiting for someone to call in at the plant. The hose was lying on the grass spraying water over the parapet of the empty tank, which was drained of sludge and had the ladder in it ready for Brusher to stand on. We fished him out of the tank and helped him to rinse the greasy scum from his face and hair. His clothing was completely saturated with raw sewage but of course, he had nothing else to change into so Bill, showing great compassion for the poor chap, said he would drive him home to get changed and have a bath. We put lots of newspaper and an old sheet over the immaculate front seat of Bill's Austin Cambridge and, when Brusher had stopped dripping sewage, sat him in the car and took him home. He was so grateful for our rescue efforts that he was moved to tears as he tried to express his thanks; it was quite touching. Nevertheless, as soon as he went into his house Bill and I fell apart with laughing. The car was stinking so we threw out all the newspapers and the sheet and Bill had it valeted later that day.

It was a while before I realised that if we hadn't gone to Hatfield Heath sewage works that day Brusher, a simple but genuine, hard-working fellow, would have probably drowned in raw sewage and nobody would have known about it. The realisation, however, came to Bill much more quickly and he took action by reporting the incident at the Rural District Council office, basically telling the Chief Engineer it was extremely unsafe and unfair for a man such as Brusher to be working all alone at the sewage treatment works with nobody to check up on him every so often during the day. The Council responded by instructing the sewage treatment foreman to go to Hatfield Heath twice a day to check on Brusher.

The next time I went to take samples at the plant I was greeted with a tirade of abuse from Brusher with much reference to fuhgn Bhill getting him into trouble. No amount of explanation would pacify the poor chap and he never wanted to stop and talk to me again. It was such a shame! Even so, I still have to laugh when I picture Brusher up to his armpits in filthy water yelling "amuh anuh abuh mnuh" and similar unintelligible sounds.

*****

Harry's diesel pump.

The town of Bishops Stortford had a sewage treatment system set up around the late nineteenth or early twentieth century, comprising a pumping station and screens close by the River Stort to the South of the town and a land irrigation area of eighty-five acres situated on a nearby hillside. Screened sewage was pumped up to the top of the hill and allowed to irrigate the land area, thus receiving natural biological treatment before discharging into a small watercourse called the Hallingbury Brook. This irrigation system originally provided adequate treatment but over the years as the town had grown the land area had become grossly overloaded and consequently became a stinking mess. The effluent caused considerable pollution to the brook and subsequently to the River Stort for quite a few miles downstream.

When I was an Assistant Pollution Inspector there was just one large electric pump that had been installed in 1935 plus an additional and more recent diesel pump for handling storm flows. The electric pump was automatically started and stopped according to water, i.e. sewage, level but the diesel pump had to be manually started as and when required. Whenever there were storm flows it was necessary to connect up a six-inch flexible pipe to the delivery side of the diesel pump before starting it up and when the flow had returned to normal it was disconnected again because the pipe's position restricted access into the pumping station. It was a difficult job because the pipe was heavy to lift and the connection was made with a six-inch flange held down by eight heavy-duty bolts. Harry the pumping station attendant, though only a slightly built man, was nevertheless quite adept at connecting up the pipe-work and as he lived in a house less than twenty yards away was always readily available to deal with the problem.

One day, following a heavy thunderstorm I visited the pumping station to see if there was any overflow of sewage to the river. The electric pump was already beaten by the incoming flow and the level of sewage was rising fast. Harry was still finishing his lunch when I arrived but on seeing me there, he rushed from the house and began frantically to connect up the diesel pump. Sewage began to overflow the pumping station while he was tightening up the bolts on the pipe flange so I readied myself with my official sampling kit in preparation to take a formal sample of the spillage to the river. Harry frantically started up the diesel engine. Sure enough, SHIT happened with gusto!

Unfortunately, in his hurry to finish the connection and avoid the possibility of a prosecution, Harry had forgotten to fit the rubber gasket on the pipe flange before bolting it down so there was no proper seal. As the pump started and revved up to full speed a circular blast of very black raw sewage belched from the pipe flange, hitting the walls, windows, lights and poor old Harry too. He collected his share straight in the face with enough force to lift off his glasses and shatter them against the wall while at the same time fill his mouth, nose and ears with the foul liquid. Luckily, I was spared a similar fate but could do nothing to help the man. I watched as he groped his way to the cut-out switch and stopped the pump.

Harry stood there for a moment dripping wet with raw sewage then launched into a tirade of abuse. "You f*****g b*****d this wouldn't have happened if you hadn't turned up. You're all the f*****g same you c***s from the f*****g River Board. P**s off before I set the f*****g dog on you."

As the dog in question was a small mongrel terrier with barely enough energy to bark my immediate reaction was to hoot with laughter at the threat but I didn't have the heart to take an official sample and drop Harry in the fertiliser.* He'd already had his punishment. Besides, as nobody was hurt it had been quite an amusing episode and everyone back at the office had a good laugh about it afterwards. In fact, some years later when I was manager of the new treatment works at Bishops Stortford, I reminded Harry of the event and he was able to see the funny side of it too!

Pollution to a roadside ditch from the Town Clerk's house.

My senior colleague Bill and I had been touring various sewage treatment works around Ware, Much Hadham and Little Hadham in Hertfordshire, looking to ensure they were producing good quality effluent and that the receiving watercourses were in good condition too. My vehicle was being repaired so we were travelling in Bill's Austin Cambridge car. He said he was getting fed up with driving and fancied something nice to eat and drink so we were making our way into Bishops Stortford to find a decent pub and have lunch.

As we drove down through Thorley, which in those days was only partially developed with just a few very nice, expensive houses, I noticed some detergent foam bubbling up in the roadside drainage ditch. There had been no rain for a week or two so the ditches were all very dry. I suggested to Bill that we should stop and investigate. Bill stopped the car and then said, "Let's go and have lunch. Come on Dave it's only a bit of soap suds, there's no factories or farmyards around here."

Nevertheless, I quickly got out of the car just to satisfy my curiosity as to the cause of the foam. I discovered that there was soapy water running down a smaller tributary ditch that drained the verge of a cul-de-sac wherein there were some very fine houses. Furthermore, the soapy water was gushing from a plastic pipe feeding into the ditch from one of those houses. This had to be dealt with so I collected my sampling kit from the boot of Bill's car and took an official sample.* Bill, albeit rather reluctantly, watched the sampling procedure and asked to whom the third portion should be served. "Well, it has to be the house owner doesn't it?" was my instant reply. "OK then," said Bill, "here she comes now so off you go, this is your show!" as the lady of the house came towards us and demanded to know, with a very haughty voice, precisely what we were doing.

"Good day, madam," I said as I proffered my warrant card for her to read. "We are from the Lee Conservancy Catchment Board, Protection of Water Department and I have just formally sampled a suspected polluting discharge coming from your property. I'm afraid that what you are doing maybe in contravention of the Rivers Prevention of Pollution Act 1961 and I must inform you that it is our intention to have the sample analysed. It will be divided into three parts, one of which will be handed to you for comparative analysis if you so desire. I would ask you to please witness the dividing of the sample."

She replied with an even haughtier tone than before.

"Never heard of your organisation! Can't see any river around here to pollute and its water from my washing machine for heaven's sake. It's CLEAN water from MY washing! Very well then, get on with it I'm extremely busy!"

I pointed out to the lady that the discharge from her washing machine should go into the sewer and she muttered something about the builders not finishing their alterations to the house yet. Subsequently, she signed the document, having witnessed the division of the sample, formal labelling and sealing of each bottle but she flatly refused to accept a portion of it for comparative analysis.

"You'll have to see my husband about that," she said snootily.

"Oh, and where may I see your husband madam?" I asked.

"At Bishops Stortford Council Offices," came the reply and she added with a broad smile and a chuckle, "As a matter of fact he's the Town Clerk". Then turned on her heels, sniffed the air haughtily as if to say, "Pick the bones out of that then", and went back into her house.

Bill and I walked back to his car and stowed the samples. "Now we're going to have lunch," he said, "then we're going to the Council office and then we're going back to OUR BLOODY OFFICE and you can tell the boss what you've done! You've dropped us both in the SHIT"!

So we went to the pub and had lunch, then to the Council office. I had been there many times before to hand over an official sample of some polluting discharge, usually, one from the sewage treatment works. The reaction from the Council engineers was always one of supreme indifference and they never bothered to get a comparative analysis done. In fact, there were so many official samples there just kept in a cupboard that clearly nobody really cared, or at least so I thought.

I was told that the Town Clerk was at an important meeting in London and therefore unavailable but one of the engineers offered to accept the sample and sign for it on his behalf. He did so with a very straight face and then said, "You know this is going to cause a frightful row, don't you? By the way, were you tipped off by someone?"

Having been assured that I wasn't tipped off he went back into the engineers' office and after a few moments, we heard an almighty guffaw from within. Well at least they all saw the funny side of it and as it happened so could I but poor old Bill was still sure we would get it in the neck* from our boss.

As it transpired, we got nothing of the kind when we returned to our office. In fact, our boss thought the whole thing was priceless and that it couldn't have happened at a better time, although strangely enough, he too asked if we had been tipped off about the polluting discharge.

It so happened that the important meeting being attended by the Town Clerk was actually with senior people and Board Members from our own organisation, including the Protection of Water Officer, our ultimate boss, to discuss how and when the polluting discharges from Bishops Stortford's antiquated sewerage system would be stopped. Amazingly it took a further five years or more before the issue was finally dealt with but even after all that time, when I had been appointed as the manager of the new works, people at the Council still reminded me of the day the Town Clerk was caught out polluting the watercourse.

Fortunately for me, that particular Town Clerk had retired and been replaced before I started working for Bishops Stortford Urban District Council.

*****

Netting a strange object.

The Lee Conservancy Catchment Board's Protection of Water Department had responsibility for the protection of fisheries as well as pollution control. Nearly all the fishery in the Lee catchment comprised angling for coarse fish and there were many angling clubs owning exclusive fishing rights on various stretches of the rivers. Sometimes these angling clubs would make complaints that their members were unable to catch many fish on their particular waters and the pollution control inspectors were obliged to make very thorough inspections to determine any reasons for a lack of fish. More often than not there was no source of pollution found but the angling clubs were rarely convinced. Contrarily the pollution control inspectors, especially one or two of us that were also keen anglers, were convinced that the reason club members didn't catch much was their lack of angling skill coupled with the fact that most of them went fishing at the weekend so there were always hordes of them causing great disturbance to each other's fishing. In addition, many of the club waters were on the canalised stretches of the rivers so there were usually plenty of boats at the weekends too, also disturbing the fishing.

On one occasion, I was asked by the Protection of Water Officer, my ultimate boss, to go fishing for a couple of days on a particular stretch of the River Lee, just to see what was there. Of course, I needed no encouragement to agree and the following day my colleague Mike and I went fishing. It was actually during the close season for coarse fishing and although, strictly speaking, it was illegal our formal instructions from the authority with responsibility for fishery protection enabled us to do it. It was pretty good too to be paid for going fishing, as I'm sure most people would agree! Mike and I actually caught quite a few fish, though nothing spectacular, and these were recorded as species, length and weight. All were in good condition and all were returned to the water. It was concluded that the reason for our relative success was that there was nobody else fishing and no boats to disturb the waters. The fishing club members, however, were still not convinced.

Following another complaint from a different angling club about a dearth of fish in the River Lee near its confluence with the River Stort, it was expected that another couple of days paid fishing would be offered. The club claimed that the effluent from Rye Meads sewage works was killing the fish or driving them downstream but we knew better. Unfortunately, I pointed out that the effluent collection channel around the lagoons at Rye Meads was full of fish and they were clearly there for two reasons at least. First was the abundance of food to be found in the effluent channel. This was in the form of tiny crustaceans such as Daphnia and Gammarus, plus many other small aquatic creatures. Second was the fact that the river water just a short distance downstream was relatively very warm due to the discharge of condensate water from the cooling towers of the Rye House Power Station nearby. This warm water would not be attractive to coarse fish of the types normally found in that river. So there was no paid fishing that time, all because I couldn't keep my mouth shut! Ah well, SHIT happens, doesn't it?

A subsequent electro-stunning exercise in the Rye Meads effluent channel revealed thousands of fish including some very large eels and many large pike. I believe the angling club eventually gave up their rights on that particular stretch of river.

A while later, the Protection of Water Department obtained a large seine net and because of my great interest in fishing, I was invariably heavily involved

31

when the netting of fish was carried out. On one occasion, we were asked by the then Metropolitan Water Board to remove the fish from one of the reservoirs in the East Warwick Group in Walthamstow, North East London. This small reservoir was being drained, I believe, for modifications and certain repair works and the fish needed to be removed. I recall the fish were used to restock certain stretches of the River Lee, which is essentially whence the water was derived for the reservoirs and therefore where the fish had originated in the first place. The one remarkable thing about this exercise was that on the first day the water was still deep enough to make our donkey jackets wet when we were working in it wearing chest waders. Several of us took our jackets off where the water was too deep and hung them on an old iron structure that was sticking up out of the muddy bottom. Little did we realise that this iron structure could have caused the most monumental SHIT happening of all time.

The following morning nobody was allowed into the reservoir complex. There were police everywhere controlling traffic and there were a number of soldiers there too. These men, it transpired, were from the Army Bomb Disposal Unit and were there to defuse and remove the same iron structure, which had been there since the Second World War. It had, of course, been dropped by a Nazi aircraft during the blitzkrieg of London and may never have even been primed to explode. It had surely disintegrated quite a bit over the years and probably bits had fallen off it because none of us recognised it as being anything like a bomb. Nevertheless, that's what it was and we had to wait for another day or two before we could complete the seine netting exercise. Furthermore, whilst netting fish afterwards we were all highly sceptical of anything we dragged from the bottom of the reservoir!

We also got to seine-net a sizeable lake at a country club called Bonnington's, near Sawbridgeworth in Hertfordshire. The proprietors wanted to turn the lake into an exclusive carp fishery as an attraction to club members but they had no idea what fish were already in the lake. Once again Mike and I had the good fortune to be sent fishing for a couple of days on full pay to find out what the lake held. Even the deputy Protection of Water Officer came along on the second day and borrowed one of my rods to go fishing. What a treat indeed. It was good weather, close to my home so not far to travel, a very picturesque lake and plenty of fish to be caught. We all thoroughly enjoyed ourselves and over the two days fished at different spots all around the shoreline. This demonstrated that more fish were at one part of the lake than at any other but we could see no reason why this should be. It was also the best area for access with the boat and the seine net so it was decided to bait-up that area and try to concentrate the fish stocks there.

Netting was scheduled for the following Tuesday, so over the weekend my wife and I took several sacks of wheat middlings, obtained from the local flour mill, to the lake and tossed it into the water as sticky wet balls that dispersed as they splashed in. Hopefully, the bait would attract the smaller fish and the predators would follow them.

Tuesday came but I was unable to take part in the fishing because it was my day at college. Shame, because it had been arranged for the BBC television news people to be there too and there was a short televised report on the event on a 'round-up' news programme with Michael Aspel that evening. Damn, I missed a part of my fifteen minutes of fame! Hey Ho – SHIT happened again!

Not a lot of fishing was done while the television people were around so the next day, we had plenty to do. My job was to feed the seine net off the stern and direct my colleague as to which way the little boat needed to be rowed. We managed several good sweeps and netted plenty of fish. They were mostly small creatures but there were some quite large perch and plenty of good-sized pike caught too. Unfortunately, there was also quite a lot of trash in the lake and every sweep of the seine produced something unexpected. Sometimes the junk made it difficult to pull in the net and sometimes it caused it to lift off the bottom so that many fish escaped. The junk included an old bicycle wheel, the remains of an old rusted wheelbarrow, the base-plate of an old radio set complete with slime-covered valves etc., plus plenty of chunks of concrete, pieces of rusty corrugated iron and lumps of rotting wood. After the remains of the wheelbarrow had been removed from the net, I made the comment, "I hope there isn't another one of those German bombs in this lake. There were a few dropped around this area you know. We've found everything else so far barring the bloody kitchen sink"!

The reply came from shore, "You're hardly likely to find a kitchen sink in the middle of a lake like this. Stop moaning and get on with the job Marpole"! as once more the boat was rowed out and I fed the seine net over the stern.

This sweep was a good one with the net describing a perfect curve and its full length was put into the water. The lake was a little deeper at this spot so the withdrawal should have been much easier. It wasn't, because the seine was badly snagged on something large and heavy. The boat was rowed out again and the net tugged up where it was snagged. I couldn't see down to the bottom but with a bit of effort, I was able to lift the offending object out of the mud. Any further effort would have probably caused the boat to sink so the whole thing had to be dragged out as the net was retrieved. Finally, with a lot of pulling and plenty of foul language from the crew, the net was fully retrieved complete with the snag. Believe it or not, it was a very large, stainless steel KITCHEN SINK, complete with draining board, waste pipe and 'S' bend attached. It was mounted in a rusting steel frame that had once had cupboard doors but now only the long hinges remained. Absolutely incredible!

A quiet voice behind me said, almost apologetically, "Well David you found the kitchen sink after all. I guess that shot me up the arse didn't it?" Everybody howled with laughter. What a pity that didn't happen when the BBC television cameras were there. It would have made excellent viewing for the whole country, I think.

The fish were used to restock parts of the river catchment and the lake at Bonnington's was stocked up with carp as intended. I don't know if they had the lake dredged first to get rid of any remaining trash but, if they did, I'm sure they didn't find anything quite so dramatic as a kitchen sink!

*****

Strange oil pollution at Harlow

Periodically, I would drive along Edinburgh Way at Harlow in Essex to inspect a pair of Flush Tanks. These were situated close to the River Stort in the middle of a sizeable industrial estate known as Temple Fields, that included a large glassworks, the town's gas holders, the town's public refuse recycling site, various engineering enterprises and a couple of bakeries. The huge rectangular concrete structures were provided to protect the river from spillages of oil or other pollutants that may find their way into the surface water sewers in the area. They were fitted with surface baffles that would trap any floating pollutant so that it could be subsequently removed with a suction tanker machine or similar equipment for safe disposal elsewhere.

Usually, the water discharging from these Flush Tanks was clean enough for the river but occasionally I did see a light, oily film trapped by the surface baffles and, on these occasions, I would contact the engineer responsible for drainage at the Harlow New-town Council and advise him to get the material removed. On one occasion, however, I found both the Flush Tanks to be badly contaminated with a black oily substance that carried a peculiar sweet smell. The water discharging from the tanks was clean but clearly the pollutant needed to be removed so I went to see the Council's engineer with a sample of fluid skimmed from the surface of the tanks. The engineer told me they had found this same black oily substance more than once recently but had no idea where it came from. They had had analysis done at the Rye Meads Sewage Treatment Works laboratory and had determined that it was a mineral oil of some type but could not identify it. Anyway, it was promised that the material would be removed from the Flush Tanks as soon as possible.

Later that day, I inspected a small stream called The Canons Brook where it crossed a popular golf course of the same name. At one point close to Edinburgh Way I spotted a small field ditch that was running with a black oily fluid with the same strange smell I had encountered that morning at the Flush Tanks. The ditch was discharging the fluid into the Canons Brook which, in turn, had a light film of the oily material over its surface. I thought this would be difficult to sort out because the pollutant was simply seeping from the ground at the head of the little ditch. There was no pipe to be seen and the nearest building was at least 50 metres away. It was unlikely to be coming from there, however, because the building actually housed the I.T.T. Company's offices and no manufacturing units. Nevertheless, I needed a formal sample of this fluid so I walked back to my parked vehicle and collected my official sampling kit. Nearby was a group of men working for the Eastern Electricity Board. They were working from two large vans and using some heavy equipment down a cable manhole that was covered by a blue and white striped tent. I more or less ignored them but one of them seemed to take a bit of interest in what I was doing. He watched me as I crossed the road and the grass bank until I reached the head of the little polluted ditch.

It was necessary to obtain three litres of the liquid so I had to use a small paint kettle to collect a number of smaller quantities to fill the official sample vessel and in consequence, the paint kettle was smeared with the stuff around the outside. As I walked back to my van the same man asked me, "What have you got there mate?" I told him it was a sample of oil from a ditch.

"Has it got a sweet sickly smell?" he asked and, when told it had, he asked to have a look at it.

"Ah, that's the stuff all right," he said after giving the paint kettle a good sniff.

"OK gents," he called to his colleagues, "the leak's definitely around here somewhere. This chap from the Rivers Department has just found it. Can you show us where it is, mate please?"

I took them to the spot where the fluid was seeping into the little ditch and they immediately began to dig back towards the road. The seepage increased and became quite a trickle so I had to ask them to stop forthwith and bung up the little ditch with soil. For the hell of it, I also produced my warrant card to show them that they could face prosecution if they caused more to flow into the watercourse. They agreed to do the job with a mechanical digger and avoid any more pollution but I still didn't know where the oil was coming from. They explained it was coming from the casing of the eleven-thousand-volt cable serving the industrial area of Harlow. The oil was used as an insulation medium but had been leaking for some time due to cracks in the casing. It was black because it had dissolved away the pitch-tape protection around the casing. Their problem was that they didn't know where the cracks were but now, they had a rough location so could expose the cable and replace the section with the cracked casing.

When I told them about the same oil having been found at the Flush Tanks their foreman asked me to show him where they were. Evidently, they subsequently traced the location of other cracks in cables' casings where the oil could seep into surface water sewers draining to the Flush Tanks. Surprisingly, I received quite a bit of praise for my efforts, both from the Protection of Water Officer, who usually never had a good word for anybody, and the Area Engineer for the Electricity Board. It was quite amazing that nobody in the Protection of Water Department had previously been aware of the vast volumes of oil used in the casings of heavy electric cables or its potential pollution threat if the casings ever became damaged.

This event gave rise to no SHIT happening for me but it certainly did for a lot of people and businesses in the Harlow area. A day or two later there were very lengthy power cuts in some areas while the leaking cables were replaced and I recall reading an account, in one of the free local papers that the cables had to be replaced because they had become saturated with oil that had leaked from the river. Clearly, some people just didn't understand at all!

<u>Inspecting a surface water sewer near Finchley, Gasworks.</u>

Finchley is a suburb of North London and, at the time I was an Assistant Pollution Inspector for the Lee Conservancy Catchment Board, it had a coal carbonising plant or gasworks close to the North Circular Road, which was and still is an extremely busy main thoroughfare around one of the world's largest cities. Most of the smaller watercourses in that area had been culverted many decades ago and their status reduced to that of surface water sewers. One, however, retained its original name, which I recall as being the Finchley Brook but where it emerged from its culvert it still flowed in a concrete channel for a considerable distance before its confluence with another tributary of the River Lee.

A film of oil had been spotted on this watercourse by Brian, the Area Pollution Inspector and now my immediate senior. Brian asked me to accompany him to the site so that between us we might discover the source of this pollution and within an hour we were at the discharge from the culvert wearing thigh-waders and overalls, ready to start our upstream inspection.

Brian was appointed to the Lee Conservancy Catchment Board on the same day as me. He was five years older and had recently completed a part-time degree in biology so was quite fairly given the senior position when it became available on the resignation of one of the older Area Pollution Inspectors. His experience of water pollution control, however, was considerably less than mine and his conception of safe working practices was pretty well non-existent. It had not occurred to Brian that we might require some form of lighting to see our way inside the culvert, nor did he consider that we might need a third person to remain outside it as a watchman if we should encounter any problems. Of course, neither of us considered gas detection equipment and there probably wasn't any available, even if we had. However, I did have a small torch with me but the battery was pretty flat and it only provided a faint light.

Into the culvert, we went, under the roaring traffic on the North Circular road. We carried sampling equipment, labels, notebooks and the little torch. We both had to crouch whilst walking in the culvert because the roof was not very high but it was possible to move fairly rapidly upstream. After a couple of minutes, all light from the culvert's exit had vanished and we were reliant upon the small torch to see anything at all. We both began to notice a smell of gas and concluded that it was probably from the nearby gasworks but it was only a faint whiff so we were not unduly concerned about it. There were also other odours occasionally, probably arising from the silt on the bottom of the stream as we disturbed it with our hobnailed waders.

Having walked a few hundred paces upstream we came across a pipe discharging from the side of the culvert. We appeared to be in a large chamber and could stand up straight so it was undoubtedly a manhole access into the culvert. The discharge from the pipe appeared to be quite dirty water and had a very oily/gassy smell to it but we were unable to see it very clearly because the battery in my torch was exhausted and indeed within a few moments the torchlight simply died. So now we were standing in pitch darkness with quite possibly the source of the oil pollution at hand but were unable to do anything about it.

Brian now had a wonderful idea. "Have you got a lighter David or a box of matches? If we can have a light for just a few seconds it will be enough for us to get a sample."

As a smoker, I always carried a cigarette lighter and indeed had one of the new butane lighters, the type that are nowadays more readily obtainable than a box of matches! It had an adjustable flame for lighting a pipe so would be ideal for giving us a light to see the offending discharge pipe. I was not, however, very keen on the idea of using a cigarette lighter within the confines of an oil-polluted culvert that smelled, albeit only slightly, of coal gas from a nearby gasworks. Brian, on the other hand, was quite sure there would never be an explosive mixture in the culvert because there was an almost continuous flow of air through it due to the passage of the water. Furthermore, he was very keen to be able to sample the suspect discharge so that we could eventually get this oil pollution stopped. Reluctantly, therefore, I gave him my lighter, handing it over very carefully in the pitch darkness and with a strong feeling that SHIT was about to happen, which of course it did.

Brian moved a few steps away and struck the flint, producing a long flame that illuminated the space admirably. Within a fraction of a second, this was followed by a tremendous BANG, BANG, BANG! The enormous din was sufficient to send us bolting back downstream like two terrified rabbits fleeing the inevitable fireball and we didn't stop until we could see daylight from the culvert's exit. It so happened that this was the point where I cracked my head on the culvert roof, tripped and fell headlong into the six or seven-inch deep Finchley Brook, getting completely saturated in the process. Brian also tripped and fell but, being rather shorter than me, managed to avoid cracking his head on the roof. But where was the fireball? It didn't happen! There was no gas explosion! In fact, there was no problem at all. So, what was the infernal din caused by? Certainly not by Brian striking the flint on my little plastic cigarette lighter. What was it?

We didn't find out until the next time we visited the Finchley Brook Culvert, which was a couple of days later. This time we were comparatively mob-handed, with two other people to act as watchmen at the culvert exit and also at the manhole access by the traffic lights a few hundred paces upstream. This was in fact where we now entered the culvert, this time equipped with powerful torches, hard hats to go with our overalls and waders, eye protection goggles and PVC gloves, not to mention traffic warning signs and road-safety cones. Indeed, on lifting the heavy-duty manhole cover to enter the culvert, we discovered the reason for the terrifying bangs that had caused our panic two days earlier. It was a rather loose fit, undoubtedly caused by wear and tear from the heavy traffic and what we had heard was probably the sound of a heavy articulated lorry's wheels hitting the cover as it was braking before the traffic lights no more than fifty metres ahead.

Down the access ladder we went into the culvert and, sure enough, there was the offending discharge of dirty, oily water, this time bathed in light and readily sampled. We knew from maps of the surface water drainage system obtained from the local Council offices where the polluting liquid was coming from and subsequently the company responsible was obliged to correct the problem or face prosecution and a hefty fine. So, another pollution successfully stopped but I shall always have the memory of the claustrophobic terror within the Finchley Brook culvert and I have never entered such a place since without proper consideration of the health and safety situation.

*****

Overflow from Vauxhall storage lagoons at Luton

The Vauxhall Motor Company was very big in Luton in those days and they manufactured a sizeable range of motor products from small cars to large lorries.

Their biggest factory was in an area not far from the airport and also close to the River Lee. It was a part of my routine duties to inspect the tiny streams in the area and the discharges from the culverted watercourses, most of which also had a number of surface water sewers draining into them.

One day, I received a radio call from the Deputy Protection of Water Officer, something of a rarity indeed, anxiously asking me my location. When told that I was at the village of Wheathampstead he seemed to be somewhat relieved.

"Listen," he said, "there's been a big spillage at the Vauxhall factory in Luton. One of their waste lagoons has burst and all the muck's running down the road! Get up there and I mean 'PRONTO'! See what's going on and call me back! Lee Catch-Board* out!"

This sounded rather nasty so I set off as fast as possible to Vauxhall's factory, which wasn't so far away, and in about twenty minutes I reached the scene of the spillage. It was one of the biggest SHIT happenings I have ever seen. A traffic policeman stopped me close to the scene and told me to take a different route around it but after seeing my warrant card and receiving an explanation of my purpose was very helpful in explaining what had happened.

Just a short distance from the enormous employee car park, the road rose up to a small ridge. Atop the ridge was an earth embankment which, it transpired, was the outer wall of three large storage lagoons. I was already well aware of the embankment but had never realised that there were storage lagoons behind it. These lagoons were used to retain wastewater from the vehicle manufacturing plant before it received pre-treatment prior to being discharged into the sewers leading to the Sewage Treatment Plant at East Hyde. The earth embankment reminded me of the wartime photographs of the Moehne Dam in Germany after Operation Chastise, the Dam Busters' raid. A great chunk of it had obviously collapsed suddenly, causing a miniature tidal wave of wastewater to roar down across the car park and probably into every surface water drain in the area. Several vehicles had been shoved aside and badly damaged by the flood, including some of the large Cresta models. Fortunately, nobody was hurt because it would seem, there was nobody around at the time except for two GPO telephone engineers, one of whom was working on the high cables while his mate was sitting in his van having a sandwich. Apparently, the van was buffeted somewhat and a nearby cable ducting was flooded but otherwise, they were safe. The drains and, more importantly, of course, the River Lee itself were not safe, however. Furthermore, there was a very real risk of imminent failure of the thin concrete wall dividing the damaged lagoon from its neighbour, which was also full. Engineers from the factory were already looking at ways of preventing another deluge because there would soon be a shift change and many people would be trying to enter or leave the car park area. They were also preparing, with the assistance of the local fire brigade, to flush away all the sediment left behind by the deluge and clearly most of this was likely to finish up in the poor old River Lee. Most of it would surely get into the ornamental lakes at Luton Hoo,* where the life expectancy of the fish and exotic water plants was dramatically reduced.

I radioed my boss and appraised him of the situation, telling him that it was more than just a big spillage, it was a catastrophe and there were going to be far-reaching effects upon the river! Although there were others already on their way from the Protection of Water Department, the news that the Fire Brigade's flushing of the area was about to start caused him to panic somewhat. "You must find a way to stop them", he said. "Do whatever you can! Talk to the Fire Chief, anything you like but you must stop them from washing all that shit into the river! That'll be where all the poisonous stuff is, in the sediment! OK, get on with it! I'm on my way up there myself now!"

As it happened the Fire Chief was not there but I spoke to the leading hand on the fire engine. He calmly pointed out that they would hose the area down as much as possible into the lowest corner of the car park at shift change time. The next shift would have to wait until the clean-up was finished before parking their vehicles and going to work. The lowest corner of the car park was already having a sandbag sump built from which the Borough Council would draw up the silt with their suction tankers. "Otherwise," he said, "all this shit will go in the river and we don't want that do we?"

What a pleasure it was to find somebody who understood that the 'drain' is not the place to chuck whatever you don't want because it probably leads to somewhere and somebody else that doesn't want it either!

By the time the other Protection of Water people had arrived the shift change was about to begin. Shortly after 2.00 pm, vehicles were being driven from the car park while controlled by traffic police from the factory's security staff. Some cars actually got a quick wash underneath as they passed a couple of men with pressure lances. Those belonging to non-shift personnel were directed back to vacant plots that were already hosed clean. An hour later the next shift's vehicles were able to park on a clean spot. The whole exercise was carried out extremely efficiently and was completed before 4.30 pm. To me, it seemed quite obvious that this was not the first time something of this nature had happened but Vauxhall's management staff insisted that it was!

The damaged lagoon wall was repaired very quickly and, I believe, lined with concrete. To my knowledge there was never a serious problem again originating from the Vauxhall factory. No doubt they would have been sternly reprimanded by Luton Borough Council and by the Lee Conservancy Catchment Board and, had the Health and Safety at Work Act been in existence the chances are that somebody would have been prosecuted but as it happened the incident was soon forgotten.

The River Lee didn't suffer too badly from the incident either. There were certainly dead fish seen and the water in Luton Hoo's ornamental lakes was a bit off-colour for a while but considering the scale of the pollution and the concentration of toxic materials in some of the samples I had taken, it was contained in a very small area. Downstream from East Hyde, there was little or no visible effect. Nevertheless, at the time it was quite a SHIT happening!

*****

Accident with Vacci tank beside the River Ash at Little Hadham

As an Assistant Pollution Inspector, I was obliged to walk along the rivers and streams searching for sources of pollution or even potential sources, the latter being noted for future inspection as appropriate. On one occasion I decided to walk the River Ash at a village called Little Hadham. The Ash is a pretty little river in places and as it was a nice sunny day, I thought a walk of two or three miles along it would be very enjoyable so I parked my vehicle near the A 120 road bridge, climbed over the style into the field and set off upstream.

Unfortunately, due to near drought weather conditions for the past few weeks, there was hardly any flow in the river and immediately upstream of the bridge it had been reduced to a couple of large pools with just a tiny piddle of water flowing into them. The pools were actually green and quite foul-smelling with hordes of insects infesting their surfaces. Furthermore, the tiny flow in the river was also very clearly contaminated and from its sickly smell, much like sweetened cow poo, I concluded that the contamination was from silage liquor.

Silage is important in Southern England as a nourishing feed for cattle during the winter months. It is made by cutting grass that has been allowed to grow long and lush and then stacking it, while still fresh and green, into a huge heap to ferment. The heap is usually made in a rectangular bay, often made with railway sleepers, and when sufficiently deep is covered with a tarpaulin. The finally fermented product looks rather like tobacco and has relatively little odour but during the fermenting period, the stink from it is quite repulsive. Furthermore, a highly polluting liquid is squeezed from the grass by the overall weight of the heap and this is known as silage liquor. On most farms, this liquor is collected in a holding pond or tank and subsequently sprayed or channelled onto the land to be absorbed as a bit of fertilizer. The spraying of silage liquor is a smelly procedure and often leads to complaints but the odour usually disappears after a day or so. Its discharge into a river, however, can cause very serious pollution, leading to major fish kills and extensive despoliation of the watercourse.

Having sampled the foul water in the river I subsequently set off with my official sampling kit in search of the offending discharge, which turned out to be almost half a mile upstream. Sure enough, there was the huge silage stack and a tiny drainage/collection channel carrying the liquor away. The channel was connected to the river via a few feet of four-inch plastic pipe. After sampling the foul discharge, I searched out the farmer (actually the Farm Manager) to formally serve him with the third portion of the sample and notice of intended action.

The Farm Manager seemed to be quite ignorant of the fact that silage liquor should not be dumped willy-nilly into the River Ash but at least agreed to do something about it forthwith. He bunged up the discharge pipe and instructed a couple of his men to extend the channel away from the river so that the liquor would not drain into it. He promised to dig a collection pit and spray the liquor over the fields with his Vacci tanker. Clearly, he was afraid of a possible prosecution because he agreed to pump out the two foul pools that had formed near the road bridge and personally went to prepare the tractor-hauled machine to do the job.

Though feeling rather proud of myself for having sorted out this nasty little pollution I was blissfully unaware of the impending SHIT happening as I walked back to my van with the official samples. These had been stowed in the vehicle and my radio report made to the office when the Farm Manager arrived with his tractor and Vacci tanker. He parked the machine on the riverbank, connected up a few lengths of a suction pipe, adamantly refusing my offer of help to hump the pipes around, and began to suck down the largest pool with the tanker, which held about five hundred gallons. I estimated that it would require five loads to empty those pools and maybe several more loads if there were similar pools downstream, which I had not yet checked for, but the man appeared to be slightly irritated by this when I told him. I ignored his irritation, however, and took photographs of the machinery and the now shrunken pool as he disconnected the suction pipe from the tanker. I had intended to photograph the spraying of the liquor onto the field but, just as he was about to drive off with it, the irritated Farm Manager ACCIDENTALLY, or so he subsequently claimed, started the thing spraying while I was standing behind it with my camera. I was sprayed from my neck to my boots with the foul-smelling liquid, probably for two or three seconds only, but sufficiently to soak my clothing right through. My 35mm camera was also saturated, subsequently needing to be professionally dismantled, dried out and cleaned, but at least I got nothing on my face or in my eyes, nose or mouth. The Farm Manager, however, came very close to having all his orifices filled up with either my fists or my boots and certainly would have done had he not apologised profusely without the slightest trace of a smile on his face. What could I do? When the river was finally cleaned of the silage liquor and the absence of further pools of it downstream confirmed, I drove back to the office to deliver the samples before going home for a bath and changing my clothes. My working suit would have to go to the dry cleaners too.

By the time I reached the office in Cheshunt, I was in a much better frame of mind. As I got out of the vehicle the Deputy Protection of Water Officer came over to speak to me.

"Christ!" he said, "What happened to you? You smell of cow shit!"

"Well you don't smell like ashes of roses either Donald," I replied, "but at least I have an excuse because I just got sprayed with silage liquor. What happened to you?"

I didn't like this man very much but at least he had a sense of humour and we had a good laugh about it. I told him I would hand over the samples and then go home for a bath and change of clothes. He would get my report the following day.

It transpired that prosecution did not materialise, though a stern warning letter was sent to the farm. I never had occasion to go there again but I shall never forget being sprayed with silage liquor. I'm sure that bastard did it on purpose.

*****

Chapter 4

Manager/Chemist and Trade Effluent Inspector with Brentwood Urban District Council

Brentwood is a sizeable Essex town on the outskirts of London. I managed to secure a good position there as Treatment Works Manager/Chemist and Trade Effluent Inspector and that was probably the best opportunity I could have had to gain experience of people-management, industrial waste-treatment and treatment-works operations. During the few years I was there, however, there were more SHIT happenings than at any other time in my career so far and most became etched indelibly onto my mind.

<u>Distilling wine at Nags Head Lane</u>

The sewage treatment works at Nags Head Lane had been extended and extensively refurbished and the work was nearing completion when I was appointed to the job. One of my first tasks was to fully equip and set up a super little laboratory to perform all the necessary routine analysis of wastewaters, trade effluents, sludge, etc. and this required a number of stills and a fractionating column. Once the distillation equipment was ready, I thought it might be a good idea to test my own capability of producing spirits. It so happened that I had been making wines from various fruits found growing in the hedgerows and, in the airing cupboard at home, I had four one-gallon demijohns of it that had finished fermenting. There was one of bullace wine, two of cherry-apple wine and one of haw wine. Unfortunately, all of them had turned sour because the bubble traps in the demijohns had dried out and let in the air. Nevertheless, I reckoned that the alcohol was recoverable and therefore took it to work and started distilling it through a fractionating column, the product being collected into a Smirnoff vodka bottle to which the label was still boldly attached.

Of course, everyone on the site knew what I was doing and a couple of the operatives actually brought in their tea mugs for a sample to taste. Both declared it to be 'bloody good grog' so I was encouraged to distil the lot, knowing full well it was in serious breach of the law. Imagine then my terror when a black car pulled up outside and an officious looking character walked into my laboratory brandishing a briefcase bearing a Royal Crest and the words Customs & Excise. "Good morning," he said, "Customs and Excise. Here to inspect your new still." I thought somebody must have betrayed me!

Well, SHIT didn't actually happen but it was as close to happening as the thickness of a cigarette paper and you can guess where the event almost took place!

"Ah, there it is," said the inspector pointing to the brand new Mannesty* electric still mounted on the wall.

"Just need to check the serial number, that's all. Don't know why we have to do it with these, you couldn't really distil anything with it except tap water."

"Y-y-yes," I stuttered in reply as my heart skipped several beats.

He checked the number, wrote it in a register and turned to leave.

"What's that evil-looking muck you're distilling there then? Smells like some kind of alcohol to me."

"Oh, it's the trade effluent from the Ilford Film factory," I burbled in reply, "It's got all manner of solvents in it from the film making."

"Well sooner you than me old chap," said the inspector, "You're welcome to that job." Then he strode to his car and left. Nobody had betrayed me after all!

I shall never know if the inspector realised what I was doing. He must have seen the Smirnoff vodka bottle, not to mention the clearly labelled demijohns still containing homemade wine and he must have seen the look of terror on my face too. If he didn't, he must have been either half-blind or plain stupid and if he did, he was either a decent fellow or a skiver, simply shirking his responsibility. Whatever it was I never took the risk again and the alcohol I produced, which was subsequently shown by analysis to be over 90% pure ethanol, was not consumed but was used to light my primus stove during a camping holiday with my wife and friends in Germany!

In retrospect, it was, of course, an absolute waste of 'bloody good grog'!

*****

47

Nags Head Lane primary tanks.

The new works was equipped with rectangular primary settlement tanks that had floors sloping from the outlet end back to the inlet end. The raw sludge that settled on the floor of the tanks was slowly scraped back to the inlet end by a full-width scraper machine running on rails along the sidewalls. The machine was used for all the settlement tanks and was moved from one to another by a transfer carriage. The inlet end of each tank was constructed with three pyramidal hoppers in the floor, each one about 2 metres deep and with a pipe connection from its centre into a separate sludge collection chamber. Each pipe finished with a vertical telescopic valve in the middle of the chamber. This arrangement enabled the raw sludge to be removed from each settlement tank without having to drain it first, thus preventing the release of foul odours, but to do so efficiently the telescopic valves had to be opened slowly. This allowed the sludge to be removed by hydrostatic head pressure without drawing a hole through it and letting water through instead. It was a good system but gave rise to the most awful SHIT happening.

Unfortunately, the operatives often opened the valves wide and then went off to have a smoke and this caused a hole to be drawn through the sludge in the hoppers and water to flow through the telescopic valves. When they returned, they saw water and assumed that all the sludge had been removed which, of course, it had not. The net result of this bad practice was that the hoppers eventually became blocked and the settlement tanks became filled with sludge. Consequently, it was necessary to pump them out one at a time and unblock the hoppers. Furthermore, the scraper machine could not be used on an empty tank so the floor of each one had to be manually cleaned with squeegees, a thoroughly unpleasant job.

The first tank was being squeegeed while the hoppers were being emptied with a vacuum tanker-lorry. The lorry was quite elderly and was extremely noisy so people had to shout loudly to be heard by anyone even close by. I watched the proceedings from the parapet of the tank and saw, to my horror, that one operative pushed his squeegee right to the end of the tank, turned around and retraced his steps exactly back up the tank floor. Clearly, he didn't realise he had walked between two of the hoppers which were only separated from each other by 60cm of the concrete floor. If he had deviated just slightly from his straight line, he would have fallen into two metres depth of foul stinking raw sludge and

48

quite possibly have drowned. I yelled to the man to stop short of the hoppers but he couldn't hear me over the noise of the vacuum tanker so, beginning to lose my cool, I climbed down the ladder to the tank floor, wearing a pair of wellington boots and a suit. Yes, a suit! The operatives were wearing hobnailed thigh-waders and overalls! Walking carefully over to the man in question I explained to him in a loud voice that he must not go close to the hoppers again until he could see their outline, i.e. when the sludge level had reached the floor. He asked me to show him roughly where that was so I walked slowly and carefully towards the hoppers, yelling, "Don't go past the-e-e-e-re!" as my non-hobnailed boots slipped on the slimy floor of the tank and sent me sliding into the hopper feet first.

Being only 1.9 metres tall I knew I was going right under so tightly shut my mouth and eyes as I went in. Fortunately, the sides of the pyramid at its centre enabled me to quickly stand upright with my feet held apart pressing on the walls and my head was clear of the sludge to just below my bottom lip. A quick wipe of my eyes and a snort down my nose enabled me to see, more or less, and breathe but I dared not open my mouth. Somebody had the presence of mind to stop the infernal noise of the vacuum tanker and I could hear panicky voices from all around. Jed, one of the operatives in the tank yelled to me to grab the end of his squeegee so he could pull me out and, in my hurry, I grabbed it and pulled. Of course, I didn't pull myself out, I just pulled him in too and then had a second ducking in the foul fluid. Worse still I realised that Jed was considerably shorter than me and I had to hold him up so he could breathe. Luckily there were other people in the tank by now and with several standing in line and holding on to each other they were able to pull Jed out with a squeegee. Next, I was pulled out but one of the others slipped over and quickly replaced me in the hopper. Fortunately, he was rapidly retrieved and we all scrambled up the ladder and out of the tank.

Wasting not a moment, we all three made a beeline for the locker room, where there were two showers. The other two started to strip off before getting under the shower but I stood there fully clothed and washed the filth off my face and hair first. Only when my eyes, ears, nose and especially my mouth were clean did I begin to remove my clothing, starting with my wellington boots. After what seemed an age, we were all tolerably clean but of course, we were all naked too. Jed lived in a house adjacent to the site so was able to get fresh clothes brought over. The other man had a clean set of overalls in his locker so was able to get decent and drive home. For me, there was a problem. The only things I wanted to salvage from my heap of clothing were my wallet, watch, car keys and fountain pen. Everything else was to be dumped. I had a lab coat I could wear but no trousers and the lab coat was not suitable for decency. Fortunately, Bob, the Plant Foreman, also lived in a house adjacent to the site so he was able to loan me a pair of trousers and underpants but Bob was a short, pot-bellied guy so the trousers flew at half-mast and had to be held up when I walked to prevent them dropping straight to the ground. Nevertheless, I managed to get home, about an hour's drive away, without further embarrassment and spent forty-five minutes in the bath scrubbing every inch of my body. I swear I could still smell sludge on me a week later!

The following day I went to work in my best, now only, suit and organised the emptying and cleaning of the primary settlement tanks, this time using fire hoses instead of squeegees to clean sludge off the floors, so nobody needed to enter the tanks. A careful analysis of what had happened that day showed that we had had a close brush with death but only a few years later did I realise how easily it could have been avoided and that was when the Health and Safety at Work Act became law.

Three weeks later I had bought a new suit for best and I just remarked on the fact during the lunch break. Charlie, the electrician at the plant told me he had a new suit too that he had found. Later he went home, his house being not far from the plant, and came back to the mess room wearing it. To my astonishment, I realised that the suit was mine, no longer soaked in foul-smelling raw sludge but clean and neatly pressed. Charlie had taken it from the waste bin, washed it down with a garden hose and then gently hand washed it with detergent, dried it on a hanger and sent it to the dry cleaners to be professionally cleaned and pressed. It needed a minor adjustment to the trousers because Charlie was slightly shorter than me but the result was a suit quite good enough to wear to the pub on a Saturday evening. I was and still remain completely amazed by that!

*****

Charlie burnt his face.

Charlie was not a well-qualified electrician but was able to cope with most of the relatively simple control technology for pumps and other machinery on the works in those days. In fact, there was hardly enough electrical work to warrant a full-time electrician so he often did other work that would normally be done by the operatives. One such task was the daily descaling of the heat exchanger's fire tubes.

When the new sludge digester plant was built, the heating system was designed to burn sludge gas, which is essentially methane but contains a large proportion of carbon monoxide and non-flammable carbon dioxide. It has a calorific value similar to coal gas and the same burners and gas jets can be used for either fuel. Since there was a ready supply of coal gas at Brentwood the system was designed to be fed either by coal gas from the town supply or by digester gas. So when the digester plant was being started up, we could use town gas until we were able to produce sufficient gas from the process. The fuel would then be changed over to digester gas.

At the appropriate time, the digesters were filled and the process was ready to be started. The town gas was turned on but we found that it burned very poorly in the new heat exchanger. It transpired that the town gas supply had been changed from coal gas to North Sea gas, which contains a very high proportion of methane and requires a higher pressure and much finer gas jets to burn it properly. We, therefore, had to have a new burner grid made for the town gas that could be interchanged with the original burner grid and that would take a month to supply. Meanwhile, we would have to heat the system as best we could if we wanted to get it started properly. We decided to burn town gas but it had to be started with a small flame and then increased slowly to get it to feed into the heater tubes. Also, it would have to be shut down every day and the heater tubes brushed out to remove the scale caused by incomplete combustion of the new town gas. Charlie had the job of descaling the tubes every day and reigniting the burners. He did the latter task in a rather crude way because he was a bit of a skiver and couldn't be bothered to light up the pilot flame first before slowly opening the gas control valve as instructed. Instead, he would light a roll of newspaper with a match and then open the gas control valve quickly while thrusting the burning paper into the gas stream. The result would be a spectacular 'whoomph' as the gas ignited, briefly causing a mass of flame that would draw rapidly into the heater tubes. As this happened Charlie would perform a kind of war dance, presumably to enhance his perceived macho image. Despite being told several times to light the gas properly Charlie would ignore the dangers and always do it his way when no supervisor was present.

One day I was telephoned by the Council's Chief Engineer, my ultimate boss, and whilst in conversation I heard a distant 'BAROOMPH'! A few minutes later my telephone conversation was interrupted by Bob, the Works Foreman, as he crept somewhat sheepishly into the laboratory.

"Charlie's burnt his face," he said in a rather matter of fact voice.

"OK," I said, holding my hand over the mouthpiece of the phone, "tell him to come in and I'll put some ointment on his face for him."

The First Aid box was kept in the laboratory and it was a frequent occurrence for me to deal with minor injuries incurred by the men on site. A few moments later, however, Charlie staggered into the laboratory with his face looking like a freshly boiled beetroot and wailing like a stuck pig. This was more than the usual minor injury, it was a SHIT happening! His eyebrows and most of his hair were frizzled and clearly, the man was in severe pain so, hanging up on the boss without any explanation, I grabbed Charlie's arm and steered him to my car, shoved him in it and drove like Stirling Moss, the famous racing driver, to Oldchurch Hospital, a couple of miles away.

On reaching the hospital, I drove straight to the Emergency Unit, parked up next to an ambulance and rushed poor Charlie into the building, where we were met by medical staff.

"What's up?" yelled one.

"Gas blowback burnt his face," I yelled in reply.

"OK in here quick," said a young nurse and I followed her, dragging Charlie, into a treatment cubicle.

Quickly they sprayed his face with a pain-relieving fluid and then gave him an injection, laid him on the bed and started to remove his overalls etc. A few moments later a senior nurse appeared and asked what was happening. One of the younger nurses replied by explaining that Charlie had facial burns and that they had administered some treatment. The senior nurse then grew two horns and a forked tail and, turning to me, said, "What the hell are you doing in here?"

"Err, I brought him in," said I.

"Get out!" said the monster, "Wait in the reception area 'till we're finished! By the way, is that your car over there?"

"Err, yes, it is," I replied rather feebly.

"Well, shift it then, this area's reserved for ambulances! Can't you read?"

Now, with hackles raised, I was ready to do battle with 'The Beast Himself' but decided instead to shift the car and wait in the reception area so that I could rebuke her properly later.

After about forty minutes the senior nurse appeared at the reception and, just as I rose to tell her off, she deflated me by apologising quite sweetly for her rudeness earlier, even offering me a cup of tea. She told me that Charlie had been admitted to the hospital and was now asleep in one of the wards. She said the burns were quite superficial and that he would soon recover but asked why he was so terribly dirty.

"Well, he works at the sewage treatment plant," I replied, "so his overalls get particularly dirty."

"I'm not referring to his overalls" she said, I'm asking why his body is so dirty? I told one of the nurses to take his socks off and she told me they were already off. His feet were still black though so what does he do at that sewage works, paddle in the stuff? I think the dirt on his face has probably saved his skin from getting too badly burnt. I've never seen such a dirty man in all my life. We had to give him a damned good bath before putting him to bed!"

I always knew Charlie wasn't too particular about personal cleanliness but couldn't believe he was as bad as the senior nurse had suggested until I went to visit him in the hospital the following evening. There, sitting up in bed eating grapes, was a considerably paler Charlie than the one I knew, albeit that his face was rather wrinkled and peeling. Even his remaining hair was several shades lighter than before and all because he had been bathed. Amazing!

A few weeks later, Charlie was back at work. His burns were no longer visible because he had a new layer of skin on his face and his eyebrows and hair had re-grown. He would not, however, go anywhere near the sludge heater and even backed away from anybody lighting a cigarette. Obviously, he had learnt a lesson and, fortunately, so had a number of others on that plant.

*****

Smoking on the digester at Shenfield

There was one man who had learned nothing from Charlie's face burning incident and that was the Cleansing Superintendent who was my immediate boss. Frank was responsible overall for refuse collection and disposal, sewerage, sewage treatment and the maintenance of the town's swimming pool. He didn't know a great deal about sewage treatment so left me alone most of the time but would occasionally walk around the three treatment works in Brentwood and, if he was concerned about anything he discovered, would ask me to meet him on site and sort it out.

One day, Frank called me and asked me to go to Shenfield sewage treatment works to look at the recirculation pumps. When I got there, I found the pumps had been turned off by the works foreman, who thought they were just a waste of power. I instructed him to turn them on again and, after explaining in great detail why they should be kept running, warned him not to make any changes to the plant operation without my express permission. Frank was satisfied but nevertheless decided to make a close inspection of the works to see what else might have been tampered with and started by inspecting the sludge digesters. That's when the most catastrophic SHIT happening of all time could have occurred, at least as far as I was concerned.

The primary digester at Shenfield had a floating gas-holder roof of seven thousand cubic foot capacity and it was full at the time. Waste gas was burning off at the flare stack about a hundred metres away so I knew the gasholder would be at its maximum pressure and there would likely be a bit of gas leakage from the sludge seal around its skirt. When we had ascended the spiral staircase to the top of the tank, we climbed down another stairway onto the floating roof which was about two metres below the concrete parapet of the tank. Here we were sheltered from the breeze so Frank, who was a very heavy smoker, to my horror put a cigarette in his mouth and lit up.

"FRANK," I yelled, "What the hell are you doing?"

"Oh, sorry Dave," he replied, "Do you want one?"

"NO, I DON'T, YOU SILLY OLD BUGGER. PUT IT OUT!" I screamed.

"Hey, don't you dare talk to me like that," said Frank taking the cigarette out of his mouth and waving it about.

"FOR CHRIST'S SAKE FRANK, WE'RE STANDING ON A GAS HOLDER! PUT THE BLOODY FAG OUT! WHAT'S THE MATTER WITH YOU MAN?"

Frank, now realising the cause of my fears, calmly announced that there was no chance of an explosion and that he always smoked up there because it was sheltered from the wind.

"Well not while I'm up here you won't mate," I replied and made straight for the staircase down, fully expecting to be launched into orbit at any second.

After a few minutes, Frank also descended the stairs and then began a detailed explanation of why it was safe to stand on top of a full-up gasholder while smoking. I asked him why then there were several 'No Smoking' signs around the digester and he actually said they were there for the operatives' safety.

"So, what about your safety and mine?" I asked and his reply was the most ridiculous thing I have ever heard.

"Well, you and I are not likely to do anything so stupid as to light up in a dangerous place, are we, Dave?"

At this point, I gave up and simply told Frank that from now on he could make his inspections of the digester systems on his own. Subsequently, I told all the operatives about the incident and warned them all not to accompany Frank anywhere near a digester or a gasholder.

*****

Near electrocution at Lapwater Hall

Brentwood Urban District Council had a third sewage treatment works known as Lapwater Hall. It was a small, conventional percolating filter works and was operated by just two men. Neither of them had any electrical capability so whenever there was an electrical problem, they would call Frank or me and we would send an electrician to sort it out for them. Sometimes Frank would go himself and would do simple jobs like replacing fuses if that would correct the fault.

One day, shortly after the smoking incident at the Shenfield gasholder, I received a request from Frank to go to Lapwater Hall and take some cartridge fuses with me because one of the recirculation pumps had failed and there were no spares on site. I duly arrived on site to find him peering into the three-phase control cabinet of the pumps. The cabinet was fitted with a safety switch so that it was not live when the door was opened.

"Got your tools?" asked Frank, "I didn't bring any with me today."

Of course, I had tools with me so I answered in the affirmative and he told me a fuse must have blown but he couldn't tell which one because they were of the non-indicative type.

"OK," I said, "I'll test them all."

"Don't know how you can do that?" said Frank, "The circuit is dead when the doors open. Why not just replace them one at a time and see if the pump will run as each one gets replaced?"

Clearly, he had no idea how to check a fuse unless it was a self-indicting type and this is what gave rise to the next altercation.

I turned the safety switch with a pair of pliers so that the panel was live, then tested the circuitry on both sides of each fuse with a tester screwdriver and determined that two had failed. Having carefully turned off the safety switch I then went to my car to get a large screwdriver and two replacement fuses. When I got back, I noticed Frank looking at my tester screwdriver with a great deal of interest.

"This is a good tool," he said and, as I pushed the big screwdriver with both hands onto the first fuse terminal, added, "It's live Dave!"

Another SHIT happening!

The shock I received felt enormous. It went right up both arms and across my chest and I also felt a weird sensation in my ears as if somebody had struck a match in each one. Furthermore, my body recoiled violently and I found myself sitting on the ground, temporarily quite stunned. Fortunately, I recovered very quickly and bellowed those immortal words, "F*****G STUPID BASTARD!" adding, "PUT MY BLOODY TOOLS DOWN AND GET OUT OF MY SIGHT WHILE YOU'RE STILL SAFE!" Frank did precisely that and, when I had calmed down, I replaced the two fuses after, of course, turning the safety switch off again with my pliers.

What the foolish man had done was to turn the safety switch to enliven the panel, then tried the tester screwdriver to check the circuitry, exactly as I had done. Evidently, he had never realised the switch could be turned with the panel door open and he had never seen a simple tester screwdriver before. I couldn't believe anyone in such a high position could be so ignorant of basic safety practice or such simple tools.

When I arrived for work the following morning, the Chief Engineer summoned me to his office and sternly asked me to explain the reason for my outburst at Frank. My response was to relate the above matter plus the previous incident at the Shenfield digester. He was absolutely flabbergasted that Frank, a man in whom a lot of trust was placed, could have been so foolish. Subsequently, it was decided that I would only receive instructions from the Chief Engineer himself in future but that Frank would still have overall responsibility for sewage treatment. Thus a very difficult, awkward and impracticable hierarchy was created and it was time for me to start looking for another job.

*****

<u>Boy getting burnt in a manhole at the refuse tip.</u>

At that time Brentwood Urban District Council disposed of the town's refuse on a landfill site at an adjacent village called Coxtie Green. The site was actually a small valley through which there flowed a tiny stream that ultimately fed into a lake within the parkland. The park with its lake was a very popular recreation area so before refuse tipping began the stream had been completely piped right through the valley, thus, it was presumed, preserving the water quality in the lake. Along the pipeline several access manholes were constructed using concrete rings and, as the depth of refuse and soil rose up to fill the valley, additional rings were added. The joints between these rings actually leaked slightly and allowed leachate from the rotting refuse to pollute the little stream so the quality of water in the lake was somewhat compromised. Eventually, the manholes were up to eight or nine metres deep but never protruded much more than a metre above the tip surface. They were all topped off with a heavy-duty cast iron cover within a heavy frame; the total weight of each cast iron lid was therefore about one-fifth of a ton. They were never fitted to the tops of the manholes because every few months they had to be lifted off temporarily to allow additional concrete rings to be fitted as the refuse tip became deeper and deeper. In any case, it was assumed that nobody could move the covers and frames without a heavy lifting machine so there was no danger of children getting into the manholes.

WRONG! Determined kids can get in almost anywhere and I know because I used to be one!

Sure enough, the heavy covers were frequently found on the ground as the local urchins had levered and inched them aside until they lost balance and dropped off the concrete pipes. They then entered the manholes and climbed down the step irons to the landing stages, of which there were eventually three or four in each manhole shaft. Their game was to make secret hideouts or camps where they could get up to all sorts of mischief while hidden from the eyes of grown-ups and other spoilsports. One Sunday afternoon, SHIT happened!

When just such a spoilsport was walking his dog across a field close to the tip, he saw two boys climbing from a manhole. Changing direction, he hurried to see what mischief they were up to and suddenly saw a sheet of flame burst from the concrete ring together with a screaming child ablaze from head to foot. Fortunately for the boy, he had the presence of mind to roll him on the ground and put out the flames then rush to a telephone and call an ambulance but despite the rapid response and subsequent hospital treatment this child suffered very serious burns and was probably scarred for life.

The following day there was the usual 'court of enquiry' at the office and as expected the people involved with the landfill site all tried to 'cover their own backsides with boilerplate', what I have subsequently called the B.P.B.C.S. (Boiler Plate Backside Covering Syndrome). "It wasn't my fault, I warned them something like this might happen," became the common remark in conversations around every corner. One comment, however, came from none other than Frank who reckoned the cause of the problem must have been a build-up of methane in the manhole arising from the leachate through the joints in the concrete rings. I had already appraised him of the pollution occurring in the stream after heavy rainfall and that the Essex River Board Pollution Inspector was demanding some action be taken to prevent it. So it was that I was instructed to determine if there was indeed methane in the manholes and at what concentration, so along I went to the refuse tip with Paul, a highly experienced and, I thought, a very sensible colleague from the Drainage Engineering Department.

While I was setting up the gas detector Paul went to inspect the manhole in question but when I looked up, he had disappeared.

"Where are you, Paul?" I shouted as, gas detector in hand, I walked to the same manhole.

"Down here at the first landing," was the reply, "I can't smell any gas."

"Well methane doesn't have a smell, Paul," I cried, "Take the gas detector and lower it down."

"Course it does, it smells like rotten eggs. Everybody knows that. I thought you were a chemist."

"I am a chemist," I shouted, "It is hydrogen sulphide that smells like rotten eggs. Now take this gas detector and check for methane!"

Paul climbed the few feet of step-irons to the surface to get the gas detector and to my astonishment, I saw he was smoking a cigarette. "CHRIST PAUL, PUT THE BLOODY FAG OUT," I yelled, "YOU'RE AS BAD AS FRANK!"

"Oh, all right," said Paul irritably, "Keep your shirt on." and casually flicked the offending object straight back down the manhole as I braced myself for an earth-shattering explosion. Fortunately, nothing of the kind happened but my estimation of Paul's experience and common sense was shattered forever.

Subsequently, we tested all the manholes for both methane and hydrogen sulphide but found no trace of either gas in any of them. What was found, by Paul, was an empty tin that had contained petrol in the manhole where the accident occurred and in addition, there was a quantity of charred wood. We concluded that the boys had been lighting a fire in their hideout and the fire must have got out of control through the use of petrol. The Council used this as evidence in their defence but subsequently were doomed to lose the case of negligence brought against them because the site had been unsafe, unfenced and unattended. I believe they settled out of court in favour of the unfortunate child.

The memory of that case served me in good stead over the years and undoubtedly helped me to prevent similar problems elsewhere.

*****

Auto-sampler marked Danger Poison Gas

There were many surface water sewers in the Brentwood Council area that discharged into watercourses managed by the Essex River Board. The local pollution inspector had complained that foul water occasionally discharged from one of them, so I was asked to investigate the matter. I had obtained an automatic sampling machine, which was a new item on the market at that time, that comprised a cylindrical container holding 24 sample bottles, each of which was connected to a suction manifold with a length of flexible plastic tubing and each connector was fitted with a spring-loaded valve. All the bottles had to be evacuated with a powerful vacuum pump before use and once emptied of air each one was closed off with its spring-loaded valve. A clockwork-powered, rotating release arm was then set to trip the valves at hourly intervals, thus collecting 24 separate samples of the water over one day. The machine was positioned beside the outfall to the stream with its suction neatly placed at the bottom of the 36-

inch surface water pipe. Just to be sure it would not be interfered with, I placed a notice beside it on a wooden post. It read "Brentwood Urban District Council" and KEEP OFF in large red letters. Of course, it would be safe.

Was I really so naïve? Did I actually believe the local louts would really leave the thing alone? Well, I certainly knew better the following day when I found the sampling machine lying on its side in the water fifty metres further downstream. It was badly scuffed and quite battered but at least the padlocks holding its cover in place were still intact. Nevertheless, several of the sample bottles inside it were smashed and of course, there were no usable samples of the surface water. Of the notice so neatly screwed onto its post, there was no trace at all. Clearly something else was required to prevent further SHIT happenings of this nature so it was reported to the local police who promised to keep an eye on it for me, provided of course they could spare the manpower from their hard-pressed, short-staffed force.

A few days later the newly painted and almost dent-free sampling machine was ready for a second try. It had been fitted with two lugs to which a stout chain could be attached and it was my intention to chain it to the safety handrails around the concrete wall of the surface water outfall so at least it wouldn't be kicked down the stream this time. As an afterthought, I had also carefully painted a skull and crossbones on the cover in bright orange paint with the words DANGER POISON GAS in large letters underneath.

Well, that kept the local vandals at bay and I was able to collect the full 24 samples the following day and indeed managed to do so for a further couple of days too. Unfortunately, however, I didn't allow for the diligence of the hard-pressed, short-staffed, local constabulary who went to keep an eye on the sampling machine for me as promised. An officer saw the sign and immediately went to the Council offices to complain that poisonous gas had been left in a large green cylinder in a public place where children were likely to play. He said it must be removed forthwith as it was a serious danger to the public. Even though I subsequently explained why I had painted the sign on the thing I was obliged to remove it or paint over the sign to avoid complaints from the local populace. One officer actually suggested I should set this portable sampling machine in concrete to prevent it being vandalised and seemed quite delighted when I sarcastically told him that with ideas like that, he could become Chief Superintendent in a couple of years!

So once more the sampler's casing was painted plain green and sure enough the next day it was vandalised again and half the sample bottles were destroyed. Almost unbelievable; I gave up!

*****

Alf's cat versus a stoat.

The treatment works at Shenfield was provided with two rather nice staff houses, one of which was occupied by Alf, the works foreman, and his family. They were the proud owners of a fat, lazy, black and white, neutered tomcat that was always lying in the middle of the works access road right in front of their house. Many times vehicles had to stop and wait for this bloated moggy to move out of the way before they could enter or leave the site and it was cursed by almost everybody except its owners. Frequently I had driven over the top of the cat and it didn't budge because it undoubtedly knew the car wheels were not going to touch it. Nobody really wanted to hurt it but I think secretly everyone wanted its tail to get squashed by somebody else's car so it would keep away from the road.

The works had sludge drying beds equipped with a monorail system for taking the dried cake to a tipping area that was sufficient for several years' storage. After this time the cake was well weathered and could be used as a soil conditioner so it was taken away by a contractor over a period of two weeks. The frequent lorry traffic in and out of the works had disturbed Alf's cat so much that it no longer loafed in the middle of the access road and instead took to its sedentary pastime next to the monorail train shed, close to the sludge tip.

As the sludge was shovelled up by the contractor's front loader, rabbits were frequently seen running away from the area as their warrens were destroyed. Indeed many hundreds of them had taken up residence in the sludge cake, which was just like a rich loamy soil and covered with all manner of green leafy foliage; ideal for the animals. Alf's cat just ignored them all. It was too lazy to chase them and probably too fat and slow to catch them anyway. It just lay there day after day, swishing its tail occasionally and only responding to its owners when they brought it food. Little did the creature know that SHIT would soon happen for it and rather painfully so!

61

One day as I was checking on the contractor's progress a large stoat was disturbed by the shovel and it ran towards the monorail train shed. It was a beautiful sleek and fast-moving creature, undoubtedly well fed and fit from its plentiful rabbit diet but it came to a sudden halt as it spotted the rounded shape of the overfed black and white moggy. The cat itself became instantly alert and for the first time in ages was seen to stand up and take notice. Alf, who was standing nearby, picked up a stone and threw it at the stoat but to no avail. Clearly, it was going for the cat and began to rear up and dance from left to right as it tried to mesmerise its opponent. But this was no timid defenceless bunny!

The stoat's lunge at the cat's throat was lightning fast but thwarted by an even quicker swipe from a fat paw full of razor-sharp claws. The resulting clash became a screeching howling fur ball rotating at high speed with blood, bits of flesh, fur, snot and sparks flying out of it for several minutes until suddenly it stopped. What a fight! The most vicious and violent I have ever seen! One of them was surely dead and the other was doubtless seriously injured as, bespattered with blood, Alf's now red, black and white cat, breathing heavily and bleeding from several wounds, limped painfully away from its fallen foe, no longer the detested bloated moggy but a well-respected fighting beast.

Alf learnt to respect the animal still further when he went to pick it up because it was still so pent up with fury that it instantly attacked its master, raking his arm severely with its claws and screeching like a miniature leopard. In fact, it was a couple of hours before the cat was calm enough to be taken to the vet, where it had its wounds stitched and required stoat flesh to be extracted from the sheaths of its claws to enable them to retract properly. Some of Alf's flesh may well have been there too because his lacerated arm was wrapped up for over a week!

Who would have thought that a place as mundane as a sewage treatment works could provide such entertainment? Fantastic!

Thereafter the fat black and white cat lazing in the middle of the access road was either carefully driven around or over very slowly so as not to harm or even disturb the 'Champion Stoat Killer' of Shenfield.

*****

Derek on the dumper truck.

It was a general policy to employ anybody who was considered fit to do the job in question and so it was that a young fellow named Derek worked at Nags Head Lane sewage treatment works. Derek was registered as being Educationally Sub-normal and therefore required fairly close supervision at all times. Nevertheless, he was a healthy and strong young man and made an excellent general labourer. When told to sweep the paths and site roads he would just get on with it until he was told to stop and do something else. The laboratory, the offices, mess-room, toilets and showers were all kept clean and tidy by Derek and he also did his share of shovelling and digging when necessary but was never allowed to touch any controls of pumps or machinery or operate any valves etc.

One summer while I was on my two weeks holiday, a rather foolish operative decided to teach Derek to drive the dumper truck so that he could have more interesting work to do. Even Bob, the Works Foreman, had considered this to be a good idea and allowed Derek to drive the machine with the other man seated next to him on the mudguard, a strictly illegal practice even before the Health and Safety at Work Act became law. Apparently, the dumper never exceeded a good walking pace and Derek began to get the hang of it after about a week of these 'driving lessons'.

When my holiday had finished, I returned to work on the following Monday and saw to my amazement that Derek was sitting on the driving seat of the dumper truck. The foreman, Bob, told me that Derek could now drive the vehicle and begged me to allow him the chance to show how well he had learnt. Reluctantly, I agreed and the next minute the other operative jumped on the mudguard beside Derek and they started to move off.

"Can't do that," I yelled, "it's illegal to have two men on a dumper like that. You'll have to get off and walk beside it." So the man jumped off and started walking beside the truck but the walk became a trot as the vehicle gathered speed downhill towards the outfall and the trot became a run as Derek began to panic.

Then SHIT really happened!

The poor chap looked around for help and just then one of the dumper's big front wheels hit the kerb, causing Derek to bounce off the seat. Now he was hanging on for dear life but was treading very hard on the accelerator pedal. The dumper roared across the site outpacing all of us running as hard as we could to catch it and all the while the terrified young man on board was screaming like a banshee. It described a great arc across the grassed area towards the sludge storage bays but came to a shuddering stop as it collided with a large raised concrete manhole. Unfortunately, Derek didn't come to a stop with the vehicle but carried on through the air for a few metres before landing very heavily on the grass.

When we caught up with him Poor Derek was a gibbering wreck, wide-eyed, dribbling and shaking like a leaf from head to foot. It must have taken the best part of an hour to calm him down sufficiently to walk him back to the mess-room, where he sat on a chair for the rest of the morning hunched up and sucking his thumb. Later on, he had returned to his normal self apart from a bruise on his shoulder caused by his heavy landing and otherwise was seemingly none the worse for wear. In the afternoon he did his job of mopping the floors and cleaning the benches in the laboratory, mess-room and locker room. He cleaned the showers and toilets and kept himself busy until it was time to go home, when he waved to everyone as he rode his bike through the gateway.

About an hour later, I received a telephone call from Derek's mother, asking where he was because he had not yet returned home and was about forty minutes late. I told her that Derek had left the site on time and not to worry because he may have met a friend or someone from the Mencap Organisation and got delayed. I was sure he would be home soon, I told her. A few minutes later, however, I received another call, this time from the hospital, telling me that there had been an accident in Brentwood High Street and Derek had been knocked off his bike. Though having only sustained a bruised shoulder, the same injury he received at work that day as it transpired, he was howling and very aggressive. It had taken a while for the medical staff to find out who he was, that he was on his way home and where he actually lived and worked. They tried to call his mother but got no reply, undoubtedly because she was calling everybody she could to find out where he was. In desperation, they called the works number. After confirming I knew Derek the nurse asked if there was anything wrong with the chap because they could find no sign of head injuries that may have caused his apparent dementia. "Yes," I said, "he is educationally sub-normal and also registered with Mencap* because he is mentally sub-normal too."

"OK," she replied, "all is revealed now. There's no need to keep him here any longer now we've calmed him down. Please just confirm his address and we'll make sure he gets home as soon as we can. By the way, is everybody at that sewage works a bit strange?"

Yes, it was the same senior nurse who had chewed me off about a year earlier when I took Charlie to the hospital with his face burnt! After confirming Derek's address, I felt obliged to tell her what I wanted to tell her before about her nasty superior attitude and her likeness to a fat, dumpy version of Hitler. She put the phone down!

Derek, or more likely his mother, decided he should stay at home, sick, for a week and before he returned to work, I frequently lectured all my staff to be aware of his condition and not do anything so silly again as to try teaching him to drive. I remain convinced it was the events of that day that caused him to have the accident on his way home and have felt rather guilty about it ever since.

*****

Strawberry crop lost.

Close to the sewage works in Nags Head Lane was a sizeable farm in those days. I recall it was a mixed farm where they kept cattle and sheep as well as growing various vegetables and cereal crops and two fields adjacent to the plant were used for growing strawberries. It was a pick your own*site, which is very popular in South East England because the public can get fresh fruit quite cheaply and enjoy picking them at the same time, often with the whole family of parents and children involved.

Unfortunately, the weather had been particularly dry and the crop was in dire need of watering but the farmer had no suitable water supply close-by except for the stream into which the treated effluent discharged. He, therefore, set up a pump powered by a tractor power take-off facility and drew water from the stream to irrigate the fields. His strawberry crop then grew very nicely but he was soon informed by the Essex River Board inspector that as he didn't have an abstraction licence, he would have to stop taking water from the stream and furthermore was likely to face a heavy fine.

The farmer was bewailing his fate to me a few days later across the works boundary fence so I suggested to him that he should take the water directly from the treated effluent channel. The flow was pretty well guaranteed, there was no need for an abstraction licence and the water quality was barely different from the stream anyway because it made up about 60% of the stream's flow during dry weather. Provided watering was not done less than five days before picking the crop it would be perfectly safe because the coliform count in the effluent was negligible. The next day the tractor and pump were repositioned and the strawberry fields received all the water they needed for the next few weeks.

It was a bumper crop that year and the farmer made a substantial profit. He was so pleased that he sent over several boxes of delicious ripe strawberries for the works staff to share on two or three occasions. It was great for us because we didn't actually have to do anything for it.

Later on, a deal was struck with the same farmer whereby his people would cut the grass on a sizeable piece of land that was within the sewage works boundary but was beyond the capability of the works staff to maintain. The Council's Parks Dept. was at full stretch and also unable to maintain this 15 or so acres so it was agreed that the farmer would cut the grass, let it lie for a while and then bale it for use as cattle feed on his own property. The field was maintained for free and the cows got several hundred bales of very cheap, good quality hay. The farmer was very happy when the area was finally cleared and he walked across it to make sure there were no places the baler had missed. When he came back to my office, however, he was pretty upset because during his walk around the field he had somehow lost his wallet from his pocket and it contained a lot of money. He searched everywhere he had walked but couldn't find it.

"Never mind," I assured him, "I'll get all the staff to look for it. I'm sure, we'll find it for you."

"Well," he said, "there's a reward for whoever finds it. Please tell them it'll be a good one!"

All the staff were organised into a line to search the field together and within half an hour the wallet was found by one of the operatives. As promised, the fellow received a generous reward from the farmer and surprisingly, the man was so honest that he hadn't even opened the wallet to see how much it contained.

Now we had a really friendly neighbour, an unusual phenomenon at a sewage treatment works because most of the neighbours usually complain about nasty smells, noisy machinery, weeds being spread from our land to theirs, too many vehicles entering and leaving the plant, ugly structures and buildings for them to look out upon etc. etc. Very rarely are people happy when there is a sewage works near their property, even though in many cases the works was there before they decided to move in.

The following year, we had another very dry spell as the strawberry plants were maturing and beginning to approach flowering, so our friendly farmer neighbour started watering them every day with the treated effluent. Everyone expected another bumper crop but after about two weeks of intensive watering, SHIT happened!

As I arrived for work on Monday morning the farmer, no longer our friendly neighbour was already waiting for me. "What the hell have you been doing with this bloody plant?" he squawked. "The effluent's gone off and all my bloody strawberry plants have died over the weekend!"

Incredulous, I suggested we should take a look and immediately went to the effluent outfall, where the water discharging to the stream was almost gin clear and attracting a lot of small fish.

"Looks pretty good to me old chap," I responded. "It was like this all last week and I can't imagine it was any different over the weekend. You haven't been putting any pesticides on the fields, have you?"

"NO, I BLOODY HAVEN'T," came the reply at a deafening volume, "IT'S YOUR BLOODY EFFLUENT THAT'S KILLED THEM! DON'T TRY TO GET OUT OF IT BY BLAMING ME!"

Feeling somewhat affronted, I asked to see the stricken crop and what I saw was absolutely incredible. There was hardly anything in the regimented rows of once-promising strawberry plants that hadn't wilted and sagged down to the soil. Clearly, the crop was ruined but I could not believe it was as a result of watering it with what was obviously a high-quality treated effluent.

"Well, I can understand how you feel about it," I assured him, "but you can't just say it's our fault or the effluent quality has gone off. You'll have to find out what's actually killing the plants before you jump to conclusions like that. Can you get some plant and soil analysis done? I'm not equipped to do that kind of testing in my little laboratory."

The farmer said he could get the analysis done at the Melton Mowbray Agricultural Research Centre, so we collected a few plants and a sample of soil that were then sent off for analysis.

Imagine my chagrin when the results were produced a week or so later and we were informed that the plants had all succumbed to Boron poisoning. Apparently, strawberry plants, among others, have a very clearly defined threshold level of tolerance to this element of just a few parts per million and when the concentration in their tissues exceeds this limit even by a tiny fraction the plants wither and die. Boron is, of course, present in most household detergents in the form of sodium tetraborate, which is used as a foam promoter.

Domestic sewage contains a lot of household detergent from everyone's washing and at Brentwood, in those days there were also two substantially sized laundries on the catchment. The detergents themselves, being biodegradable, would have been broken down by the treatment process but the boron would have remained in the effluent from the works. Thus there was no doubt that the strawberry crop was destroyed that year by watering it with our otherwise first-class treated effluent. There was nothing we could have done about it but the farmer never forgave us and remained, for some peculiar reason, convinced that we had done it deliberately.

So remember that if you grow strawberries in your garden and there's a drought, don't water them with the wastewater from the family washing machine because you're likely to kill them!

*****

U.K.O.P. helicopter stopping next to sewer construction.

When I worked for Brentwood Urban District Council the Ford Motor Company had their British and, I believe, their European head offices in Warley, which was within the Brentwood U.D.C. area. Their Experimental and Design centre was also there, making a huge combined office and laboratory complex. Frequently helicopters would be seen taking off or landing at this complex and people began to think that every helicopter seen flying in the Brentwood area was on its way either to or from Ford. Every day a helicopter would be seen at around 11.00 am flying almost straight over the sewage treatment works in Nags Head Lane at quite a low altitude and there would nearly always be the comment made by someone, "Ford executives on their way to Dagenham!" Ford at Dagenham in Essex was at that time one of the biggest factories in Britain and the only place in Southern England sporting blast furnaces for the smelting of iron, in this case, to manufacture steel for making cars.

The Council was having a new sewer constructed at the edge of the Warley district and I frequently drove past the construction site offices. Occasionally I would go to the site just to see what progress had been made and how much closer the new pipeline was to its junction with the main sewer into Nags Head Lane treatment works. One day, while chatting with Maurice, the Senior Drainage Engineer for the Council, the 'Ford' helicopter came thumping along,

68

presumably on its way to Dagenham, but on this occasion, it circled and then hovered directly overhead for a minute or two. It then circled once more and continued on its usual route towards the Dagenham factory.

"I wonder what that was all about," remarked Maurice, "perhaps he lost his bearings for a minute!"

"That's a bit unlikely Maurice!" I replied. "He comes that way virtually every day so he must know his way by now. It's hardly a long-distance flight, is it?"

The matter was then forgotten.

Maurice came to the treatment works a few days later to pick up some drawings and he told me that the helicopter had circled and hovered two or three more times on its way over the sewer construction site but nobody could figure out what the pilot was doing. How strange!

The next time I drove past the construction site, I particularly wanted to ask Maurice about some issue at the treatment works and just as I reached his site office the helicopter came over again. Sure enough, it circled and hovered for a minute or two and then to everybody's astonishment it began to descend and landed less than 100 metres from the site huts. Its engine was cut and the rotor blades finally came to a stop as a man alighted from the aircraft carrying some rolled-up papers. He made straight for the site office and Maurice strode out to meet him.

"Good morning," he said proffering his right hand, "I'm the Line Inspector from U.K.O.P. Are you from the Council?"

"Yes, I'm from the Council," replied Maurice, "Who the hell's U.K.O.P. and what are you doing landing a helicopter on this site?"

The Line Inspector pointed out that he didn't land the helicopter, the pilot did! U.K.O.P., he explained, stood for United Kingdom Oil Pipelines. "Those pipelines are of special strategic importance to the nation and are inspected frequently from the air," he said, "in this particular case on a daily basis at the moment."

Apparently, the sewer construction was getting very close to this U.K.O.P. line and he needed to know precisely where it was going. Very special permission was required to cross the U.K.O.P. line and it would have to be crossed from below rather than from above so it might not even be possible to do it with the gravity sewer that the Council was building. He also pointed out that if the line was damaged it could cost up to a million pounds for every hour it was unserviceable. He, therefore, asked for full details of the sewer's planned route and Maurice was told that our construction works could not pass a particular line shown on a diagram of the area that he left at the site. Telephone numbers were exchanged and the Line Inspector returned to the helicopter, which once more roared into the skies and disappeared from view.

It so happened that the new sewer would not interfere in any way with the U.K.O.P. line but the Council received no detailed information as to its exact position, depth or size. The only information received was that it was under great pressure when in use, that it was of all stainless-steel construction and that it carried all kinds of oil to various locations.

We subsequently discovered that the routes of U.K.O.P. lines are marked for aerial recognition by special coloured cones that may be located beside roads, railway lines or even farm gateways. Their strategic importance was clearly demonstrated at the time of the national strike by oil tanker drivers during the Thatcher Government years. The strike had absolutely no effect upon fuel supplies for power stations, airports and the like.

And Ford? Well, we now knew that the daily helicopter flight across the treatment works was not going to the Dagenham factory with their executives after all. In fact, most of the Ford helicopter services, I believe, went to Stansted Airport, where Ford had an international check-in desk all of their own.

*****

Chapter 5

Sewage Works Manager at Bishops Stortford Urban District Council

The Council had been advised by the Lee Conservancy Catchment Board to appoint a manager for the new treatment works long before the completion of the project in order for him to become properly acquainted with the new plant, the temporary treatment facility and the remaining irrigation system. Their reasoning was that transition to the new treatment systems should be performed under the instruction and guidance of an experienced manager to ensure there would be as few problems as possible. Fortunately for me, I was recommended for the job by none other than the Deputy Protection of Water Officer of the Lee Conservancy Catchment Board and, after my interview at the Council, was offered it and therefore started work at Bishops Stortford in late 1971.

*****

My mother's innocence of condoms at B/Stortford Oxidation Ditch.

When I was appointed as Sewerage and Sewage Treatment Manager at Bishops Stortford Urban District Council, the new treatment works was still very much under construction. A large, temporary treatment unit had been built to deal with approximately sixty per cent of the incoming sewage but the remainder was still being treated by land irrigation. The temporary treatment unit comprised a butyl rubber-lined split-channel oxidation ditch based on the Dutch 'Pasveer'* system. Aeration was provided by two 'Kessener' brushes* that rotated in the common channel. In addition, there were two large sludge digester/thickener tanks which were lined with paving slabs. The temporary unit was cheaply constructed but efficient in its operation and effectively freed up a large proportion of the land area for construction of the new works over a period of two years or so. At that time the archaic pumping station, however, with its single electric pump and diesel-powered standby pump, remained in use together with its completely inefficient screens. In consequence, the oxidation ditch was inundated with trash and the Kessener brushes needed frequent inspection and clearing of it.

Over the Easter weekend, due to staff holidays, there was nobody available to inspect the brushes so I volunteered to do the job myself on both Saturday and Sunday. On Saturday, there was quite a lot of trash on one brush and in consequence, I spent almost an hour clearing it off; a rather distasteful job but very necessary to ensure reliable operation of the machine.

It so happened that my mother was visiting my wife and me for the weekend and she asked me what I had needed to go to work for so I thought that rather than try to explain to her what it was all about I would take her there on the following day and she could see what I was doing and also get a chance to look at the new plant that was under construction. I thought she might actually be impressed.

Sure enough on the following day, my dear mother was almost agog when I showed her the partially built laboratory and explained what would be done in it. She was equally enthusiastic when I walked her around the treatment plant and tried to explain to her what would eventually be happening in the half-built concrete structures.

"And what's it all for then?" came her searching question.

"To treat the sewage from that town over there and turn it back into clean water," I replied, "to stop pollution of the River Stort."

"What? You mean everyone's lavatory will be emptied here then?" she asked in an astonished tone.

"In a manner of speaking," I told her, "it will actually be pumped up here from the collection sewer."

I then took my mother to see the temporary oxidation ditch, which rather, fortunately, had no sign of trash on either of the aeration brushes so required no action on my part.

"There you are," I said, "all that dirty water comes in here and after it's been in this aeration tank for several hours it gets settled in that other section and goes out over the weir as clean water."

"Oh, I say," said my mother, "that's wonderful. I didn't know they did things like that with it. I thought they just shovelled it all up!"

Although the remark elicited a slight snigger from me, I decided not to continue the discussion to find out where on earth she, and very likely most other people too, thought they shovelled it to and what they did with it after shovelling. The 'crack of the day', however, came a little later as we were walking back past the aeration brushes on the oxidation ditch.

"Aah, look at all those little ducks swimming about around that machine," she said.

"Ducks? Where Mum? I can't see any ducks," was my reply in disbelief as she pointed to the end mounting the drive motor and gearbox for one of the brushes.

"Look, they're bobbing up and down where the water's all swirling around," she persisted.

Now realising what she was looking at, though how my mother could have mistaken them for a group of ducks swimming about I have no idea, I just had to enlighten her that they were actually sheath contraceptives that had collected a bit of air in the end and were floating around in the turbulence of the aeration paddles.

"WHAT?" she said, "You mean those rubber 'dooly' things that men use? How do they get in here? Surely, they don't throw them down the lavatory, do they? It's disgusting, there should be a law against it! There must be some filthy people around here!" Then came the expected remark, "David why don't you find a different job?"

Though bursting with laughter at my mother's outburst I could still almost feel her disappointment that I wasn't running a little chemist shop like old Mr Gower had. Ah well, c'est la vie as they say in France!

*****

Harry has arm just out of the pump as I start it up.

Before the new works was completed at Bishops Stortford much of the sewage flow from the town came via a pumping station in Southmill Road. The pumping station was close-by the River Stort canal and directly opposite a large pub that had a sizeable car park in front of it.

I had noticed a considerable reduction in the incoming flow to the works for about an hour and decided to have a look around the town to see if there was anything obviously wrong; Southmill Road pumping station was the obvious first port of call. As I parked my car next to the pumping station, I noticed that the Operative's car was parked in the pub car park. Harry was possibly having a sly pint while doing his rounds!

The pumping station door was not locked so I walked inside, only to find that both the pumps were switched off. The sound of overflowing water was quite loud and drowned out any other noises from the pumping well. I presumed that Harry must have nipped out for a quick one at the pub and forgotten to turn the pumps on again. There was no notice hanging on the control cabinet doors to say that the pumps were under maintenance and no sign of anybody downstairs, although I had not actually descended the ladder to have a good look around. "Harry!" I yelled, "What's going on down there?" but received no reply, confirming in my mind that Harry was indeed in the pub. Therefore, I turned to the control cabinet and switched on the Number 1 pump, only to miss a catastrophic SHIT happening by a tiny fraction of a second.

Harry was not in the pub but in the pumping well. Furthermore, he had heard my yelling and had actually answered me but his voice was drowned out by the sound of overflowing water. He was actually unblocking the Number 1 pump and had literally removed his arm from within the machine a split second before I switched it on. The terrified scream that subsequently issued from his lips, however, was not drowned out by the sound of overflowing water. Indeed it was loud enough for me to hear well above all the other pumping station noises, including the sound of the newly started pump. In some state of shock, I stopped it again and rushed down the ladder to the pumping well, half expecting to find a bloody mess of poor old Harry. Instead, I found him chalk-white and almost frozen to the spot with shock but otherwise, fortunately, unscathed.

Of course, there was an immediate exchange of foul language between Harry and me and indeed there had been some carelessness on both sides, not to mention some downright stupidity that should never have happened. Yes, I should have gone down into the well and checked if Harry was there before starting the pump but Harry should have hung the CAUTION signs on the pump control panels to indicate that someone was working on the pumps. Furthermore, he should have removed the starter fuses and/or locked the power switch OFF before sticking his arm in the bowl of the pump. It could so easily have been chopped off above the elbow! In any case, the Number 2 pump had already been unblocked and could easily have been started again so there would have been little reason for me to go to Southmill road in the first place. The door to the pumping station should have been properly secured to prevent anybody else entering the building while Harry was working on the pumps.

To be fair to poor old Harry, he, like many others in those days, had never received safety training and was therefore quite contemptuous of the new rules associated with the Health and Safety at Work Act that had only recently been introduced. It was my job to put that matter right, not only with Harry but with all my other staff and thereafter I held regular Safety Meetings to ensure everyone knew his responsibilities.

When Harry had finally calmed down after his close brush with disaster, I asked him why his car was parked in the pub car park. "Because it's easier to get out of there onto the main road," was his immediate reply, "and because I often have my lunch in there when I'm finished here." That seemed a good excuse to take him into the pub, have lunch and a pint, so drawing a line under a somewhat frightening event.

Subsequently, the pumps at Southmill Road became blocked again but the cause of the blockage was now identifiable. It was caused by the contractors who were rebuilding parts of the sewerage system in the town, allowing debris on a large scale to be washed back into the sewer feeding the old pumping station. They were duly instructed to take away the trash, bits of broken concrete and brickwork etc. properly in future instead of washing it down the pipeline!

Eventually, Southmill Road pumping station was bypassed and what was really an old eyesore vanished from sight.

*****

Row over smoking at B/S Council Public Health Committee Meeting.

At Bishops Stortford Urban District Council, as with most district councils before the formation of the Water Authorities in England and Wales, sewerage and sewage treatment came under the auspices of the Public Health Committee, which was a committee made up of lay councillors under an elected chairman.

It was necessary for certain Council officials to attend the regular committee meetings and as the Sewerage and Sewage Treatment Manager, I was obliged to attend them if called to do so. On one occasion I was called to attend to discuss potential staffing levels for the new treatment works which was expected to become operational sometime during the next financial year. This discussion item was near the bottom of the agenda so I knew I was in for a pretty boring evening listening to discussions about numerous other public health issues about which I knew little or nothing and cared even less about. Little did I know that I would be the one to cause a SHIT storm that would turn the evening into a thoroughly entertaining event.

It started with an issue about a fish and chip shop that had been forced to close down because the proprietor had no facilities for washing his hands when handling food. The Chief Public Health Officer was berated by one of the councillors for being unfair to the shop owner by not giving him time to sort the problem out. The retort came that the shop had been operating for over a month with no facilities even though the proprietor had been warned about closure weeks beforehand. And so it went on, with people getting hot under the collar and polite insults being exchanged between those councillors supporting the shopkeeper and those supporting the Chief Public Health Officer. Meanwhile, there were two reporters present from the local press, who were feverishly scribbling notes the whole time in preparation, no doubt, for some sensational publications on the matter in that week's local papers!

More discussions ensued with more arguments between the councillors until a point was reached where the Committee needed to go into private session. Members of the press were asked to leave and there was a ten-minute break before resuming the important business of the evening.

As the group reassembled, I noticed one of the councillors was smoking a cigarette and feeling the need for nicotine myself I lit up a Capstan Full Strength and inhaled deeply. Ashtrays were provided all around the table so I could not imagine there would be any objection to me smoking. The discussion droned on but after a minute or two, a piece of paper was passed around the table to me. It was from the Deputy Clerk of the Council and read: "Mr Marpole, please put the fag out. You're not allowed to smoke in Public Health meetings."

Now feeling a bit miffed I was moved to write a reply. "Why me? What about the councillors? One of them is smoking too."

When she received the reply the Deputy Clerk handed it to the Council's Nominated Doctor,* a woman in this case, who had been quietly sitting in the meeting so far without showing any interest in the proceedings at all, presumably only concerned about receiving her fee! The note woke her up, however, and SHIT subsequently happened very vociferously. The doctor immediately rose and asked the chairman to stop the discussion for a moment, which he did. She then launched into a tirade about smoking in the Public Health Committee meeting, banging the table and shouting that it was not allowed; I dogged out my cigarette immediately.

"Who the bloody hell says so?" replied the smoking councillor at the top of his voice. "There's no rule that says we can't smoke in this meeting or any other bloody meeting! How dare you tell me what I can or can't do, you're not even an elected councillor, you're only a bloody hired help!"

The chairman tried to calm things a little by saying, "Language sir, language. There's no need for swearing!"

"And there's no need for bloody Doctor Dolittle over there to interrupt a formal discussion in this committee just because she doesn't like tobacco!" yelled another councillor. "My colleague's right. I've sat on this committee for a number of years and I don't remember any rules being introduced about no smoking. Who does she think she is eh?"

At this, the doctor all but exploded, "Don't you ever call me Dr Dolittle again!" she squawked, "I don't have to be here with morons like you! I can quite easily resign you know!"

"Best thing you could do too. There's plenty of other medics to take your place!" came the acid reply.

At this, the chairman stood up. "Gentlemen, gentlemen, doctor, please, please stop this! Let's resolve to bring up the matter of smoking in committee meetings with the full Council. We are here to conduct public health business and there is still a lot to do tonight. What I propose is that we leave things as they are right now. If you wish to smoke a cigarette please do so but I would ask you to consider the other people present and try to keep the smoke away from them. Are you happy with that?"

Grunted OK's came from all present except the Nominated Doctor, whose reply was a mumbled, "Just this once then but we must bring it to the full Council!"

After the verbal fracas, the public health matters were discussed in their order but interestingly, there were now two or three councillors who lit up cigarettes and one even lit a small cheroot. One of them even gestured to me that I should smoke a cigarette too if I wanted to. My reply was to silently mouth to him, "After the meeting, thanks."

When we finally dispersed from the meeting my boss, the Chief Engineer sidled up to me and asked for a cigarette. "I didn't bring any with me, David," he said, "and I was about to scrounge one off you when the shit storm started. Didn't dare ask you after that!"

Just a few days later, I went to the Post Office in the centre of town to renew my car tax for the year. There was a sizeable queue and I had to wait for about fifteen minutes to get to the counter. By then I was completely disinterested in my surroundings and took absolutely no notice of the person behind the counter.

"Want a fag mate?" he asked as I handed the documents over. It was the councillor who had called the Nominated Doctor Dr Dolittle. "That was quite a schimozzle the other night, wasn't it?" he said. "Silly old cow making all that fuss about someone having a smoke. Whatever next?"

I didn't disagree with him at the time but on reflection, I think she was the more sensible one. For sure there would be a rigid NO SMOKING policy in such a meeting now, not only in an English town council but more or less anywhere in the world.

*****

Chapter 6

Group Manager Bishops Stortford
with Thames Water, Lee Division

In April 1974, the Water Authorities were formed and took over responsibility for sewage treatment from the local councils. My area of responsibility was enlarged quite dramatically and I was now titled Group Manager for a number of treatment works and pumping stations together with two hundred miles or so of sewerage pipelines. There were several SHIT happenings to come!

*****

<u>Sludge spilling all over the road just as I pass in my car.</u>

The new Sewage Treatment Works at Bishops Stortford was finally up and running, although there was still a substantial amount of construction work to be completed. The incoming flow was gradually diverted to the new units and after a week or so the temporary oxidation ditch was no longer required. It was necessary therefore to remove its contents by pumping into the temporary sludge digester/thickening tanks which were equipped with dewatering facilities so that separated water could be diverted back to the inlet of the new works. Thus we were able to concentrate the disused activated sludge from the oxidation ditch and store it in the thickening tanks until the new digesters were completed and ready for operation.

At about the same time the new Water Authorities came into being and the local councils relinquished responsibility for sewage treatment, in this case to Thames Water. In the reorganisation, I was promoted to Group Manager and took responsibility for the operation of a further fourteen treatment plants plus their terminal pumping stations plus all the sewerage and its pumping stations too. The extra responsibilities made it necessary to travel around the area frequently because no additional supervisory staff had yet been appointed. Instructions were therefore given to the charge-hand at the Bishops Stortford plant, rather aptly named Wally, to keep an eye on the pumping and dewatering operation to ensure the sludge thickening tanks were not over-filled. Meanwhile, I went to sort out a problem at another works.

In the early afternoon, I was returning to the Bishops Stortford works via the Hallingbury Road alongside the now disused irrigation area. It was a sunny day in late May and the heat haze was causing a mirage effect on the road ahead. The car windows were open and I was calm and relaxed when suddenly SHIT happened with a vengeance.

Just as I reached the mirage, I realised it was nothing of the kind. Instead, the road surface was covered in water that was flowing down from the old irrigation area. I braked quite hard but there was another vehicle coming in the opposite direction that did not appear to brake at all. It was a Land Rover towing a trailer and we both hit the water at the same time, more or less as we passed each other. The other vehicle had much bigger wheels than my Ford Cortina so the spray from each of its three axles went much higher than the spray produced by my car, high enough to pour through my open windows. Of course, it soaked me completely as well as the inside of my car and that's when I discovered that it wasn't water! It was rancid activated sludge from the old oxidation ditch!

In just a few minutes, having driven onto the treatment works, I was the laughing stock for all the construction workforce and undoubtedly some of my own staff. Not for Wally the charge-hand, however, who was the recipient of my wrath and full verbal fury. What a 'wally' he was to forget about a roaring, six-inch diesel pump! Quickly he fled to turn off the pump and, with four other men, rushed to the irrigation area with spades and sandbags to divert the flow of sludge away from the Hallingbury Road. Fortunately, the diversion was completed in record time before the local schools closed for the day and thereby avoided cars, mothers and children getting sludge-coated which would otherwise have given rise to a stream of complaints.

To be fair, Wally the 'wally', as I now addressed him, did offer to clean the inside of my car for me but I decided to have it done by a professional valeting service close to my home. There was also a nearby dry cleaners where my work suit could be de-sludged.

Why did we always wear suits in those days? I must have spent thousands having the damned things dry-cleaned. They were always getting splashed with some form of shit! On this occasion, even though I had the jacket on a coat-hanger at the back of my car it still got coated in sludge! No wonder people tend to dress more casually for work these days.

*****

The Ehrwig (1)

The preferred method for the disposal of treated sewage sludge during my days in Thames Water was by spreading it onto farmland for use as a fertiliser or soil conditioner. The digested sludge was spread as slurry from special tanker vehicles and the treatment plant at Bishops Stortford was provided with a new type of tanker to do the work. One of these machines had been on loan from the manufacturers as a test unit. It was called The Ehrwig and was a self-loading, tractor-towed, tanker vehicle fitted with a special E.H.R.*slurry pump, powered by the tractor's power take-off facility. The pump had a lever-operated, three-way valve system whereby it could suck slurry into the tank, circulate the slurry within the tank or pump the slurry out of the tank via a high-level spreader nozzle at the rear of the machine.

The Ehrwig was successfully tested for a week on fields adjacent to the treatment plant and proved satisfactory except for its small capacity of only eight hundred gallons. This would cause time wasting if the machine was used on land much further away so it was decided to buy a much larger one of two thousand four hundred gallons capacity. The bigger machine required a far larger tractor to pull it so a seventy-five horsepower International Harvester machine was ordered too. Before the order was finalised the local suppliers asked us to test the new, revolutionary, automatic version of their tractor with the new Ehrwig and subsequently the machine was delivered to site, accompanied by three smartly dressed salesmen equipped with a very fancy cine camera.

The automatic tractor was duly put through its paces towing the empty Ehrwig around the site roads. The Operative driving the vehicle, a real country lad named Trevor, declared it to be a wonderful machine, better than any tractor he had ever driven in his life. The senior salesman was so pleased that he invited both of us to accompany them to lunch at a posh restaurant in town. Great! It just remained for the tractor to be tested and filmed filling the Ehrwig, pulling it full up and spreading the slurry on an adjacent field. This was my bright idea but necessary, I decided, to properly justify the additional cost of the automatic gearbox.

Whilst the Ehrwig was being filled Trevor and I stood close by the tractor, each relaxed and smoking a cigarette. It suddenly occurred to me that the tanker must be nearly full and I quickly climbed on top to look into the inspection manhole; it was about to overflow! I yelled at Trevor to stop filling and in his panic to turn the three-way valve to the circulate position he pulled the lever too far and instead opened the discharge line.

SHIT happened big time!

As the pump was running at top speed the discharge from the spreader nozzle became a thick, black, fan-shaped fountain of digested sewage sludge covering an arc twelve metres wide and ranging fifteen metres behind the Ehrwig. The blast of sludge was accompanied by screams from all three smartly dressed salesmen who were standing precisely in the spread zone, one of them actually operating the fancy cine camera which he immediately dropped and probably broke it. To say they were coated from head to foot would be an understatement because they were actually soaked right through to their underwear!

The pump was stopped after a few seconds and for a moment silence reigned. Suddenly that silence was shattered by howls of laughter from a dozen onlookers, all untouched by the sludge and their guffaws were of course accompanied by the foulest language ever heard from three smartly dressed salesmen. I approached them trying desperately to keep a straight face and asked if they were all right. "**!##@##!**!##@##**" was their only response and I was slightly taken aback. My feelings were restored however when Trevor, the Operative quietly said, "I expect it'll be my sandwiches for lunch then!"

After a remarkably quick rinse of their faces and hands, the salesmen got into their car and drove off, presumably to get showered, change their clothes and probably have the car valeted too! Everybody else just split their sides for the next hour or two.

It turned out that we found the automatic tractor was not really suitable for the job anyway so we had the manual gearbox version instead! The tractor had to be modified with an air braking system to serve the Ehrwig for use on the public roads. These air brakes were extremely fierce and undoubtedly contributed to the next SHIT happening involving this machine.

*****

The Ehrwig was in use transporting and spreading digested sludge onto cattle pasture fields a couple of miles from Bishops Stortford treatment works. One day Trevor telephoned me and said, "We've got a big problem with this Ehrwig. You'd better come down to Hallingbury and see for yourself." So I drove the two miles to see what had gone wrong.

I found a scene of absolute chaos. The Ehrwig was stuck in the middle of a small country lane into which it had been turning. The offside wheel bogey had been wrenched off by the force of severe braking and the lower edge of the tank had dug itself into the road surface, leaving the machine at an angle of about thirty degrees. There was a car travelling from the opposite direction with its front wheels in the roadside ditch and the thoroughly irate and extremely 'toffee-nosed' female driver of it complaining loudly to a policeman. It was actually her incompetent driving that had made Trevor apply the brakes very hard and this had caused the damage to the Ehrwig. There were two police cars parked up and two other policemen there. One of them was a more senior officer with a fancy uniform and he was marking a detailed checklist held on a clipboard. He was inspecting the Ehrwig very closely while muttering something about Construction and Use Regulations and when he saw me, he spoke with a very officious tone, "You the Works Manager?"

I replied in the affirmative with an equally officious tone.

"Well, this thing must be moved Mr Works Manager," he snapped, "and I mean right now!"

"Well, Mr Policeman," I replied, resisting the urge to call him Mr Plod*, "the trailer's full up and it weighs about twelve tonnes so it isn't going to be moved until it's emptied!"

"I don't want to know your problems," he bellowed, "just get this thing off the road and quick about it!"

Fortunately, discretion triumphed over my desire to tell Mr Plod where to go and instead I arranged for the sludge collection tanker-lorry to come and empty the Ehrwig.

About half an hour later the collection tanker arrived, driven by a slightly scatty Irishman fondly known to all as Ted the Tank. I asked Ted to connect his suction to the Ehrwig's filler pipe and empty out the sludge so we could get the machine lifted and moved. "Can't do that," said Ted, "it's a different fitting.

Mine's a Bauer type and that's a different pattern but never mind I can empty it from the manhole at the top." With those words Ted shinned up the access ladder quick as a flash and opened the inspection manhole. SHIT happened once again but this time it was even worse than before!

The Ehrwig had obviously been filled to the brim and as the manhole opened thick black sludge belched out of it across the sloping top of the tank straight over Mr Plod, his fancy uniform, his clipboard and the Construction and Use documents, which were completely destroyed. His face was black and sludge dripped from the peak of his cap. It couldn't have happened to a nicer person!

The other two policemen, howling with laughter, fled to their separate cars and locked themselves in. Ted ran to his lorry and scrambled into the cab while Trevor concealed himself behind a hedgerow so I decided it must be time for me to head back to the plant and I did so at a rate well in excess of the speed limit. Well, wouldn't you?

A couple of hours later Ted and Trevor returned to the treatment works in the collection tanker and with tears rolling down their faces related the rest of the story. After I left the scene Mr Plod had almost burst a blood vessel through hysterically screaming at the convulsive constable in his car until the man, still busting his gut with mirth, eventually opened the door and let him in before driving him back to the police station. Everyone witnessing this maniacal ranting of the sludge-soaked inspector, for that is what Mr Plod turned out to be, had aching sides from the jolly spectacle. Even the toffee-nosed* female who caused the accident deigned to giggle about it as her BMW was lifted unscathed from the roadside ditch.

Later, the remaining policeman arranged for a heavy breakdown lorry to lift the stricken Ehrwig, now devoid of sludge, to a level position and support it while it was very carefully towed off the public road. Fortunately, there were no repercussions from the incident. Nobody was injured, nobody's car was damaged and the Ehrwig was subsequently modified by the manufacturer. It gave excellent service for several years.

Mr Plod's failure to pursue the matter probably arose from a justifiable fear of ridicule by the rest of the local constabulary but for a while, I lived in trepidation lest I should be confronted by him following some minor infringement of the traffic laws.

*****

Theft of pay packets from my office.

When Thames Water took over sewage treatment from the local councils there was an immediate change to the way wages were paid to the workforce. All of them were paid weekly and hitherto had to go to their respective council offices each week to collect it or had alternatively received their pay packet at their place of work, either from their foreman or a pay clerk. The Water Authority was a vast organisation split up into various divisions; my group was within the Lee Division, the Head Office of which was a considerable distance away in Cheshunt. Payment of wages was, therefore, a massive exercise and each Division used special cash delivery companies with armoured vehicles toting money around to the various operational centres. The Loot Cart, as it was fondly known, used to arrive at roughly the same time every Thursday afternoon and stop outside my office. One man, wearing a protective helmet, goggles, padded clothes and Kevlar vest, would step from the cab and usually adjust the hang of his long truncheon while furtively looking around. He would then bang on the side of the vehicle, the chute with the loot would be opened from inside and he would bring a bag of pay packets into the office. These would be tipped onto my desk, counted and signed for, whereupon the man would go back to the vehicle, readjust the hang of his truncheon and climb back into the front cab ready to leave. All this would occur in the space of just a few minutes and hardly a word would be spoken.

The pay packets for those at the Bishops Stortford plant would usually be taken around to the workforce by the Assistant Manager/Chemist a Czechoslovakian fellow named George Jellicka, who was one of the most conscientious people I ever knew. I would always distribute the rest of the pay myself by driving around to the other treatment plants in my group. It was a real nuisance and, I suppose, not devoid of risk because there would have been a large amount of money in my car sometimes and there were many people that knew it, one or two of whom were rather unsavoury-looking characters, to say the least! The plant and the new sewerage system in the town were not yet completed so there were many contractors to-ing and fro-ing the site. Quite a few of these contractors were single-man businesses, comprising a tipper-lorry driven and operated by its owner; it was common knowledge that many of these characters were operating on the borderline of legality.

One Thursday, there was a rather nasty SHIT happening, the shockwaves from which rumbled for a very long time within Thames Water.

On this occasion, I was off-site at a small plant two miles away when the Loot Cart made its delivery to Bishops Stortford. I actually passed the vehicle on its way to the main road, undoubtedly heading for the neighbouring group at Hatfield. Most likely George had received the wage packets and would be awaiting my return, which was only a few minutes later. As I entered the office building, I heard the gent's toilet being flushed. I looked for George in the laboratory but saw it was empty and then the toilet flushed again. The door opened but it wasn't George that emerged from it. Instead, it was one of the tipper-lorry drivers, a particularly foul-mouthed individual, who appeared quite shocked to see me.

"Only went fer a piss mate! Sor right i'nit?" he mumbled as he hurried past me.

"Yes, I suppose so!" was my reply but I wondered for a moment why he had flushed the toilet twice after only a pee! Going to the door of my office I found it to be unlocked but surprisingly there was the sign-off sheet for the Loot Cart lying on my desk with George's signature on it. However, there were no pay packets. Just then George arrived holding the sign-off sheet for the plant's employees.

"Hello, George. Where did you put the pay packets old chap?" I enquired.

"Left them on the desk," came his reply. "I've paid everyone on the works. Look", as he handed me the sign off sheet.

"Well, they're not on the desk now George, are they?" I said, "Don't sod about. Where did you put them?" George looked at me with a wry smile on his face, "This is a joke David isn't it?" he asked.

"No, it bloody isn't, George!" I snapped, "WHERE'S THE BLOODY MONEY? YOU DIDN'T LOCK THE OFFICE DOOR! SOME BASTARD'S NICKED IT!"

Poor George, now ashen-faced, stumbled to my desk and tried to open the drawers, which were always kept locked, then pointing to the desktop squawked, "I LEFT THEM THERE! HONESTLY DAVID, JUST THERE! Oh my God!"

Throughout these few moments, there had been big tipper-lorries rumbling past the office and it suddenly occurred to me that I should check the gent's toilet, though what I expected to find there I did not know. As it transpired there was nothing unusual to be seen, all was tidy and there was nothing to see in the toilet pan.

George was now a gibbering wreck, asking what we should do and would he have to pay for the loss.

"Only if you pinched it, George, then they'll probably send you back to Czechoslovakia," I quipped but it was a little unfair because that was the biggest fear of George's life. He had escaped from the then Communist regime and eventually arrived in England having been a political refugee, first in Italy and then Sweden before coming to England to follow his Swedish girlfriend.

"I didn't steal anything David, please, please believe me!" he wailed.

"I know that you daft bugger!" I reassured him and then dialled 999 to report the theft to the police. This was followed by a call to the Divisional office to give them the news and a few calls to other works to inform the affected workforce that their pay would be delayed until tomorrow morning at least. As anyone would imagine, this news was received with a fair amount of blasphemy, even from the well-spoken people!

Although Bishops Stortford is actually a Hertfordshire town the Sewage Treatment works is located in Essex, as indeed were most of the plants in my group at that time. The first policeman to arrive was the local Sergeant from Hatfield Heath whom we knew well through previous dealings but this was the first time he had attended a crime scene at this site. Firstly, he took off his cap and asked if it would be all right to light his pipe in my office. I agreed and both George and I joined with him by smoking cigarettes.

"Any idea who took it?" He asked after being presented with all the facts.

"Not really," I replied, "but that little bloke who was in the toilet when I got back to the office has got to be on the list of possibles!"

A few moments later, I was able to point him out to the policeman, who instantly recognised him along with two or three other well-known dirt-lorry drivers that were obviously on his list of possibles too.

"Well this has got to be a job for the C.I.D," he said and promptly called in to Harlow Police Station, the largest one in the immediate area. He then knocked out his pipe, replaced his cap and went outside to speak to the drivers he had recognised, telling them all to remain on the site until the C.I.D. officers arrived, which they did after about fifteen minutes. Our local Sergeant had by then left the scene.

Into my office burst the most ill-mannered lout of a policeman, I have ever come across. He grabbed a chair, sat down and asked, "OK then, who's nicked the wage packets?" My response was to ask him who the hell he thought he was bursting into my office like that, where was his warrant card and when he thought he might learn some manners! This prompted him to stand up immediately, introduce himself as a C.I.D. sergeant and show me his warrant card. He then apologised for bursting into the office in such a rude way. I also threw in the comment that if I knew who had stolen the money it wouldn't be necessary for the C.I.D. to be involved. Subsequently, George and I related all the facts again and several of the tipper-lorry drivers were questioned. My list of possibles suspect was actually searched and his cab too but of course nothing was found. A monkey would have had time to hide the loot by then!

Nothing was found, no fingerprints were taken, nobody was arrested and nobody seemed to care except for the driver that was searched. When the police left he came to the window of my office and hurled a tirade of abuse at me in the foulest language possible but was told in no uncertain terms to shut up and get on with his work or he would be off the job by another owner-driver, with whom I had occasionally had a pint in my local pub over a game of darts. That fellow was the undisputed Mr Big of the tipper-lorry people in that area.

The following day, a car containing three men from the wages section at the Divisional office came to the site with replacement wage packets and insisted, for some strange reason, in taking me to the other treatment plants to pay the men concerned. Subsequently, manual employees were encouraged to have their wages paid by credit transfer to their bank accounts just like all non-manual staff were obliged to but although one or two opted for the change it was not made compulsory until after the Water Industry's National Strike several years later.

*****

A colleague's mate's dead rat placed on a bar in Hatfield.

When I was Group Manager at Bishops Stortford my neighbouring Group Manager, Roger was based at Mill Green, Hatfield. We were not particularly good friends but as work colleagues with similar daily issues and problems to face we got on well enough with each other. Occasionally, all the Lee Division Group Managers would be called to a meeting in one of the groups and it would be up to that GM to arrange for lunch at a local pub. When it was my turn, I took them all to a very nice pub in Great Hallingbury, just two miles from the treatment plant at Bishops Stortford. Roger, who thought of himself as a bit of a gastronomic expert, declared it to be excellent and subsequently often found some excuse to come over to my area so that we could go there for lunch.

Roger's problem was that he was a real Yorkshireman and he followed his County's motto as closely as possible:

'Ear all, see all, say nowt;
Eat all, sup all, pay nowt;
And if ever tha does owt for nowt –
allas do it for thysen.

Of course, I know that doesn't apply to Yorkshiremen any more than it does to any other people but in Roger's case, it was spot on. Several times I almost had to shame him into buying a round of drinks and on two occasions he claimed to have forgotten his wallet. Other work colleagues actually referred to him as Fish Hooks, even occasionally to his face but he remained unfazed by it.

There was one occasion, however, when Roger did the unimaginable thing of inviting me over to his Group in order to see some new equipment he had acquired for servicing large grass mowers. He suggested that we should have lunch together at the pub he called his local, which was in the middle of Hatfield and nowhere near his home. To my astonishment, he even offered to pay for it because I had paid for his a few times when he came to my patch with insufficient funds. How could I resist?

I looked at the new machinery for servicing mowers but was unimpressed by it because the mowers in my Group were serviced only once a year and were done using ordinary tools in the main workshop. I couldn't see any point in buying such equipment; after all, I was not operating a landscape gardening company. Roger then suggested we should go to lunch so off we went to his local and I soon realised why he had been so keen to take me there. One of the barmaids, quite an attractive lady, was clearly very friendly towards Roger and it was obvious that Roger, who was newly divorced and single again at that time, was keen on her. He introduced me to her and we chatted for a few minutes until she became busy with the lunchtime customers. Our food arrived and we consumed it sitting at the bar, largely because by so doing he could talk to the barmaid whenever she had a free moment.

"What do you think of her Dave?" he asked. I told him she seemed very nice and wished him luck but why he should have asked for my opinion I shall never know.

Just then a man came to the bar and, very rudely, stood between us, even though we were still in conversation. He slapped Roger on the back and slurred, "Allo mate, 'aven't seen you for a while." Obviously, the man was drunk and I felt sure he was going to cause trouble, which he certainly did. Firstly, he nearly knocked my drink over and I had to tell him to be careful. Then he reached into his pocket and pulled out a large object wrapped up in a couple of paper serviettes, which he placed on the bar. He continued to slur some almost indecipherable conversation at Roger who, becoming embarrassed by the drunk's presence, excused himself and went off to the gents' toilet.

The man then turned to me and in a very loud voice made a comment about Roger saying, "He works with shite you know!" I told him that Roger was a Wastewater Treatment Manager, the same as me.

"So you work with shite as well then!" he retorted louder than ever. At this, the landlord of the pub called out to the man to keep the noise down and mind his language.

"We don't like that kind of talk in here," he said, "there are ladies about!"

At this point, Roger returned and asked what all the fuss was about. "Just your mate getting a bit lairy that's all!" I told him, "It's time we left!" Whereupon the drunk begged to know if we ever saw big rats on the treatment plants. "Not really," said Roger. "Only the two-legged variety," said I sarcastically.

"Well there's a bloody big one in 'ere!" bellowed the man as he whipped the paper serviettes off the object he had placed on the bar, causing an immediate SHIT happening of some magnitude.

The object was, in fact, a very large, dead and rather bloody, brown rat, the site of which caused the barmaid to squeal loudly and recoil in horror, sending a couple of glasses crashing to the floor at the same time. A few other customers recoiled too but rather more in disgust than in horror. For my part, the reaction was surprising really because I thought the parcel wrapped in serviettes was his lunch but who knows? I may have been right!

The landlord reacted very differently, however, as you may well have guessed. He came from behind the bar like an express train, grabbed the drunken loudmouth in a half-nelson and marched him very quickly and forcefully out of the pub, with the words, "OUT, OUT, OUT! AND DON'T BLOODY WELL COME BACK! YOUR'E BARRED! COME BACK IN HERE AND I'LL CALL THE POLICE!"

Roger and I, not wishing to be in any way associated with the uncouth fellow, quietly left the pub through the car park entrance and drove back to the Mill Green Treatment Plant. "Nice pub, Roger," I told him, "the barmaid's nice too and the food's pretty good. Don't go much on your mates though," I added sarcastically.

He replied that the man was not his mate but was, in fact, a friend of John, the Union Steward at Mill Green, who just happened to be universally considered as one of the most objectionable cretins in the whole of Thames Water.

Not surprisingly, Roger never invited me over to his group again. I really didn't care!

*****

My filled trousers at Hatfield Heath P/S

One Saturday morning I got a call from the Divisional Duty Officer to say that a complaint had been received from Hatfield Heath that sewage was overflowing from a manhole in someone's front yard and spilling into the Pincey Brook. Unable to raise my standby crew on the telephone I decided to drive to Hatfield Heath to find out the cause of the problem. Sure enough, there was a serious pollution of the stream arising from the overflowing manhole so I went to inspect the pumping station on the opposite side of the watercourse. The wet well was full to the brim so obviously, the pumps were not working. On entering the pumping station however, I found both pumps running flat out and making a lot of noise; there had to be a blockage on the suction side of the pumps. What could I do? The standby crew and probably the suction-tanker lorry would be needed to clear a blockage and I could not contact them (this was before the days of mobile phones and there was no telephone at the pumping station at that time).

This station pumped up a fairly steep hill rising probably 80ft over a distance of less than a quarter-mile so there would have to be a good head of water in the rising main. I therefore decided to stop both the pumps and then lift their reflux (i.e. non-return) valves in turn, to flush out the suctions backwards. Having stopped the pumps, I entered the dry well via the tiny access ladder attached to the wall. There was barely enough space for me to turn as I climbed over the delivery pipes to reach the reflux valve levers but eventually, I was positioned between them and, using all my strength, lugged one of the levers upwards.

SHIT happened with a loud bang as the retaining nut on the other end of the 1-inch spindle fell off! The spindle shot out of its hole taking the lever arm and its heavy counterweight with it, hitting me quite hard in the belly and, fortunately, turning me around slightly. The spindle was followed by a 1-inch-bore jet of foul sewage with 80ft head pressure behind it and would have hit me fairly in the testicles had I not been turned by the lever. Automatically I turned my back on the jet and the sewage literally filled my trousers from the outside and within a couple of seconds was spilling over my belt and through my shirtfront. Realising the tiny space I occupied and the force of the water coming in, there was a moment's panic, a rarity for me I'm proud to say but nevertheless, there was a real fear of drowning and I scrambled out of the chamber much quicker than I had entered it!

Once atop the tiny ladder, it was possible to take stock of the situation. Even the 1-inchbore deluge would not fill the well all that quickly so there was plenty of time to close the upstream service valves and stop the flow, which is what I should have done in the first place! This done I was able to check the other pump's reflux valve, force it open and tie it up with a rope then open its service valve and flush out the suction. Once restarted this pump worked fine and the overflow to the stream was quickly stemmed. It only remained for me to get to the maintenance people at the Bishops Stortford plant before they knocked off at 1.00 pm and this I did after laying an old donkey jacket over the seat of my car to avoid soaking it with sewage.

It was a little after midday when I squelched into the workshop at Bishops Stortford. The radio was turned up very loud and listening to it were two maintenance fitters, a maintenance electrician and THE STANDBY CREW!

"Where the hell have you blokes been?" I asked them. "I tried to call you about Hatfield Heath pumping station and couldn't get anybody. I had to go myself and got saturated in shitty water as a result!"

Everyone was staring at me open-mouthed and could see the mess I was in. Clearly, they sensed my seething rage and no doubt feared the wrath of Caine was upon them. However, I could see the funny side of things really. After all, I was not hurt and it's not every day one gets to see one's manager drenched in sewage. "Come on, gents," I said, "at least have a good laugh about it," which they did. Occasionally, they all reminded me of it too for a very long time afterwards!

It transpired that the standby crew had already been called out to clear a serious sewer blockage when I first called them but had I called the sewage works first I would have probably found them there and needn't have done the job alone anyway. They had returned to the works with the jetting equipment and spent an hour or so cleaning it before I arrived. Looking back on such occurrences really demonstrates the value of mobile telephones for everyone, like we have today! If they'd been available to us then a decent pair of trousers wouldn't have been ruined, I wouldn't have been saturated in filthy sewage and I wouldn't have wanted to bathe in hot water for half that Saturday afternoon either!

*****

Bedspread blocks pumps.

Some bright spark in Thames Water (Lee Division) had the idea to put a signboard on every pumping station and sewage treatment works in the division giving its name, the Thames Water logo and displaying the local Group Manager's name too. Originally the idea was to display the individual's telephone number as well but, to a man, all the Group Managers refused to allow it, lest they should be disturbed when off duty by somebody complaining about their sewerage rates or some other triviality.

One Monday evening just as I was about to walk to my local pub for a pint with my old friend Tom, the telephone rang. The lady told me she could see sewage bubbling up outside her house in Cannons Mill Lane, Bishops Stortford. She said it had been happening all afternoon and she had rung the Council but nobody had done anything about it. I told her she should have called Thames Water and her reply was rather acidic.

"What do you think I'm doing now then, you idiot? You're the manager, aren't you?"

"Yes, I am, madam," I said very icily, "but where did you get my number from?"

"From the phone book of course," was the reply, "there's only two with your name and one's in Bury St Edmunds. That's too far away to be Thames Water."

She had read my name on the ridiculous Thames Water sign affixed to the control pedestal of the pumping station. The number at Bury St Edmunds was actually my brother's! I asked her never to phone my number again but said I would organise somebody to sort out the problem and subsequently called out the standby crew. Then I decided to go along to the pumping station with them just to satisfy my curiosity as to the cause of the problem.

Sure enough, there was a substantial spillage from the pumping station and I determined that both pumps had tripped and would not restart; probably there was a blockage of both pumps, which were of the submersible type. The standby crew arrived and jacked up the very heavy, concrete-filled, iron covers to the pumping well, which was almost in the middle of the road, and attempted to lift one of the pumps. Two men could not lift it so I gave a hand and found that three men couldn't lift it either, all of us being big strong people! Normally pumps of this size can be lifted by one man with a bit of effort and by two with relative ease. We tried to lift the other pump and again it was impossible but I noticed that as we tried to lift one pump the chain on the other was being moved at the same time. Clearly, the same object(s) had fouled and blocked both pumps so they had to be lifted together, a task beyond the strength of the three of us. So barricades were erected around the opening, lights were affixed, as it was getting dark, and tripod winches were obtained from the treatment plant.

After quite a struggle, even with the winches, we managed to lift both pumps out of the well and to our amazement found that they were each completely blocked by opposite ends of a king-sized candlewick bedspread. An hour later, after much cursing and partial dismantling of both pumps, they were cleared and put back into the well. Both operated perfectly thereafter so the well covers were replaced, barricades etc. removed and the huge bedspread, bedecked with every foul thing you would expect to see in a sewer, was thrown in the back of the truck.

At this point, a very attractive lady came out of the house beside the pumping station dressed in the uniform of an airline stewardess. "Have you finished now?" she asked.

I recognised the voice as the one who had telephoned me hours earlier and so introduced myself to her and told her all was now OK. She apologised for her rudeness on the telephone and, when I told her I had missed my evening at the pub for this week, immediately went and found three bottles of beer for the standby guys and me to share. She then very elegantly climbed into a smart car, keenly aware of the three of us watching every movement she made, and drove off to work, presumably on a late flight from Stansted airport. So, it wasn't too bad a SHIT happening after all! Before leaving the site, however, I carefully removed the offending sign with my name on it!

The next day, I obtained the sewerage maps from East Hertfordshire Council and found that no sewer feeding to that little pumping station was bigger than 150mm bore. There was no property with a sewer connection bigger than 100mm bore served by that particular system and so I have never been able to determine how on earth a king-sized candlewick bedspread could ever have entered the pumping well. The only way it could have entered would have been via the huge Elkington Gattick concrete-filled cast iron covers over the pumping well which were so heavy that they required a hydraulic jack on rollers to lift them and move them aside. I cannot believe anybody would have lifted them to dispose of a bedspread even if they had the means to do so. The matter remains a complete mystery!

*****

Ted and I disturb 'friends'.

Little Hallingbury is a village on the Herts and Essex border and had a small sewage treatment works located in farmland at a respectful distance from the nearest dwellings. It also received wastewater from the village of Great Hallingbury and its treated effluent discharged into a tributary of the River Stort. The treatment works had holding tanks for sludge, which was collected regularly in a 2000-gallon road tanker-lorry and transported to the larger treatment works at Bishops Stortford for treatment in the digesters.

One morning, I happened to be driving to this little sewage works to inspect some repair work on the trickling filters and saw the road tanker in front of me. It turned left from the narrow country lane and I followed it into the even narrower access lane to the works. The access lane was about a hundred metres long and was bordered by field hedgerows covered in brambles so I could see nothing ahead of me except the huge rear end of the tanker. After about eighty metres the lorry stopped. Ted, the Irish driver, jumped down from the cab and walked back to speak to me; he had of course already noticed my car behind him several minutes earlier.

"There's a car in front of the gates," said Ted, "I expect they're probably picking blackberries."

People often stopped in the access road to pick these blackberries but usually only at weekends. It was particularly dangerous because it was impossible to turn a car around on such a narrow little road and reversing out into the equally narrow country lane was extremely hazardous.

Ted and I both walked to the car, actually a small Ford van, but there was no sign of anybody by the hedgerows so, presuming they were picking on the other side of the hedge we passed the van to squeeze between the boundary fence and the end of the trees to have a look.

SHIT happened when a startled squeal from inside the vehicle revealed a young couple, both completely naked, making whoopee on the passenger seat! Ted and I tried to avert our eyes, though probably not too hard because the woman was particularly well formed, and nipped to the back of the van. I banged on its roof and shouted that they would have to move. The reply I received is unprintable except for the final three words, "f***ing peeping toms!" It came from the woman, not the man! After a few minutes of frantic scrambling within the van, the young man emerged looking quite sheepish.

"Christ, I didn't hear that thing turn up!" he said, "You might have sounded the horn!"

"Well if you couldn't see and hear a bloody great lorry like that mate," I replied, "you must have been rather preoccupied! By the way aren't you building the new houses near where I live in Sawbridgeworth?"

"Could be," was the response. "Now can you back up and let us get out!" he snapped very irritably. I told him it was not possible for my car and the huge tanker to reverse out into the narrow little country lane and that we would all have to enter the treatment works so that he could turn around and drive out forwards. Thus said, I went to open the gates and let him drive in. All three vehicles entered the works and with some difficulty the van was turned around and driven out again but all the time the young woman was holding her head down in embarrassment and hiding her face with her hand. After they had gone Ted and I had a good chuckle about the whole incident.

"Do you know the man?" asked Ted.

"Yes," I said, "he's building four new houses in a little cul de sac close to my house. I'd better make peace with him next time I see him!"

After a while, Ted had filled the tanker and driven off and I had finished my inspection of the repair work so went to have lunch at the village pub. Imagine my surprise when, having ordered my lunch and a pint at the bar, I turned around and saw the same young builder fellow sitting at a table staring gooey-eyed at the young woman who lived, with her husband, next door to me. No wonder she had struggled so hard to hide her face an hour ago! On seeing me they both blanched.

"Oh hello," I said to them, "nice little pub this isn't it?" The young woman stared up at me with a kind of pleading expression.

"Look," she said, "we're just friends, OK?"

Stifling my laughter, I replied that it was none of my business and professed to have seen nothing, whereupon I went to find a table as far as possible from them to have my lunch but all the while wishing I could have 'friends' like that! It so happened that after just a few weeks our next-door neighbours split up and their house was sold. I never saw the young woman again but frequently saw her young builder 'friend' and at least remained on nodding terms with him.

*****

Man digging a hole for fence post hits a cable.

In the little village of Hatfield Broad Oak, there were several small sewage pumping stations for which I had managerial responsibility. One of them served a small housing estate that was built either just before or just after the Second World War. When Thames Water took it over it was perfectly functional but the building was festooned with ivy and the fence surrounding it was quite rotten and needed replacing. There had been complaints from the neighbours that the pumping station was an eyesore. A local contractor was therefore engaged to get rid of the ivy and decorate the walls of the building, paint the window frames and doors etc. and replace the rotten fencing. I also asked for the single gate to be replaced by a double gate to allow access by the maintenance vehicles so it was necessary to install new concrete gateposts.

Power for the pumping station was derived from an electricity substation immediately next door to it and this was fed via an underground cable from the other side of the road, where it dropped down from an overhead supply at eleven thousand volts. The law in England, according to the Public Utilities and Street

Works Act, requires that when excavating in such an area the contractor must seek information from the utility suppliers, i.e. water, gas, telephones and electricity before digging to ensure the services are not damaged. Water we knew, telephones were overhead, gas did not exist at that spot and electricity was deeply buried and, according to the local Electricity Board's information, fed directly to the substation. The contractor was, therefore, able to dig new holes for concrete gateposts without difficulty and so started to dig them about three quarters of a metre deep to accommodate the big new posts. As you will have guessed, SHIT happened and it could so easily have cost a life.

The contractor's foremen telephoned me to say he had struck the cable feeding our pumps while digging with a spade but the hole he had dug was so far only thirty centimetres deep. I therefore hurried to the site and, sure enough, there was the foreman standing next to the shallow hole wearing a thick woollen cardigan and brandishing his spade. A quick look down the hole revealed nothing to me except wet clay soil.

"So, where's this cable?" I asked.

"Bottom of the hole," came the reply. "Look, I'll show you." With that, he pulled the sleeve of his cardigan down over his hand and, holding the steel shaft of the spade whacked it into the hole. There was a flash and plenty of sparks and the blade of the spade had a sizeable piece burnt out of it.

"Crikey, don't do that, mate you'll stop the pumps!" I exclaimed. "They're three-phase motors so four hundred volts at least. You'll get a hell of a shock from it if you're not careful."

A quick examination of the pumps showed that they were operating correctly and a somewhat more careful inspection showed that they were fed directly from a transformer within the substation next door. So what could be the cable producing all the sparks and flashes at the bottom of the gatepost hole? Clearly, we needed the expertise of the Electricity Board, so I telephoned them and an inspector was immediately sent to the site. He quickly determined that the cable was, in fact, the eleven-thousand-volt feed to the substation but it was not where it was shown to be on the record diagrams. Subsequently, it was found that the cable had been laid at a time when a machine gun pillbox was there to protect a temporary wartime fighter station, of which there had been many in that part of Essex, and had been laid to avoid the pillbox. On the record drawings, however, it was shown to be several yards further away and recorded as being at least a yard below the ground surface. Obviously, the exigencies of wartime had overridden the need for accurate records. Furthermore, the pillbox, though overgrown and filled with refuse and other unsavoury items, was still there and was also a substantial distance from where it was shown on the records.

The feed cable was subsequently replaced and laid directly to the substation. Power was cut off for a few hours while the work was done and we had a tanker vehicle standing by to ensure the pumping station did not overflow while there was no electricity supply. Later the contractor was able to complete the refurbishment of the fencing around the pumping station and all was well thereafter. It is nevertheless quite remarkable that the contractor's foreman could have jabbed a sharpened, heavy, steel-shafted spade into an eleven-thousand-volt cable while standing on damp grass and with only the sleeve of an old woollen cardigan around his hand for insulation. He never got a shock and was quite prepared to do it more than once to demonstrate to me that the cable was live. He must have been the luckiest man on earth at that time and quite possibly the silliest too!

*****

<u>Labourer removes fuses from the sludge pump control panel.</u>

For a number of years, there was a keen ornithologist and member of the Royal Society for the Protection of Birds who had been given permission to net and ring birds at Bishops Stortford treatment works, where there was still a huge area of wild land that had previously been used for sewage irrigation. Jack, as he was known, was a life assurance salesman for a big company but he was able to spend every Thursday following his favourite pastime at the plant and would set up his mist nets and trap all kinds of birds, ring them, measure them, weigh them and record various other data before releasing them unharmed. He had amassed an enormous amount of information over the years concerning bird migration, breeding success rates, etc. and had on many occasions recorded very rare species passing through. Having more than just a passing interest in birdlife, I frequently chatted with Jack during his weekly visits and a friendly rapport developed between us.

One day, Jack came into my office and told me he was very worried about his son John. He was Educationally Subnormal and had recently lost his job as a labourer through some misdemeanour and was consequently unemployed and

99

potentially unemployable in that locality. Jack asked me if there was any chance of a labourer's job at one of the sewage works. He told me his son could read and write but was just very slow; he was physically sound and had always been brought up to do as he was told, could use a broom and shovel properly and could also operate a simple motor mower. It so happened that there was a requirement for another pair of hands at the Stansted Mountfitchet treatment works so I agreed to take on John as a labourer, with the proviso that he would have to serve a three months probationary period. He started work at Stansted Mountfitchet the following week and, remembering the fiasco years earlier involving Derek at the Nags Head Lane works in Brentwood, I made it very clear to the other staff that under no circumstances was John to be allowed to drive the dumper truck or the tractor, which were the only two vehicles associated with this site.

After three months, it was necessary to make an assessment of John's performance and it was reported by the works foreman that although he was rather slow, John always did as he was told and was in all respects a worthwhile employee, albeit for only the simple jobs on the treatment works. Consequently, he became a permanent employee and Jack, his father, was very pleased.

Sometime later, there was an electrical fault with the raw sludge pumps at Stansted Mountfitchet which was dealt with by a bright young electrician from the Bishops Stortford maintenance group. The electrician, Steve, told me that John had been very helpful whilst the repairs were being done, fetching and carrying tools and helping to lift the pumps out and hose them clean etc. He also told me that John showed a great deal of interest in the electrical work and was continually asking questions about what was being done and why. Steve's comment was that John seemed to be quite intelligent and didn't show any sign of being educationally subnormal. He even suggested that John should have a more challenging job than being a labourer at a small treatment works because he would otherwise become bored and may become a skiver. It was a remarkably prophetic comment, as was to be demonstrated by the next SHIT happening, which occurred after only a few weeks.

A while later, the raw sludge pumps failed again. They simply stopped working and the sludge well was on the point of overflow into the treated effluent channel when John closed the valve and avoided a serious pollution of the river. The pumps could not be restarted. Steve, the electrician, was called to the works to correct the electrical fault but could not find anything wrong with the circuits. No fuses had blown and as soon as the pumps were reset to the automatic operation they self-started and worked perfectly well. There were no further problems for a few days but then the same thing happened again. Once again a serious pollution was avoided when John closed the valves feeding to the sludge pumping well. Again the pumps could not be restarted and the electrician was called. When he arrived, he found that the circuits were all normal and as soon as the pumps were switched to automatic control they self-started and worked perfectly. Steve was completely mystified.

When the same thing happened a third time the foreman at Stansted Mountfitchet became very scathing about Steve's capability and demanded that somebody else should look at the pump control panels, so another electrician attended instead of Steve. On this occasion, however, the plant foreman stayed in the sludge pumping station to make sure that the control panels were properly inspected, even though the man had not the faintest idea what was inside an electrical control panel. The inspection revealed that two of the three cartridge fuses were missing from each pump control circuit. Clearly, someone had deliberately removed them but where were they?

At this point, John reached the top of the panel and, producing the four fuses, said, "Are these what you are looking for?"

"How did they get up there?" asked the electrician.

"Don't know," replied John, "They're always there when the pumps fail but when they go back the pumps work again."

When this was reported to me it was quite obvious that John was having a game, a very dangerous game, playing with the control panels, so he was ordered to keep away from the sludge pumping station and subsequently to come to my office the following day.

In order to be fair to this unfortunate young man and also to be seen to be fair, I arranged for his union steward to be present at the meeting, having first informed the man of John's E.S.N.*condition and my almost certain knowledge of what he had been doing. I started by simply asking John why he had been removing fuses from the sludge pump panels. His reply was quite remarkable.

"Don't know why I took them out," he said, "but I always put them back again afterwards. And I always turned them off at the mains before I did it."

I asked him how he came to know how to remove fuses from the panels.

"By watching Steve," he said. "I want to be an electrician one day Mr Marpole. I get fed up being a labourer at that little works at Stansted!"

Having told John that he had been very stupid I issued him with a written warning; in view of the seriousness of his actions it was actually a Final Written Warning and I explained to him that any further wrongdoings of that nature would result in him being dismissed. I also explained that there was no possibility of him becoming an electrician but agreed to transfer him to the works at Bishops Stortford, where there were more people for him to talk to but, more importantly, more people to keep an eye on him. His union steward was rather less gentle, however, and after the meeting, he berated the poor chap for about ten minutes while using extremely foul language too. John was subsequently so upset that he sat and cried for quite a while.

Later I telephoned his father Jack and explained to him exactly what had happened. Jack was grateful that I had not sacked John and promised me there would be no further trouble from him because he would read the Riot Act to him that evening. Amazingly the following day John came to my office as soon as I got to work and, like a chastised schoolboy in front of his headmaster, profusely apologised for what he had done, promising never to misbehave again. He was good to his word too and was always a solid, reliable worker thereafter. When his father died a few years later he asked permission, which was granted, to plant a Japanese flowering cherry tree on a corner of the works as a memorial to Jack who had spent some of the happiest days of his life on that site bird-watching. I hope the tree is still there!

*****

Chapter 7

Group Manager Deephams

Upon the retirement of the first Works Manager at Deephams the position was advertised internally within Thames water so naturally, I applied for the job. To my astonishment, I was subsequently offered the position (now known as Group Manager) the day after being interviewed and that was one of the highlights of my career. I had started work at Deephams at the age of sixteen, regarded by all as the most junior employee but now I was going back there as the most senior and I felt that I had achieved something special.

A week or two after my appointment, I took my old Mum to see the treatment works. She was amazed by the flowerbeds and neatly clipped lawns and could not believe the place was a sewage works. I took her into the power station, where the noise disturbed her somewhat, and she asked me if we were allowed to be there. At that moment one of my Shift Charge Engineers, a Burmese gentleman named George came over to say hello to Mother and she actually asked him if it was permissible for us to be there. George replied, "Of course it is my dear, David's the Group Manager. He is the boss here."

Finally, she realised that I did not have to shovel shit for a living and made the comment, "Oh, you've got a good job then and all these years I was hoping you'd be running a chemist's shop one day."

I declined to comment!

*****

Dead fish in Lee at Edmonton.

One morning, having just arrived at Deephams works, I spotted Robin, the Works Chemist, striding towards the laboratory with a full sample bottle in his hands. Robin was always a cheerful fellow but on this day, he had a grin from ear to ear.

"Get a load of this," he said, brandishing the bottle, "you won't see a better final effluent anywhere. It's almost good enough to drink!"

The sample was indeed very clear and almost sparkled in the sunlight. Obviously, the plant was operating very well and it all made a good start to the day.

Just a few hours later, I received a telephone call from the Divisional Office to say that people were complaining about the enormous number of dead fish in the river downstream. I replied that it couldn't be anything from the sewage treatment works because the effluent was like gin today and well within the standards. An inspection downstream was obligatory, however, so in company with Robin I walked down to the outfall to take a look.

Just upstream of the effluent outfall was the confluence with the storm bypass which, during dry weather, was still full of water at the same level as the effluent channel. It was full of fish, all looking active and healthy but there were far more fish there than usual. A glance at the effluent channel showed something was wrong because there was no sign of a fish in it, even though it was almost crystal-clear water just like the morning's sample that Robin had been so proud of. Then, a little further on, we came to the outfall into the Salmon's Brook. Upstream the brook had a few fish visible that appeared to be healthy but downstream it was almost choked with dead ones all floating belly up. A further inspection where the brook joined the River Lee revealed very large numbers of dead fish of all types to be found in those waters.

SHIT had happened for sure but how? What could have caused such an enormous fish kill? Had somebody poured something into the works effluent? Surely not, why would anybody at Deephams do such a thing?

Well, the Pollution Control Dept. of Thames Water had already collected samples of the dead fish and were taking them to the Government Laboratories in London for analysis to determine what could possibly have killed them. Our own laboratory analysis of the works effluent was almost complete and nothing untoward had been shown. We would have to wait and see!

A day or two later, it was revealed that the fish kill had been caused by selenium poisoning, which had to be a very rare occurrence. Selenium is an element that is generally used in small quantities in, for example, light-sensitive battery cells of the type found in calculators and other pocket electronic

104

equipment. It is present usually as selenium oxide. The material is not regarded as being particularly toxic but it so happens that fish have a very clearly defined tolerance level to it. Most can survive in waters with a selenium concentration up to a few parts per million but if this level is exceeded by the tiniest fraction the fish will die. (Rather like the strawberry plants and their tolerance to boron). Subsequent analysis of the treated effluent showed that there was indeed selenium present but only one or two parts per million, which is below the toxic threshold for fish.

The Trade Effluent Inspector, Colin, knew all the industrial premises draining to Deephams extremely well. There was one company that specialised in precious and semi-precious metal recovery from all types of industrial waste shipped in from overseas and Colin went to see them as soon as we received the Government Laboratory's report. Sure enough, they did recover selenium from various waste products from the electronics industry and they produced the recovered material on a plate filter press. They had indeed lost a sizeable quantity of the selenium compound when the press had burst a couple of filter membranes and the material had gone into the drains.

They did not report the matter, however, because there was no limit on selenium concentration in their discharge licence so they were unaware of any possible consequences of the failure except their own financial loss. Of course their discharge licence was rapidly amended to include a very strict limit on selenium concentration and they were obliged to compensate for the cost of restocking the river with various coarse fishes.

Although the river system recovered after a year or two it was still very much a shame for me because I remember as a boy in the nineteen fifties that stretch of the river being pretty worthless as a place to go fishing. After the construction of the new Deephams works, however, and the various other pollution control measures that were taken in the following decade, it had become a very attractive area for north Londoners to cast a line for recreation. It could have been destroyed purely through our lack of knowledge. I fear there could easily be much more SHIT of this type just waiting to happen.

*****

<u>Colin and I working the screens at Deephams: bursting condom.</u>

In the political climate of the times, it was inevitable that the Water Authorities' employees would go on strike when called to do so by their Trades Unions. At Deephams there was a one hundred per cent turnout of all manual employees; operatives, mechanical fitters, electricians and even the gardeners, cleaners and canteen staff. In fact, everybody was on strike except for the laboratory staff, office staff, the shift charge engineers and the management staff. The people continuing to work were mostly members of a different Trades Union that did not support strike action and many were able to perform their usual duties without interruption. It was necessary, however, to have certain essential works carried out that these people would normally have nothing to do with and in the interest of public health and safety I was obliged to ask for volunteers to do those duties. Although one or two refused to do manual work there were sufficient to do all the really essential jobs but nobody was prepared to perform the most undesirable job of all, which was the daily manual raking of the low-level coarse screens.

The low-level coarse screens were sixty feet below ground level on the end of the low-level incoming sewer, which was a six-foot diameter pipe delivering sewage from a substantial area of North London. The screens, which were installed solely for pump protection, were six-inch spaced steel bars set at an angle of only fifteen degrees from the vertical and reaching down about two and a half metres into the discharge chamber. To rake them, one needed to stand on a platform, drag a metre-wide rake up the screen with all its load of foul trash and then drop it into a bin for removal via the lift to ground level. The job was somewhat strenuous but not overly so and although it was visually unpleasant the atmosphere was not foul because there was an effective forced air ventilation system in place. The wearing of overalls, eye protection and gloves was nevertheless essential but the only difficulty with the job was caused by the low ceiling in the discharge chamber. This necessitated the rake being turned at an angle when it was dragged up the screen to avoid the end of its handle hitting the ceiling. As a consequence, some of the foul trash would sometimes drop off the rake onto the platform and would then need to be shovelled into the disposal bin, a rather unpleasant task.

Since there were no volunteers to rake the low-level screens, I was obliged to take on the job myself but the Trade Effluent Inspector, my close friend Colin, agreed to do the job with me as it was necessarily a two-man task. Phil, one of the administrative staff, agreed to be the 'top man' for us each day lest there should be some emergency sixty-foot below ground level.

Both Colin and I regularly wore a suit to work in those days but Colin was always turned out as if he had just come from the tailor's shop. We both went to the screen chamber each day wearing wellington boots and a boiler suit over the top of our suit trousers, smart shirt and tie. It was inevitable that there would be a SHIT happening to us and sure enough there was. It was awful!

On the second day of our manual duties, Colin dragged a particularly large and heavy load of trash off the screen with his rake and as he turned it over to avoid hitting the ceiling with its handle half of its load fell onto the platform. "Watch out Dave!" cried Colin, for within this load of foul trash was a round, pink coloured, bouncing object that fell towards me, just a few feet away. Boing, boing, boing, SPLAT it went as it bounced and exploded within inches of me, showering me from head to foot with its disgusting contents. Colin received a small share too!

Close examination of the now deflated object revealed it to be a sheath contraceptive which had undoubtedly been urinated into and then tied in a knot before disposal in some obscene individual's lavatory. Both of us were on the point of vomiting but being used to seeing disgusting things on a regular basis fell instead into uncontrolled laughter.

"What filthy dirty bastard would do that?" yelled Colin.

"Don't know mate," I replied, "but if that happens regularly it's no wonder our blokes are on strike!"

With that, we left the low-level chamber and fortunately never had such a revolting experience there again. Our overalls thrown in the wash and in my case a thorough cleansing of face and hair was an end to the matter but Colin and I have often had a good laugh about it over the years since.

Despite my somewhat sympathetic feelings towards the striking workforce, I was subsequently very much aggrieved by their attitude when pickets arrived at the works entrance from the North London Water Treatment Plant. As I arrived for work the following morning, I was greeted by a mob of louts who had already threatened physical violence against one of my staff. One of these louts actually said he would kick my car if I went into the works but when I told him he'd better phone for an ambulance first he backed off rather sheepishly. The threat, however, was sufficient for me to ask for a police presence at our gate to ensure no violence occurred and this was granted. It actually took the form of two female police officers, both of them hefty buxom women who would clearly tolerate no nonsense from picketing louts and there was no further problem throughout the strike period.

There was, however, a rather amusing incident when one of the WPCs decided to warm her bottom next to the coke brazier that had been provided for the pickets. Little did she know that at least twenty men and half a dozen women in the office building could see her knickers and bare thighs as she lifted her uniform skirt to combat the chill around her buttocks for about half an hour. Nobody told her!

*****

Security fencing disappearing at Deephams

Deephams Sewage Treatment Works was at one time incorporated into the Greater London Council along with the refuse incinerator plant next door that disposed of a substantial percentage of North London's rubbish. When I became manager of the sewage works there was no discernible boundary between the GLC's refuse plant and Deephams that belonged to Thames Water. There needed to be a proper boundary fence between the two. Furthermore, there was a real need for security fencing around the sewage works because there had been numerous incidents of theft, suspected to be by Gypsies encamped nearby. In those days there were very many Gypsy encampments on the Lee fields and marshes in that part of North London and those people were, rightly or wrongly, blamed for almost every criminal activity that took place there.

Money was available at the end of the financial year for security fencing so it was decided that Deephams would be fully fenced off and properly secured from all possible intruders. The two-metre high, galvanised steel, palisade fence separating the plant from the railway and the nearby recreation centre would be extended to enclose the whole plant and this was done by a suitably reliable contractor during March of that year. The fencing was excellent, proof against anything short of a tank and durable for 30 or 40 years without maintenance. It carried a substantial pair of gates across the road link between the sewage works and the GLC's incinerator and I issued a general instruction to the management staff that these were to be kept securely locked at all times.

A week or two later, there was a visitor to Deephams who was actually one of the senior managers at the main North London water treatment plant. He had come to discuss a couple of issues arising from the recent monthly meeting with the local union stewards, which we were both obliged to attend. I had been waiting for him to arrive and remarked that I hadn't seen him drive in through the main entrance gate.

"No David," he replied, "I came through the incinerator plant, it's much quicker."

"Who opened the gate for you then John?" I asked.

"What gate's that then? I've never seen a gate on that road," was the unexpected reply.

"It's a new pair of gates, a part of the new security fencing," I explained.

"Well, I didn't notice it," said John. "I must have been half asleep!"

So, I concluded that John was indeed half-asleep and that somebody had driven out via the incinerator plant and been too lazy to close the gates behind them.

After our brief discussion, John drove back the way he had come in and I followed him to make sure he could actually exit the treatment plant, in case whoever left the gates open had returned and locked them again, and to make sure the gates were properly locked after he had gone. I never expected SHIT to have happened, but it had!

Imagine my shock to find that there were indeed no gates across the road and furthermore that eight fencing panels were also missing! Clearly, they had not been knocked down by a tank either, they had been cut off neatly with a disc-cutter. Even the support posts had obviously been cut off and taken in the same way.

The matter was, of course, reported to the police but they were not able to do much. Fingerprinting produced nothing of value and there was no sign of tyre marks, even though the fence thieves must have used a lorry and probably one with a loading crane on board. The matter was brushed off as being the work of Gypsies and although the police would have a look in the local camps, they expected to find nothing because the fencing would have already been totted as scrap metal anyway. For my part, I always suspected that the fencing was not stolen to be totted as scrap but for use as security fencing somewhere else, probably with the connivance of my own staff or staff from the incinerator plant next door. It would even have been no surprise to find the original fencing contractor's people had been involved. Subsequently, there was always a chuckle from somebody when security fencing was mentioned.

"It'll only be taken away as scrap metal anyway," was the usual comment.

Sometime later an incident at one of the North London reservoirs involving intruders resulted in a child fatality and this brought the issue of security fencing to the forefront once more. The stolen fencing at Deephams was replaced and this time, security cameras were fitted too. It may well be that they are still there!

*****

Sludge eruption from pumping main at a Gypsy encampment in Walthamstow.

Deephams Sewage Treatment Works was originally constructed without facilities for drying and disposing of the treated sludge from its digesters. Sufficient land simply was not available for this purpose at Edmonton. A decision was made, therefore, to retain one of the smaller treatment works scheduled to be abandoned when Deephams was finished and to use the land area of that plant to construct a sludge drying and storage facility. A twin line sludge pumping main was constructed adjacent to the main London-East Anglia railway line to a site known as Rammey Marsh, nearly four miles north of Edmonton and close to the River Lee at Enfield Lock. For several years the daily make of digested sludge was pumped via two Wilde ram pumps to Rammey Marsh where it was fed up to nine inches deep into drying beds and allowed to dry naturally into a cake. When the cake was sufficiently dried, it was stacked for eventual use as a soil conditioner on farmland. Some of the liquid sludge was simply lagooned and periodically dewatered so that in time it could be transported off-site and used in the same way.

Some years later, in the days when Greater London Council had responsibility, Deephams Sewage Treatment Works was extended and its treatment capacity considerably increased. The sludge plant at Rammey Marsh was now inadequate and could not be extended, therefore a plan was conceived to construct a new twin pumping main to Beckton Sewage Works, which was the largest such plant in Europe. The pumping main, with several crossover points, followed the course of the River Lee and eventually the main Beckton sewer to the plant, where it was dewatered and subsequently shipped to sea to be dumped in an area known as The Black Deep. There were two large Whitehead

110

and Poole twin-cylinder ram pumps housed in a separate pumping station at Deephams. It was known as the Beckton pumping station but there were cross-connections with the Rammey Marsh pipelines that could allow these pumps to withdraw sludge from the digesters and pump to Rammey Marsh or Beckton or alternatively draw from the Rammey Marsh lagoons and pump to Beckton; it was a complex system of valves etc.

The twin pumping main to Beckton passed through heavily industrialised and heavily populated areas and at several points crossed the river but there were also areas through which it passed in those days that were not heavily populated or industrialised. Those areas were known as the Lee Marshes and as the name suggests used to be subject to occasional flooding during prolonged wet weather. Flooding, however, had been rare in modern times, i.e. from the mid-1930s onward, due to the construction of huge flood relief channels down the Lee Valley from Enfield Lock to the River Thames.

The Lee Marshes in the area of Walthamstow became the magnet for bands of Travellers, invariably called Gypsies in England though most likely there are very few of them that are actually derived from the Romany people who, I believe, came from Egypt in ancient times. Wherever they originated, there were a lot of these folk and they used to park-up their caravans at certain times of the year in that area, particularly in the late autumn and winter months. At other times there were fewer of them because they would travel away to the numerous fairgrounds that crop up traditionally all over Britain and where many of them make their living. Rightly or wrongly these people were unpopular with the local residents and were always accused of causing unnecessary trouble and stealing.

The so-called Gypsy Camp was quite crowded at a time when there were significant problems on the sludge main to Beckton. There had been alarms recorded that the pressure in the sludge main had risen to near maximum for the safe operation of the pipelines and investigations were carried out to determine precisely where the problems lay and what those problems could be. At crossover points between the twin pipelines, the valves were changed to allow the flow to pass down the alternative route for a time to see if the pressure readings would change, thus indicating where there may be a restriction. Nothing was determined as to the cause of the high-pressure alarms.

The location of the problem was revealed suddenly and spectacularly, however, when there was an eruption of digested sludge, some described it as being more like an oil well strike, right in the middle of the Gypsy encampment.

Allegedly, a spout of sludge burst from the ground and shot very high into the air. The surrounding area was liberally sprayed with black digested sludge for several minutes until the alarms at the Deephams site had been responded to and the pumps shut down.

A SHIT happening indeed of the first order, causing distress, disorder and a great deal of mess to a number of the traveller people on the site!

These folk were, of course, quick to complain, were very vociferous in their complaints and some also made stupid claims that the SHIT SPOUT, as it became known, had been caused deliberately to move them off the site. This certainly was not true but if it had been it would have been quite successful because a great many of those Travellers found alternative places to park their caravans in future. I do not recall the reason for the failure of the Beckton pipeline but I know it took quite a time to fix it and retest. Deephams staff attending to the problems frequently complained that they were verbally abused by the Gypsies and there was more than one complaint that dogs had been set upon them. True or false there was very little support from the Metropolitan Police, who tended to regard the Gypsy sites as No Go areas, a most unsatisfactory situation.

*****

Chapter 8
Group Manager Luton

Following yet another reorganisation within Thames Water I was transferred from Deephams to East Hyde, near Luton and took responsibility for the Luton Group. This had been extended into the River Colne catchment when the Eastern and Northern divisions of Thames Water were amalgamated. The new Luton Group proved to be something of a challenge. It had been poorly organised for a long time and most of the workforce responded well to the change of management. Indeed I made one or two lifelong friends from my new work colleagues. There were, however, a number of SHIT happenings as well as some amusing episodes.

*****

The East Hyde Stinks Campaign & being a Belisha beacon.

The major sewage treatment works serving the industrial town of Luton was built in times of austerity, largely by Italian prisoners during the latter part of the Second World War. It was constructed adjacent to the River Lee at the village of East Hyde, just a few miles south of Luton where the river is little more than a small stream. The plant had done a sterling job over the years but after roughly four decades it was ready for replacement. Similarly, the treatment works at Harpenden, just a few miles downstream, was also due to be demolished and the flow pumped to the new works at East Hyde.

With the reorganisation in Thames Water, I was moved from Deephams Sewage Treatment Works in North London to take over as manager of the Luton Group, based at East Hyde. I was unhappy about the move because it was in effect a demotion that was completely undeserved and undoubtedly caused by a clash of personalities between myself and the new Senior Manager; it was just another SHIT happening that had to be endured! The staff in my new Group, however, were in the main competent, responsible and pleasant people and I got on very well with them indeed.

The treatment works at East Hyde was a different matter. The office building and the laboratory were reasonable places to work but the sewage works itself was, in general, a stinking and repulsive place. There was no sludge digestion and the raw sludge was treated with lime before dewatering and in consequence, it gave off a substantial odour when it was stored on site. A portion of the incoming flow was treated on rectangular percolating filters which, although they were not particularly odorous, were the source of a considerable fly nuisance in the village of East Hyde during the summer. Surprisingly, there was a thriving Sports and Social Club on the site with a well-designed, licensed bar that was very popular with the local villagers as well as Thames Water employees. It had been stopped from opening during the lunch periods before I arrived there but it was still open every evening. In addition, there was a well-maintained football pitch on the site but this was only used by female footballers belonging to a local club that had been allowed to use the facility, largely because many of the women were also members of the Sports and Social Club, though not even employees of Thames Water. Indeed, none of these women were even related to Thames Water employees so how they were allowed to use the facilities I did not know. The whole issue of the Sports and Social Club was to cause serious problems in the near future.

For the time being, however, the biggest problem I faced as Group Manager was from an organisation that had recently moved into the village, made up from extremely vociferous and rather masculine women who, it was rumoured, had played a significant part in the anti-nuclear disturbances at the infamous Greenham Common airbase a year or two before. Their organisation was known as The East Hyde Stinks Campaign and they regularly placed derogatory notices on the boundary fences of the treatment works and displayed them through the village. I was told that occasionally they toured the area with a loudspeaker van trying to gather local support but I never saw or heard it myself. Fortunately, none of them tried to enter the plant to cause mischief like the women at Greenham Common airbase had done but I think that was purely because aircraft and nuclear warheads are rather less repulsive to interfere with than tanks full of sewage and piles of stinking sludge-cake! Nevertheless, they did have a point to make. East Hyde did stink and I had some sympathy with anybody who lived within smelling distance of that treatment works. It was horrible!

Plans were afoot, however, for a new works and construction work began after a year or so. The East Hyde Stinks Campaign women had been informed of this but they, like many other people I'm sure, could not grasp the fact that it would take a very long time to build a new treatment works on the same site as the existing one, particularly when the existing works was still in full operation. Consequently, the news that construction had started did not dim their campaign and they began to get the local newspapers involved. Badly written, factually incorrect articles in local rags had absolutely no effect upon the progress of construction, however, so attempts were made to get the national newspapers involved. Little attention was paid to the campaign by the national newspapers but I did get a telephone call one day from somebody purporting to be a journalist working for the Independent Newspaper. The questions he asked me were silly, to say the least and I concluded that he was probably not a journalist at all. In any case, I had been instructed not to answer queries from the news media but to refer them to our Press Officer at Reading. The man said he had already spoken to our Press Officer and that he had referred him to me, which was, of course, an absolutely obvious lie, so I told him politely to "go forth and multiply" and put the phone down.

Some weeks later, I received a call on my mobile telephone just a few minutes before I left work for home. The caller said he was from a local radio station, BBC Bedfordshire or something similar I think, saying that the East Hyde Stinks Campaign leader would be interviewed shortly and asked me a couple of questions about the treatment works. I told the caller I would not speak to him on the matter and again advised him to contact our Press Officer at Reading. He accepted my reply and then told me the broadcasting wavelength for his local radio network and the time of the broadcast. He refused, however, to tell me how he had obtained my mobile telephone number and I never did find out. I tuned in and listened to the broadcast as I was driving home.

The interview was a pretty one-sided affair with the interviewer allowing the East Hyde Stinks Campaign leader to ramble on about things she clearly knew nothing about and to make silly statements suggesting that everybody in the area could be struck down by some airborne disease from the smell at the treatment works. She also said she had evidence that Thames Water was hiding the truth about potential diseases. When she had finished this ridiculous rambling the interviewer actually stated that a spokesman from Thames Water, presumably me, had refused to comment when he had been questioned just a few minutes earlier.

"So, perhaps the campaigners are right," he said, "and there is something to hide."

That was enough for me. I turned the rubbish off!

The following day I contacted our Press Officer, who indeed seemed to be very professional, and related the story of the previous evening. He told me not to worry about it because the Press office was well aware of what the campaigners were up to and didn't expect it to last much longer. He pointed out that they had started with notices and placards, then involved the local press, the national press, that evidently had printed a small article but I cannot remember which newspaper it was in, then the local radio network. They would finish off by getting national television involved but that would be when Thames Water would retaliate and the campaigners would have shot their bolt.

"The TV people will come to the site and you will have to show them around and answer questions," he told me, "but don't worry I'll be there to tell you how to handle it. It will be a piece of cake."

So, feeling completely reassured, I forgot about the whole thing.

A week or two later, the Press Officer called me and told me to prepare for the BBC Television News crew to arrive at the site in a few hours. They were coming to interview me on site after they had interviewed the East Hyde Stinks Campaign people. The Press Officer was already on his way to the treatment works and would quickly give me advice as to how to conduct the interview etc. and what to show the cameraman.

I quickly went on site and advised my own staff to make sure they were all wearing hard hats near the construction areas and to be looking busy whenever the camera was aimed in their direction. I asked the Irish foreman of the construction crew to make sure all his men were suitably attired and to have an excavator doing something in view of the camera while the interview was taking place, even if it was only loading broken concrete into a lorry.

"Please don't let any of your men do something daft like a wave at the camera. This will be serious stuff," I told him. He assured me that all his men would be seen working hard or they would be getting their arses kicked!

The Press Officer arrived and briefed me what to do, which was basically to answer the first question with a very long answer so that the interviewer had little chance to ask anything else. The interview would be limited to just a few minutes, so I should just keep talking.

The television crew arrived and, in their wake, came a bunch of the East Hyde Stinks Campaign women, all of whom were asked to leave the site forthwith, which they did and were locked out. The BBC crew consisted of three people; a cameraman with his big shoulder-camera, a sound technician with a big fancy microphone and recorder and an attractive young female interviewer, a girl of Caribbean origin I believe. First, I told them they would all have to wear a hard hat but the cameraman complained that it would interfere with his camera. I told him that was the rule and if there was no way to work the camera it would have to be switched off. This elicited a nod of approval from the Press Officer. So, they all donned their hard hats and I followed suit. Mine, for some reason, was bright yellow with Thames Water in blue letters at the front. I had to have that one because all the others were too small for my rather large cranium!

When we got to the interview point there was plenty of activity from the construction crew, with two excavators working and several dumper trucks being loaded with rubble. Excellent for the camera. The young lady said that the campaigners had complained about the stink at East Hyde and asked what Thames Water was doing about it. I replied with a wave of my hand to the activity behind me that we were spending many millions of pounds constructing a new plant that would have new facilities for treating sludge that would produce no odours, new facilities for producing even better quality final effluent for the river, a larger capacity to include the flow from Harpenden so that the old, unsightly and inefficient works there could be done away with, better-looking structures that would not be an eyesore to the public, etc., etc. until the interview had almost overrun its time. At that point, the interviewer thanked me, turned to the cameraman and told him she would do the nod. This turned out to be a short clip of her seemingly nodding in agreement to whatever I was saying and pretending to understand it and look interested. I almost howled with laughter as I realised that all TV interviewers must do that. What a con!

The cameraman, who unlike the young lady interviewer was very experienced, had a quick quiet word with her and obviously told her she should have asked more questions. She then suggested to me that we should do the take again from a different angle but our Press Officer was far too cute for that.

"David," he said, "You're going to be late for your meeting with the County Council if you don't hurry up! Come on now!"

"Oh crikey, I mustn't be late for that!" I exclaimed and thanked the television crew for their efforts, wished them goodbye and asked them to leave their hard hats at the office as they left. The press officer and I then hurried to his car and we drove a mile or two up the road to have lunch in my favourite pub. A job well done!

That evening, I watched the local newsreel avidly on the television but there was no coverage of the East Hyde interview. I concluded therefore that the whole thing had been a washout and thought no more about it. The next evening, I didn't watch the local news at all but one of my son's friends did. Young Ian came round to our house and announced that he had seen me on the telly a few minutes ago.

"Really Ian?" asked my son, Adrian, "What did you think of it?"

Ian told us he didn't understand what I was talking about and that his father said I looked like a lollipop because of the yellow hat I was wearing! Well, that was worth a laugh at least.

The following day, however, I was inundated with phone calls from people I knew in Thames Water. One or two congratulated me for my efforts, others made sarcastic remarks about it but all of them commented about the bright yellow safety helmet. It must have shown up particularly well on the television. One lady, a clerical employee at Deephams Sewage Treatment Works, put the icing on the cake for me by telling me that she and her husband had almost fallen apart laughing when they saw me looking like a Belisha beacon*. She said the only difference between me and a real one was that the yellow bit on top didn't flash! So SHIT happened even to my few minutes of fame!

Subsequently, the East Hyde Stinks Campaign was more or less unheard of, just as predicted by Thames Water's Press Officer. Clearly, that fellow really was a professional!

*****

Man collecting false teeth at East Hyde

There were several occasions over the years when people telephoned the Treatment Plant or even turned up at the offices to report the loss of some valuable item, either accidentally washed down the sink or flushed down the toilet. Most commonly it was a case of the lady of the house, having removed

118

her ring whilst cleaning the kitchen sink, subsequently washing it down the drain. It was usually their bejewelled engagement ring that was lost because most women rarely remove their wedding ring and always wear their engagement ring as a second decoration on the same finger. The diamond or other stone in the ring would make it more vulnerable to being spoiled doing the housework or washing the dishes so would be temporarily removed. Sometimes the call to the treatment works was the last resort after the local plumber had been hired to retrieve the valuable item from the 'S' bend or, much worse, the drainage manhole outside and had found nothing.

I recall one lady telephoning the office at Deephams to see if we could try to find a diamond earring she had accidentally washed down the bath drain. She described the earring in detail and even offered a reward if it were recovered. She was quite disappointed, however, when I explained that this tiny item would be getting flushed along with the sewage from a population equivalent of eight hundred and fifty thousand, amounting to over forty million imperial gallons of wastewater per day in dry weather and several times as much if it was raining. It would be coming down a sewer six feet in diameter and sixty feet below ground level before being pumped into one of several tanks holding over a million imperial gallons each. The chances of finding such a tiny object, however well described, were several thousand times less than the chances of winning the top prize on Littlewoods football pools. Nevertheless, I assured her that if the earring should miraculously be found and reported to me, I would make sure it was returned to her. Finally, I suggested that she should get somebody to check the bath drain 'S' bend, where it just might have settled. She confessed that she didn't know what an 'S' bend was but she would get someone to have a look for her. I subsequently told several of my operations staff about the lady's call and her offer of a reward; to a man, they all hooted with laughter and most remarked how ignorant the general public were of the sewerage and sewage treatment system that they all had to pay for in their rates.

This little tale actually had a happy ending, as I was to discover a few days later when a personal letter arrived on my desk. It was from the same lady to inform me that she had asked one of her neighbours to check the 'S' bend from her bath and amazingly the lost diamond earring had been discovered there. Apparently, it wasn't flushed away because the 'S' bend needed a good clean out and as a result, the water flowed from the bath very slowly. Whatever the reason for its entrapment she was absolutely overjoyed that it had been found because the pair of diamond earrings had been a present from her late husband. Well, for once there wasn't a SHIT happening and I was quite pleased for her!

Just once in a while, a valuable item would be found at the treatment works or perhaps in the collection system. The smaller sewers frequently had blockages that the duty operatives would have to clear and there were a few places that became regular call-out areas. These were places where the sewerage pipework had been infested with tree roots, or where they had been built with inadequate fall to keep the liquid moving fast enough to prevent settlement of heavier solids such as sand or grit. Eventually, these sections were cleaned on a regular basis using a high-pressure water-jetting machine, which amounted to a small tanker/trailer fitted with a diesel-powered pump and feeding through a reel of pressure hose to a powerful nozzle. Behind the nozzle were fitted retro-jets to propel it through the pipeline. Once the hose had been blasted from one manhole to the next it was retrieved with the powerful water spray still running and effectively washed the flow-restricting deposit to a point where it could be removed by a suction-tanker vehicle, or sometimes even by using hand tools. At this point, the deposits were washed clean enough to see the glint of metal and occasionally coins would be found or, rather more rarely, something reasonably valuable such as a ring, earring or some other small item of jewellery. As the chances of finding the owner of this treasure were virtually nil, the items were never reported to the police and the crew shared whatever they could make from selling the goods, which actually wasn't very much at all. There was one occasion, however, when a gold cigarette lighter was found and this certainly was reported at the local police station upon my insistence. It was never claimed by anybody though and after the requisite length of time, it was returned to the finder and subsequently sold to a local jeweller's shop. The jetting crew all had a drink on that one!

Towards the end of my career, I worked for United Group PCL in New South Wales, Australia, and was seconded to the Town Council at a place called Tamworth, where I managed the operations of a newly constructed wastewater treatment plant; it should be noted that 'sewage' and 'works' were words I never heard used in Australia! A portion of the incoming flow to the new plant was directed through an old percolating filter unit, which had been kept operational to deal with industrial waste from nearby abattoirs. The original screening machinery on this old plant remained in service, trapping all kinds of rubbish that required frequent removal from the collection bin, a rather unpleasant task.

On one occasion an Operative emptying the bin discovered a fifty-dollar note that had obviously been in the sewer for a day or two. Australian banknotes, being made from plastic these days, display some disadvantages when they are in your wallet or being counted because they tend to crinkle somewhat and often stick together but their superiority over paper money really shows when they have been dropped into a sewer! Unlike paper notes, that would disintegrate, they remain virtually undamaged and can be readily washed clean with only a little effort. This particular one was indeed washed clean and was soon spent at the local shop, the finder being generous enough to treat his workmates to a few snacks and soft drinks. Without a doubt that was the best find of all!

The most remarkable recovery, however, occurred at East Hyde when a man arrived at the site to see if there was any chance of finding his false teeth. Apparently, he had lost his denture down the toilet when he had been the worst for wear after a party. It so happens that dentures are frequently trapped on screens at wastewater treatment plants but at East Hyde, some Operative wags thought it was amusing to line them up on the concrete wall of the grit channels. In fact, it may be that the man had heard of this from somebody before visiting the plant. He was told that there were several sets of gnashers on display at the Inlet Works and was subsequently taken there to have a look. Remarkably he spotted an upper plate that looked very much like the one he had lost and without further ado picked the obscene object up and put it in his mouth, much to the horror and disgust of his escort, who happened to be one of the young chemists from the laboratory.

"It hasn't been washed mate!" was his plaintive cry to the man. "It's been in the sewer with all the shit for Christ's sake! Take it out of your mouth!"

"Never mind son", came the reply, "it fits and even if it's not mine it'll do me. I'll take it, OK?" With that the man removed the denture, put it in his pocket and had a good spit, mounted his bicycle and left the site.

Unfortunately, or otherwise, I did not witness the event but it was the main subject of conversation at the site for a long time. It might be that the denture did indeed belong to the man, who knows? But how anybody could pick up an unknown set of false teeth and shove it in his mouth, let alone one that had been all through the sewers of Luton and then sat on the concrete wall of the grit channels for days on end, I shall never know. This guy was either totally ignorant of hygiene or, alternatively, had the stomach of a rhinoceros. Whatever it was, the whole episode really was AMAZING!

*****

Club secretary gasses himself in his car at East Hyde

I had been working at East Hyde Sewage Works for only a few weeks when I received a visitor from a debt collection agency. The young lady came to my office accompanied by two huge, middle-aged thug-like men, quite obviously ex-policemen, who stood either side of her almost as a protective shield. "Do sit down," I invited them but only she sat. Her two 'rottweilers' stood, arms folded, by the office door as if to bar any escape on my part.

"What can I do for you?" I asked.

She told me that she was from a debt collection agency and she had come to collect a sum of money that the East Hyde Sports and Social Club had been owing to a brewery for several months. I told her that the Sports and Social club was nothing whatsoever to do with me and that she should conduct her enquiries with the Club Secretary, whose name I gave her.

"But you're the Works Manager," she said, "You have overall responsibility!"

I assured her that I did not have any responsibility for the club whatsoever and that I wasn't even a member. I asked her for the details of the debt and said I would refer the whole issue to the Divisional Head Office immediately and that there would surely be a full investigation. After she and her companions had left, I asked the works foreman to send the Club Secretary to my office but he was not in work that day. In fact, he had apparently been off sick for three days and was not expected to return to work for a few more days yet. Subsequently, I referred everything to the Divisional Manager and suggested that the Sports and Social Club should be closed pending enquiries and this was agreed. When we then started looking in the clubhouse, we found a great deal of evidence of wrongdoing, including a number of cheques that had been made out to the Club and obviously cashed over the bar but some of them were many months old and, I suspect, were never going to be paid into the bank.

A gathering of works employees was called on Friday and I told them that the Club would be closed for a time until the problems were sorted out. Nobody seemed to be particularly concerned, which I thought was rather odd, but subsequently, it was pointed out that the Club was now used largely by people from the surrounding villages rather than by Thames Water employees.

Furthermore, it was sometimes difficult for the shift operatives to get the gates shut late at night because customers were reluctant to go home at closing time.

The following day there was the most dreadful SHIT happening which I was not made aware of until I got to work the following Monday morning.

The Sports and Social Club Secretary decided that he could no longer face the pending enquiries into the Club's affairs and so committed suicide. He did it by connecting a length of hose onto the exhaust pipe of his car with the other end of it pushed through a rear window. He sat in the car with the engine running and poisoned himself with carbon monoxide fumes. Precisely where this awful event occurred, I don't know but I believe it was not on the treatment plant. The man was found dead in his car and presumably, the police were informed but there were no questions from them as to what may have been the reason for the suicide.

After that event, the East Hyde Sports and Social Club was closed down permanently. Its assets, largely in the form of unsold beverages, glasses, bar equipment and the like were sold off and the outstanding debts were settled, presumably by Thames Water. I do recall that the cheques we found in a drawer in the bar were all presented to the bank and one or two people complained that they were unable to pay the outstanding amounts but that became an issue between them and their own banks.

My last encounter with the Sports and Social Club came a week or two after the above event when two very large and extremely butch women came to my office to ask if they could still use the football pitch on the treatment works site to play matches against other women's teams. I told them that the area would be used as a storage area during the construction of the new plant and would ultimately be used for storage of the digested sludge when the new plant was finished.

"In any case," I told them, "such facilities, if they do exist in future, will only be available to employees of Thames Water and their family members." I believe those women subsequently hated me with a deep loathing!

*****

Paul Heiney from BBC at East Hyde

Sometime after my transfer to East Hyde, I received a telephone call from an ex-colleague of mine that I had worked with at the Lee Conservancy Catchment

Board. He was still doing the same job in the same organisation but that was now a part of Thames Water too. Bob told me that the BBC would be doing a radio programme about the River Lee. They did these programmes weekly and covered all sorts of places, features and interesting issues all over the country. The River Lee, being the River Thames's largest tributary flows through North East London and its own tributaries flow in Bedfordshire, Hertfordshire and Essex, all counties steeped in history. Since East Hyde Sewage Treatment Works is close to the source of the Lee at Luton, the BBC wanted to include it in the radio programme. Bob said I would be receiving a telephone call from the programme-makers in a day or two and sure enough I received a call from Paul Heiney. Paul said he wanted to include a small feature on the Sewage Works and would like to have a guided tour, so we arranged a date and time to meet at my office.

I remembered Paul Heiney from a BBC Television programme called That's Life, wherein he was a member of a team headed by Esther Rantzen and he always struck me as an intelligent and amusing character that delivered his contribution to this light-hearted programme rather well. I, therefore, looked forward to his visit to the treatment works, which turned out to be a pleasure indeed.

Paul arrived at my office at 9.00 am for an early start because, as he explained over a cup of tea, he had several other places to visit that day. I was rather surprised that he came alone, because I was expecting at least a sound recordist to be with him but he explained that it wasn't necessary, because he had the latest recording machine and microphone with him that he could operate perfectly well on his own. Paul needed to tour the sewage works with me and, through question and answer sessions, demonstrate what was being done at this point on the River Lee. He had already completed his programme's introduction and the first section about the river, from its source, then through the town of Luton and down to the Luton Hoo estate, that is situated just upstream of the works.

So off we went to the Inlet Works where I quickly described the structure, the machinery and explained what was happening.

"Right then," said Paul, "let's get started," as he switched on the recorder and readied the microphone.

"I am standing at the inlet of the Luton Sewage Treatment Plant at East Hyde," he said, "with the Group Manager, Mr David Marpole and we can see a large volume of sewage from the town rushing into the plant. There doesn't seem to be much of a smell Dave, why is that?" as he moved the mike over for me to speak.

My reply was quite a natural one, delivered with a chuckle but ill-conceived under the circumstances.

"You should be here when they're desludging the primary tanks, Paul. The stink's enough to blind you on a bad day!"

"Oh look, Dave," said Paul testily, "you can't give me answers like that! This is a documentary type of programme; I need an explanation as to why this sewage isn't smelly like I thought it would be!"

I apologised of course but asked Paul to either tell me the question beforehand or at least give me a clue as to what it might be, allowing for the fact that his own words were more or less impromptu anyway.

The starting sequence was repeated and my answer this time was that the sewage was still quite fresh and probably not yet devoid of oxygen so it wouldn't have started to decompose too much at the point of entry into the plant. That was acceptable and we progressed to the primary settlement tanks and the rectangular percolating filters, the distributors on which, despite their obsolescence and worn-out appearance, were a superb example of British mechanical engineering in their own right. Machines that could trundle backwards and forwards continuously with the minimum of maintenance, just a drop of oil and a dab of grease, for years without any other form of power than that derived from a syphon-driven water wheel. Paul was impressed by this fact and described the machines cleverly in his commentary.

I then took him to the other section that treated the flow by aeration of Activated Sludge and as we stood upon the footpath around the tanks Paul resumed his talk.

"We are now standing next to some large, elevated concrete tanks that are being churned and mixed with air. They are filled with a filthy brown material that, although there is no smell from it, looks absolutely disgusting. What do you call this, Dave?" he asked.

"We call it SHIT Paul, what would you call it?" I replied as I almost convulsed with laughter.

Paul also saw the funny side of it and admitted that he would have probably given the same answer to such a poorly worded question.

"OK, I'll give you that one mate but please remember I'm getting pushed for time. We're not on That's Life unfortunately," he pleaded.

The sequence was repeated and this time the question was, "What do you call this process Dave?" All was well and I briefly explained the Activated Sludge process as best I could in layman's terms.

The remainder of the tour went without a hitch and Paul expressed his thanks very kindly. He said he'd thoroughly enjoyed his first-ever trip to a sewage works and had a good laugh too. Finally, he reminded me of the anticipated broadcast date for the documentary programme about the River Lee and I was subsequently able to tape it. I still have the tape somewhere but unfortunately, never had it converted to DVD and can no longer play it because my old cassette recorder has long-since failed to function. Shame, because it would be fun to play it to my offspring.

*****

Dead man found by Police.

The Secretary/Administration lady at East Hyde always kept me informed of anything strange or unusual happening on the site. Her office window gave her a splendid view of the Inlet Works and much of the rest of the treatment plant, whereas all I could see from my office window was the tiny River Lee and the road to Luton.

One day, Debra came into my office with a very worried look on her face.

"There are policemen all over the Inlet Works!" she said anxiously. "I think they're looking for something!"

So, I strolled over to the Inlet Works and asked one of the policemen what was going on.

"Police business, sir!" was his curt reply.

"Really?" I asked, "I think I'd already worked that out, Constable. Where's the senior officer please?"

There came another curt reply from this particularly rude young man.

"Why, who wants to know?"

Hackles raised, I now exerted a bit of my own authority.

"I do, Constable! You people have just invaded a Thames Water treatment works that I happen to be the manager of, without so much as a 'by your leave' a 'kiss my arse' or anything else! Now please tell me where the senior officer is!"

Looking somewhat startled the constable deigned to apologise.

"Oh sorry, sir. Look, here he comes now, our Inspector." "Excuse me, sir," to the Inspector, "this is the Works Manager, he wants a word with you."

There came another curt reply.

"What about?" asked the Inspector whilst still looking straight at the constable.

I intervened by asking him what was going on and why nobody had had the courtesy to tell us that policemen would be entering the site. He said, rather dictatorially that there had been nobody available but soon changed his attitude and climbed down off his pedestal when I told him the offices had been fully staffed since 8.00 am.

With his new attitude, the Inspector informed me that a passer-by had reported a dead body leaning against the inside of the boundary fence next to the road. The police had arrived with a number of forensic officers to gather information and support evidence to determine the cause of the man's death. An ambulance was on its way to collect the body and meanwhile, he didn't want anyone, other than police, to enter the area. In fact, the gateway was already being taped off. I pointed out that the Plant Operatives would need to attend to the inlet machinery etc. throughout the day and the only reason they were not there at the moment was because they were having their morning tea break, which was almost finished. I also reminded him that there was even more good reason for having the courtesy to inform us what was happening, which he grudgingly agreed with. I could hardly imagine how this dimwit of a policeman had risen to the rank of Inspector!

The ambulance arrived with two paramedics and after a brief check of the dead body, it was quickly put on board. The Inspector did ask me if I knew the man but I didn't recognise him at all. He also asked a couple of the Plant Operatives who came back to work on the Inlet Works when their tea break had finished. They declared that he was not an employee at the Treatment Plant, nor was he a resident in the village of East Hyde. They guessed that he had entered the Inlet Works via the gate, probably at night when only the shift personnel were on site and was therefore unlikely to have been seen.

After a few hours, the police tape was removed from the gateway and all the officers left the site. This time the dimwit Inspector did have the courtesy to inform me first and furthermore promised to send me sufficient details of the incident for me to write a suitable report to the Divisional Manager. Of course, the moment the police left the site just about everyone from the Treatment works, myself included, had to traipse all around the area where the dead man had been found to satisfy our own curiosity. Had that happened earlier, any clues or evidence as to the cause of death etc. would have probably been destroyed so the Inspector should most certainly have informed us what was going on beforehand.

It transpired that this was only a minor SHIT happening. The unfortunate man had died from completely natural causes but the mystery remained as to what he was doing at the Inlet Works of East Hyde Sewage Treatment Works, particularly when it was confirmed that he had left his home in the North of England several weeks earlier and, until found dead beside our boundary fence, had disappeared without a trace. I gave instructions that the access gates to East Hyde were to be kept locked thereafter at all times outside normal working hours.

*****

Chapter 9

The Reorganisation-Mad Thames Water Did It Again

This time, my title became Group Manager (Small Works) and a little later became Group Manager (Small Works North East). This gave me an enormous area of responsibility.

Spillage of sludge from new digester at Nags Head Lane

The new job title of Group Manager (Small Works North East) was something of a mouthful but acceptable, I thought. There was a list of Sewage Treatment Group Managers and my name appeared on it as D. Marpole (SWNE), which was the address heading for all internal mail that arrived on my desk. Unfortunately, some wag decided to put a letter I between the W and the N on one occasion, and it stuck but though amusing for the first time the joke wore a bit thin after a couple of years! (Yet another SHIT happening!)

The reorganisation, however, did give me back managerial responsibilities for a number of treatment works that I had managed before, including the Nags Head Lane works at Brentwood, which was the only one of the Brentwood Urban District Council's sewage treatment works that was transferred to Thames Water; the other two were transferred to Anglian Water when the Water Authorities were formed.

A year or so earlier, it had been decided to make some modifications to the Nags Head Lane works and one of those modifications was the construction of a second digester which, in my opinion and by my calculations, was completely unnecessary. The original digester had more than adequate capacity to treat all the anticipated sludge load at the works for at least a further ten years. Furthermore, the new unit was much smaller than the existing digester, being only a third of its capacity, and I could envisage difficulties arising in the future through unequal loading of the two digesters together. The thing had been built, however, and it was necessary to commission it and test its operational capability so start-up feeding of the new digester was put in hand.

SHIT happened, although not in any way as might have been expected. The new unit had apparently already been filled with water and checked for leaks. The heater circuit and associated pumps had all been tested and all the external valves had been checked. Some of the water had been removed to make space for sludge to be pumped in and it was decided to fill the new unit with digesting sludge from the currently operating unit, i.e. to seed it so that start-up could be achieved much more quickly. The sludge was therefore transferred under gravity from the old digester's overflow pipe whilst it was being fed with raw sludge from the primary tanks. It was a simple operation but because the new digester had been tacked on to the existing pipework system, the valve arrangement was somewhat complicated. The Operatives were not familiar with it, nor did they realise that some of the pipework had clearly not been properly tested, which became apparent as a massive circular spray of very warm, black, digesting sludge burst from the upper flange of the external feed valve mounted on the side of the new steel tank. No gasket had been installed! The sludge was not very thick so it travelled quite a distance under the head pressure of several feet that was pushing it. Three Operatives and one of the contractor's engineers were liberally soaked but the flow still had to be stopped, and quickly. The new valve arrangement was too complicated, so it had to be done at the gushing feed valve!

It is amazing how, when faced with complex adversity, the human mind can instantly dream up a solution to the problem and in consequence of this I have a picture now etched into my memory of two men standing at either end of a large sheet of shuttering plywood, each holding it as high above his head as possible with both arms while a 'tropical thunderstorm' of black SHIT was raining down on the plywood. A third man was standing underneath the board closing the feed valve as fast as he possibly could. I had to admire them for their ingenuity but still hooted with laughter at them being drenched with sludge. One of the Operatives holding the plywood was Jed, the same man that fell into the raw sludge hopper alongside me more than a decade earlier. He looked at me, scoffed and said, "I always get covered in SHIT when YOU'RE around! BUGGER OFF!" He then trudged off with the others to have a shower and change his clothes.

After a frightful verbal exchange with the contractor's agent and Thames Water's Site Engineer about the standard of work, I insisted that the missing gasket be installed immediately and the pipework PROPERLY checked. This was done but when the incident was included in my monthly Operations Report it elicited a surprise visit from the Water Authority's Operations Director, who used some pretty harsh words to both of those people. I suspect they were considerably more attentive to their inspection work after that.

The new digester subsequently went into service successfully but it was soon proven to be completely unnecessary and after a month or two was shut down and emptied. It was never put into operation again during the remainder of my time with Thames Water and, for all I know, it may never have been used again since.

*****

The stink of sludge gas affecting Toy Store Manager's house.

Another reorganisation within Thames water had me responsible for sewage treatment works in the County of Berkshire for a while. One of those plants was at Maidenhead, which had been recently rebuilt and extended to serve a substantial increase in population over recent years in that area. The new treatment works was based on an oxidation ditch system but was also equipped with primary settlement tanks, final settlement tanks and an anaerobic sludge digestion system. The gas from the digesters was not used for power production at that time so any surplus was wasted to atmosphere via a flare stack that stood upon a raised area roughly in the middle of the treatment works. The gas produced seemed to be of a particularly high quality, because it was difficult to see the flame burning at the top of the stack. Often, the only visible evidence of the flame was the heat ripples in the air that could be seen against the background of a cloudy sky.

Maidenhead Sewage Treatment Works was neatly kept. Grassed areas were properly tended, the site roads were swept clean and there was no dried sludge storage on site. In fact, all the liquid sludge was transferred, after digestion, to the bigger plant at Slough. Mature trees and shrubs grew around the boundary fences, some within the site and others outside in neighbouring land and gardens, making it a reasonably pleasant place to work.

One day, however, I received a telephone call from one of the Maidenhead staff asking me to respond to a call he had received that morning from one of the neighbours, who was concerned about odour nuisance. He had refused to discuss the matter with the Plant Operative because he had been told by our Public Relations Office that he should discuss the matter with the Group Manager (Small Works North East.) The Public Relations people, for some reason, had no idea where I was based at that time or what my direct telephone number was, so had given him the number of the Maidenhead plant. When I called him back, he was, as expected, rather curt. He told me he was having a very large wedding reception for his daughter, to be held in his garden where a marquee would be erected. It was going to occur in two weeks' time and would be very expensive so he didn't want it to be spoilt by a stink of pooh from a filthy sewerage farm. I tried to reassure him that the plant was not filthy or smelly but he didn't want to discuss it further.

"Well if you don't want to discuss the matter what on earth are you doing wasting my time with your telephone call?" I asked him, telling him also that I was very busy dealing with far more important matters.

He said that he wanted me to look at the location and advise him whether or not to proceed with the celebration at his home so a couple of days later I arrived at the front gate of his luxurious home, which was actually quite close to the treatment works.

This time our neighbour was very polite and showed me his beautiful garden and lawn where the marquee was to be erected. I couldn't give him any guarantees that there would be no odour nuisance but I did take him to the works for a quick tour. I noticed he sniffed a lot and obviously was unable to detect any nuisance so was clearly reassured that his big party would not be spoilt. I did promise him that if anything untoward should happen during the next week or so leading up to the event I would let him know straight away and do everything possible to minimise any nuisance. He then admitted to me that he and his family had only moved into the area about a year earlier and they had never experienced any problems arising from the treatment works. In fact, he only very recently became aware that the site was a sewage treatment works when one of his invited guests warned him about the filthy, stinking sewerage farm nearby that used to cause a lot of nuisance. This was why he had called our Public Relations Office. Anyway, the day before his big party I called him and wished him success with the wedding reception. I also told him that my staff at Maidenhead were on alert to make sure nothing went wrong at the treatment works which, I'm glad to say, it did not.

SHIT did happen shortly afterwards, however, when the Public Relations people told me of a serious complaint from another neighbour of the Maidenhead works. He was claiming that the stench from the plant was absolutely ruining his life and he wanted it stopped forthwith or else! That sounded like a good challenge for me so I called the number given to me by the Public Relations lady, only to find it was for a very large American toy dealership that has branches all over the country. The threatening neighbour turned out to be the manager of the store in Reading and his first words to me on the telephone, spoken with pure venom, were:

"I forbid you to reveal to anybody who I work for! Do you understand that?"

My response was equally blunt.

"Please change your attitude and address me politely. I'm not the slightest bit interested in what you do for a living, I'm calling about a complaint you made! Do you understand THAT?"

There was silence for a few moments, then came the abuse.

"It's that filthy f*****ng sewerage thing you shitheads are running near my home. It f*****ng stinks all the time. STOP THE F*****NG STINK!"

I put the phone down! Later I checked with the Operatives at Maidenhead and they assured me that nothing was wrong and there was, as usual, no significant smell emanating from the works. I decided, however, to visit the place the next day just to be sure all was indeed well. So the following day, having had a good look around the treatment works and detected no real trace of a f*****ing stink, I once again called the complainant. On this occasion, I asked the telephonist to tell him I would not tolerate any foul language or verbal abuse. Clearly, she did tell him because his first words to me were:

"Sorry about yesterday, I was upset."

My reply was as blunt as before.

"So, you should be sorry! We are not shitheads and this is not a filthy f*****ing sewerage thing we are running. Any further remarks like that will have your cover immediately blown as to where you work. OK?"

This elicited a rather more grovelling apology and I smirked to myself as I said, "All right Mr X, apology accepted! Now let's get to the bottom of this problem and sort it out."

He told me that the appalling sickly smell drifted across his house and garden for hours at a time and then disappeared. His next-door neighbours also got the problem and it had to be from the sewage treatment works because there was no other possible source of such a stench in that location. Seeing the homes in that area convinced me that he was probably right about the likely source, but how? As I told Mr X, I was standing in the middle of the works and had sniffed every inch of it for the past hour and couldn't smell anything that foul. Finally, he told me that his Swedish girlfriend with whom he lived was so fed up with the stink that she was considering going back to Sweden, hence the reason for him being so upset the previous day. (One may presume therefore that Swedish SHIT is odourless!) I asked for his address and said I would go around there to see if I could detect anything myself. He then asked me not to reveal to any of his neighbours that it was him that had complained. Clearly, there's something fishy about this bloke, I thought to myself!

His very nice and spacious home was at the end of a cul-de-sac containing about ten other houses, approximately $^1/_4$ mile from the treatment works. Incidentally, it was in the completely opposite direction from the house where the wedding reception was earlier held. I left my car and walked around the cul-de-sac close to Mr X's house when suddenly I inhaled the foulest stench imaginable. It was absolutely disgusting and I must have shown it upon my face, not to mention my blasphemy as I caught the whiff.

"Jesus Holy Christ!" I said to myself, "That's bloody sludge gas!"

Just then the door to Mr X's house opened and a smart-looking young woman, very obviously Scandinavian, came out and spoke to me.

"Excuse me, you are from the Council, no?"

I introduced myself and told her I was from Thames Water and investigating the cause of the stink.

"Oh, my man said you would coming, it dreadful every time. We have to closing window or it make house smelly too!"

I assured her I knew what the problem must be and would deal with it straight away.

"How long has this been happening?" I asked her.

She said it had been for about a month. I bade her goodbye and promised the nuisance would be gone very soon, then, hackles raised somewhat, I rushed back to the sewage works.

Arriving at the treatment works, I collared the Leading Plant Operative and the mechanic/electrician, telling them that I had just discovered the reason for the complaint about odour.

"It's bloody sludge gas!" I told them, "We must have a leak somewhere and a bloody big leak too! Christ I nearly puked outside that bloke's house. The smell is diabolical!"

They both assured me, however, that there couldn't be a leak because we would smell it on the site.

"Is the flare stack lighting?" I asked.

"Seems to be," was the reply but I insisted on having a look. Sure enough, the heat ripples were clearly visible over the top of the flare stack but try as I might I couldn't get even the slightest glimpse of a flame. I told them my doubts about it burning and between us, we came up with an idea to make sure that it was. We would light the flame from the ground! This, however, would have needed an ignition system on a long pole because the flare stack was pretty high at this plant. None was available but, not to be beaten, I thought of a method to light it, or assure us that it was already alight, by flinging a lighted ball of rag on a stick up to the flame area. An old sack was duly found, wrapped around an old rake handle and then soaked in diesel fuel. Being the tallest of the three of us I was naturally expected to fling it and duly lit it with my cigarette lighter. The other two stood back as I tossed the 'Marpole cocktail' into the air. It was a weak, lousy toss and proved nothing. The second try, however, was a complete success and elicited an enormous WHOOOOMPH at the top of the flare stack. The flame was unbelievably huge and we all felt the phenomenal heat from it for a second but a serious point had been proved. The automatic ignition system and pilot flame on the flare stack had not been working. For how long, we did not know but for sure it would be working thereafter. An electrician was brought in from Slough Wastewater Treatment Plant and, along with the two men at Maidenhead, instructed to "PLEASE GET THAT BLOODY THING WORKING AND KEEP IT WORKING!" I didn't want to hear another complaint about stink! Subsequently, at Maidenhead I never did. Fantastic!

I often wondered about Mr X. Why was it that he didn't want anyone to know his employer? He had been such a nasty person until cut down to size that I secretly wished the Swedish female had indeed gone back home. Maybe she did and hopefully took him with her!

Problem wearing a hard hat.

When I took responsibility for Slough Sewage Treatment Works there was some modification work in progress on the activated sludge plant. A sizeable crane was required to lift materials and equipment in and out of various tanks and this crane was permanently on-site for many weeks. A large area was therefore cordoned off and designated a Hard Hat or safety helmet zone for anybody entering it. Since most of the plant remained in operation, there were always Thames Water employees within the Hard Hat zone as well as the contractor's workforce. Around that period the Health and Safety at Work Act was making people far more aware of safe working practices so people in positions similar to mine were very keen to ensure that the new rules were obeyed and standards properly maintained. As I remember it the Slough workforce was as good as any other within Thames Water so complaints over work-ethics or infringement of rules were rare. Elsewhere there had recently been many cases where managerial staff had been criticised for not enforcing the rules and indeed there had been cases where managers in other industries had been prosecuted so I became quite vigilant.

There was one occasion when I considered a safety rule was being flagrantly broken and furthermore it was being broken by the electrical foreman who also happened to be one of the Trades Union stewards. This man was a perfectly good worker and, so far as I was aware, was well trained and experienced in his job, hence the reason for him having been appointed as a foreman long before I met him. He was always polite and sociable and we got on well enough with each other. The problem was that he was working inside the Hard Hat zone without a safety helmet. The reason was because he was a Sikh and always wore a turban. No safety helmet was available to cover a Sikh turban and, in any case, this gentleman considered he had head protection enough. Therefore, he thought he should be able to do whatever work he had allocated to himself within the cordoned-off area in precisely the same way as he did in any other part of the works. I disagreed with him and gave him an instruction that he wasn't to go into the Hard Hat zone in future because he was obliged by law to wear a safety helmet but he couldn't. He would have to get another electrician to do the work within the cordoned-off area. He then told me that he thought I was ignorant of the law because Sikh people were allowed to drive a motorcycle without a crash helmet but that law was universally known. I had to reiterate that despite changes to the road laws there was still a requirement for EVERBODY to wear a safety helmet within a designated Hard Hat zone. Finally, he shrugged his shoulders and said, "Ok, if that's what you want but don't blame me if things don't get done properly!" I told him that if he wasn't the man doing the job wrongly there was no way he would be held responsible. It was left at that but clearly, he was disgruntled.

About a week later, I received a telephone call from a female at the Thames Water Head Office telling me that Mr Hoffman, the Chief Executive at the time, wanted to see me in his office straight away. I pointed out that it would take me about two hours to get to Reading at that time of day, to which she snootily replied, "Rubbish! It's no more than twenty minutes from Slough!"

"Yes madam," I replied, "but I'm not at Slough I am at Rye Meads."

"Oh!" she said, "He won't be pleased at that just get here as quickly as you can!" I asked the reason for the summons and was told it was an order! I then asked if I could speak to Mr Hoffman and was very rudely told; "Certainly not! You have your instructions!" and the phone went dead.

Whoever that woman was I vowed to teach her some manners someday and resolved to report the matter to the Chief Executive! But what was it all about? It had to be some very serious SHIT happening! Throughout my drive to Reading, I tried to think what could have gone wrong.

Precisely two hours later, I was waiting in trepidation outside Mr Hoffman's office. His secretary, who was not the rude woman I had spoken to earlier, invited me in.

Mr Hoffman asked me very bluntly, "Are you racist?" I replied that I was not. "The Trades Union people are saying you are! You'd better not be because I won't tolerate it!"

I repeated that I was not racist and asked what the hell this was all about. He then related some drivel about receiving a complaint from a Senior Trade Union official that I had verbally abused a Sikh electrician at Slough treatment works because he didn't wear a crash helmet. So, I carefully explained precisely what had passed between the electrical foreman and me and declared that if he, Mr Hoffman himself, had been in the cordoned off zone I would have told him to wear his safety helmet or get out of the zone. Never had there been any verbal abuse and I was quite sure the Sikh gentleman himself had never made such an accusation. I was quite certain, however, that I could point the finger at the lying, trouble-making Senior Union Official that had because he worked in my group. Mr Hoffman accepted that the abuse issue was probably invented but said I was wrong about the wearing of safety helmets.

"These Sikh people do not have to wear them. I know it!" he said.

I pointed out that nobody could be FORCED to wear them but EVERYONE working inside a Hard Hat zone MUST wear them by law. If people cannot or will not wear them, they WILL NOT be allowed in a Hard Hat zone on a plant I manage. There was not yet any exception to the rules! So far, Sikh men had been excluded from the requirement to wear a crash helmet when riding on a motorcycle. Nothing else! Despite the twaddle reported by the Senior Union Official this was not an issue about crash helmets or motorcycles! The secretary was then asked to check out the fine print of the Health and Safety at Work Act and talk to the Legal Department about it. I was told I could leave now but should expect further discussion on the matter shortly. This prompted me to complain about the rude woman on the telephone earlier, which he promised to deal with.

When I reached Slough, I confronted the electrical foreman about this issue. He was flabbergasted that I had been accused of racial abuse and apologised wholeheartedly. He said he had raised the matter at a Union Stewards meeting but had never intended it to go any further. He promised to send a letter to the Chief Executive denying that he had accused me of racism. I told him I would let him know what Mr Hoffman's secretary found out and that a decision would be made according to the Health and Safety at Work Act.

Subsequently, I was proven right but the law was about to be changed anyway so within a few weeks it didn't matter. I did, however, receive a memo from the Chief Executive congratulating me for holding my principles. That was rather pleasant but it would have been better to see the trouble-making Senior Union Official disciplined. As for the very rude woman on the telephone, I never heard a thing!

*****

Trying to enter Chequers with an arsenal aboard.

A number of people in Thames Water were interested in shooting. One or two belonged to game-shooting clubs and were owners of rather fancy shotguns, while others were more interested in Clay Pigeon Shooting and had tried to form a club at the Rye Meads Sewage Treatment Works where there was a great deal of open space. Most of the open space, however, particularly in the final effluent lagoon area, was a listed nature reserve. The Royal Society for the Protection of Birds had a ringing station there and members of the organisation had freedom to conduct wildfowl surveys and other bird watching activities without interference. The site was therefore useless as a Clay Shoot. An alternative site was found, however, at an abandoned treatment works known as Epping Northern, which had become disused when a new sewerage system was built in the area and the flow diverted to Rye Meads. The treatment works had been demolished but only to just below ground level so there was still a lot of the old concrete structures left behind. Furthermore, a storm overflow was retained on the site for use under very high flow conditions so the place was useless for farming and therefore could not be disposed of by Thames Water. Access to the site was via a shared farm track through arable land, it was essentially out of sight, far enough from the nearest road to make it safe and no houses were close enough to it for noise to be a nuisance. It was ideal for use as a clay shoot and Thames Water, the local police and the next-door farmer all approved. The Thames Water Clay Pigeon Club was duly formed and I decided to join too. Subsequently, because the site had a storm overflow and therefore remained in my management area, I was elected as Club Chairman. Our membership wasn't all that many so to make the club viable we were obliged to allow people from outside Thames Water to join and we also frequently invited guests along for a Fifty-bird Shoot. I was able to scrounge a twenty-foot long sea container from one of the contractors at the Luton, East Hyde, treatment works. The roof was rusted through in places and some of the contractor's material had been ruined, so he bought another container. The truck that delivered it was used to take the old one to our shoot and a Thames Water four-wheeled crane returning from another job, was 'shanghaied' for an hour to lift it into a perfect place on some disused railway sleepers somebody had, allegedly, found. One of our members was a welder so with a few bits of steel he was soon able to make the container watertight and my son subsequently painted it, for a bit of pocket money. The dark green chlorinated-rubber paint was scrounged from my painter brother in law in exchange for a free Fifty-bird Shoot! In the container, we were able to securely keep all the clay traps, several boxes of different sized clay targets, tools for maintaining the site, two gun racks and assorted folding chairs for spectating.

Guns were kept at home of course and cartridges were invariably purchased in just sufficient amounts on the day before a shoot. The club met on alternate Sundays throughout the year from 9.00 am to 12.30 pm, whereupon most participants went for a pint or two at a local pub before going home for Sunday lunch. It was a perfect set-up for those people interested in clay shooting and for a few years we spent many a pleasant Sunday morning harmlessly blazing away at clay discs, sometimes in competition with other groups but always enjoying the company of like-minded souls.

A club competition was organised for one particular Sunday, so a couple of boxes of cartridges were required. It so happened that I had taken all my guns to have the stocks lengthened by an inch or so because their recoil was causing bruising of my cheekbone; they were ready to collect from the gunsmith so I volunteered to pick up the cartridges from there rather than leave it to the Club Secretary, my friend and colleague Luigi. That evening I collected my three guns, two over/under, double-barrelled, 12 bore pieces and a super little 9 mm single-shot garden gun. The latter had an extension to its barrel to make it legal in UK and it looked rather like a silenced 0.22 rifle. I also collected five hundred 12-bore cartridges and fifty of the little brass-plated 9 mm shells too. It was nearly 7.30 pm when I arrived home and by the time I had eaten my evening meal, read the paper, watched the news and had my shower, it was time for bed.

The following morning, I arrived at my office to find an authorisation to enter Chequers, the official country home of the British Prime Minister. I had arranged for the application to be made because Chequers has a small sewage treatment works in its grounds and it so happened that the maintenance of this unit was performed by Thames Water. It was visited on a weekly basis by a maintenance crew that worked for my group so obviously, I should see what their duties were and determine if they were being performed effectively and efficiently. The maintenance crew and their vehicles were all known to the security people at Chequers but everybody entering the site required authorisation as well as a Thames Water identity card. At that time the responsibility for security was in the hands of the armed forces and was alternated, I believe, between the Army and the Navy, although for what reason I have no idea. The authorisation was evidently granted by a female Naval Commander, who presumably sailed a desk somewhere in Whitehall.

Having been advised by my staff of the route to the place and the appropriate entrance I set off for my first and, as it transpired, my only trip to the famous country estate. I found the entrance and stopped at the security checkpoint. I don't recall the guards being in any kind of Navy uniform but they were pretty smart characters. I was asked the purpose of my visit and for I.D., authorisation etc., then asked to get out of my car and open the boot for inspection. That's when I realised I had forgotten to empty the car the previous evening. EEK! A MONUMENTAL SHIT HAPPENING WAS UPON ME!!

"Before I do that," I blurted, "I have to tell you that in the boot there are three shotguns and five hundred and fifty rounds of ammunition! The guns are all in slips and are not loaded! Everything's legal I assure you!"

"WHAT? GET OUT OF THE CAR AND STAND BACK!" snapped the guard. "QUICKLY NOW, QUICKLY!" as he motioned to two others to join him.

I did exactly as I was told. These guys were going to take no nonsense at all! One took the keys from the ignition and opened the boot of my car, while the other started looking around inside it and took my briefcase off the back seat.

"Open this please!" he called and stood clear as I did so.

Although the first guard had already frisked me, I was asked to empty my pockets too. All three began to relax after that and I was allowed to replace things in my pockets, close my briefcase again and put it back in the car. My guns had all been carefully examined and the car was inspected underneath with a mirror, which it probably would have been under normal circumstances anyway. I was then obliged to sit down in the office where a document was handed to me. It was my shotgun certificate, which I had used when I collected my mini arsenal from the gunsmith's shop the previous evening.

"This is yours, sir. Good thing we found it." I was told. "That little Anschutz nine millimetre looked like a silenced rifle to us at first. Very dodgy!"

I was then asked to explain how I could have been so damned stupid as to arrive at a place like this with enough artillery to start a small war. My explanation was given with a sincere apology, whereupon I was allowed to leave but was not granted entry to the estate.

My Thames Water I.D. card was returned to me but the authorisation document was not and I was just too embarrassed to ask for it. Probably, it was shredded! Under no circumstances was I going to make a new application because if it were to have been refused there would have been an unholy fuss made in Thames Water, so I just quietly forgot all about the whole thing. Although I didn't know it at the time, my career as an Operations Manager within

141

Thames Water would soon be coming to a close anyway, so it hardly mattered.

*****

Chapter 10

The Umpteenth Reorganisation
Makes Several People Redundant

The reorganisation mania within Thames Water continued and on the sewage treatment side, it was decided that the groups were too big. The answer was to break them up and make the junior managers into group managers while making the senior, experienced people redundant; about the silliest thing, they could ever have done. In order to retain experience within the company a number of people were offered consultancy work doing their original job. One colleague of mine finished up on Friday and accepted redundancy with all its payments etc. for long service and started the following Monday as a consultant, being paid a far higher rate than ever before to do the same job at the same desk that he left three days earlier. Perfectly ridiculous in my opinion!

In my case, I was offered work in Thailand, initially while still officially employed by the Company but later on, after redundancy, in a consultancy capacity. I also worked as a freelance consultant and obtained plenty of work through agencies, far better paid than within Thames Water and was able to draw upon my superannuation accrued over more than thirty-four years of reckonable service. Not too bad in the end!

*****

Snake rising up in grass at Lat Krabang

I first arrived in Thailand at 06.30 on a Sunday morning, feeling unbelievably tired and cramped after the longest flight I had ever made in my life so far. I did not sleep on the aircraft and had not really slept much the previous night, probably due to the excitement of making my first trip to the Far East. Having spent what seemed an unbelievably long time at the Passport Control I finally collected my luggage and got a taxi to my hotel, the Grand Pacific on Sukhumvit Road, Bangkok. It was and still is a high-class hotel providing super service and I was soon fast asleep in my very comfortable room.

Imagine my chagrin at being awakened by the bedside telephone after only a couple of hours or so to hear the dulcet tones of my Thames Water colleague Ernie.

"Did you have a good flight?" he asked. "Is the room all right? Any problems need sorting?"

"Yes, yes and no," I replied whilst failing to stifle a massive yawn.

"Oh sorry, did I wake you up?" asked Ernie and before I could reply added, "I'll send my driver to pick you up in about an hour. His name is Montri. OK, see you soon!"

The phone went dead and I cursed my luck at getting no proper sleep. Never mind, another shower and this time with a shave too, followed by a strong cup of tea had me ready and waiting for Montri, who turned out to be an amiable, witty, competent bilingual, Thai gentleman, who was also a very good driver. The car was an almost brand-new Land Rover Discovery, perfect for the road and traffic conditions at that time in Thailand.

Montri took me for a drive of no more than half a mile and we arrived at Ernie's flat, where he was ready and waiting. We had never met before and the only conversation we had had was the one of just an hour or so earlier. Nevertheless, we appeared to have an instant rapport and subsequently got along famously with each other. Explaining my exhaustion from the flight etc. to Ernie elicited but little sympathy and his response was simple.

"Never mind you can sleep all night tonight. I thought you would want to have a look at the plant at Lat Krabang because it's where I want you to concentrate for the first week and I have to go there this afternoon anyway."

Ernie was a clean-water man who knew very little about wastewater treatment and had asked for me to go to Bangkok because, on paper at least, I was the most experienced person available in Thames Water at the time.

"I've got to sort out a problem with one of my staff," he told me, "so you can lose yourself for an hour or so on the plant and get an idea of what needs to be done with it to make it work properly."

Well, that sounded all right to me so off we went to Lat Krabang Industrial Estate, about thirty kilometres away.

As we alighted from the car, Ernie's staff member was ready and waiting to discuss the problem, so I was free to wander around the treatment plant. The only problem was that I couldn't really see it because the vegetation growth surrounding it was extremely unkempt and in places was taller than me. It was rather sparse at ground level however, so it seemed easy to just walk into it and try to find where the various structures were and off I went. After a minute or two, a final settlement tank was visible and I was making my way towards it when SHIT happened in a rather terrifying manner.

I heard a click, followed by something like an asthmatic wheeze and looked down to my right to follow the sound. There, fully reared up and looking extremely nasty, was a large sandy-coloured cobra with its hood extended and obviously displeased at seeing me in its territory. My instant reaction was to 'leg it' and put as much distance as possible between me and the serpent. Unfortunately, however, I did not appreciate the direction in which I was running and suddenly found myself up to my thighs in a channel containing rather poorly treated sewage effluent. While cursing loudly with a good many expletives, my aim was still to get as far as I could from the offending reptile so soon cleared the vegetation and reached the site road, where Montri stood open-mouthed and looking rather worried.

"What wrong Mr David?" he asked, "Why you run like that?"

"Cause there's a bloody great thing like this in there!" I replied, making a snake-like shape with my arm and flattened hand.

"Really? How long is he?" asked Montri, "And why you all wet?"

"Well I haven't got a ruler with me so I couldn't measure it Montri and I jumped in the shitty water just for fun!"

"Oh, I see," said Montri but clearly he did not. He was still unfamiliar with English black humour and it took him quite a while to understand. The penny dropped eventually, however, and both Ernie and I were intrigued to know why Montri should suddenly start laughing out loud during the drive back to Bangkok.

"Oh, that very funny joke about the snake, Mr David!" was his explanation.

"Well it wasn't very funny to me mate, I can tell you," was my response and I am convinced Montri never did understand that, even though Ernie and I both chuckled about it.

Ernie was unhappy about venomous serpents roaming around the Lat Krabang treatment works and gave instructions to get the vegetation cut down as low as possible and keep it so. Nevertheless, I never walked around that plant again without a broom-handle sized bamboo staff in my hand, lest some malevolent creature should be waiting in ambush.

*****

Men standing barefoot in raw sludge.

After my experience with the cobra at Lat Krabang, I spent a couple of days at the Thames Water office, basically to get to know some of the staff and also the people to whom we were responsible in Thailand. These were from a company called Berli-Jucker, an entrepreneurial organisation that Thames Water had entered a partnership with in order to operate the various treatment plants as consultants/contractors. The Thames Water office was in fact within the Berli-Jucker building.

The other value in spending a couple of days at the office was that the vegetation at Lat Krabang works could be completely cut down by the next time I went there, plus I had the chance to meet my driver who would thereafter chauffeur me wherever I had to go or wanted to go in Bangkok. He was a nice young lad but a completely useless driver. He would stop unnecessarily to allow other vehicles to go in front and then 'cut them up' and force his way in front of them at the first opportunity. Frequently I had to tell him off for his dreadful road manners and eventually would only ride at the rear of the car when he was at the wheel because Death Seat (i.e. the front passenger seat) no longer appealed to me.

On Wednesday morning, he drove me out to the plant at the Lat Krabang Industrial Estate, where I spent all day making an assessment of what was needed. The plant was not very large considering the number of factories at the estate but I discovered later that, subject to whatever industry the wastewater is derived from, many companies in Thailand are obliged to fully treat their own wastewater before discharging it into a watercourse. In this case, therefore, the bulk of the incoming flow was similar to domestic sewage and should not have been difficult to treat. The vegetation had been mown down to just a few inches and I was assured by the senior Plant Operative that there were no snakes around, although I still kept my long bamboo stick with me just in case!

A careful inspection of the plant demonstrated that the Operatives had very little idea of what they had to do to run it properly. The circular settlement tank scrapers were unable to rotate because there was too much sludge in the tanks. Nobody was aware that the tanks should be de-sludged on a regular daily basis! A quick dip with my anti-snake stick revealed that the tanks were more than half full of very thick and septic sludge, great rafts of which were floating at the surface. It was impossible to drain it from the tanks because it had completely blocked the withdrawal pipes. Clearly, these tanks had to be emptied but the method for doing so was not easily conceived. Suitable slurry pumps were not available and, in any case, there was nowhere on the site to pump such a large volume of sludge. Also, it would require a lot of watering down before it could be withdrawn from the very bottom of the tanks, so would create an even bigger volume for disposal.

My colleague, Ernie came up with an answer after discussion with people from Berli-Jucker. The sludge would be removed from the tanks with an excavator fitted with a suitable shovel. It would be loaded onto a tipper lorry, fully lined with heavy-duty polythene sheeting to prevent road spillages and taken away to be tipped onto a large open space where it would dry off and eventually be absorbed into the soil. The land was scheduled for building in a year or two anyway so it seemed like a good idea to me!

The following morning, I arranged for the Operatives to pump as much of the liquid portion as possible from one tank and prepare for the sludge portion to be removed by the excavator, which was due to arrive that afternoon accompanied by the tipper lorry. The Operatives achieved this very quickly, by ingeniously hanging a submersible pump from the handrail of the scraper bridge and regularly lowering it, as the level dropped until it could pump no more. The tank was left with a layer of thick, black, septic sludge about 75 centimetres deep at the outer edge of its sloping floor. The scraper blade was revealed at that point too, having been severely bent upwards by the force of pushing this muck around the bottom of the tank; obviously, there was going to be a significant amount of repair work after the tanks were emptied!

I went to inspect the sludge-dewatering machinery and confirmed my suspicions that it hadn't been used for a long time. It was a belt-press machine and the belts were extremely clean. There was a stack of paper sacks containing suitable polymer chemical but no sign of it having been used. Nevertheless, the machinery all seemed to be operable so I concluded that the Operatives had never been shown how to use the plant and this was later confirmed. In fact, the whole treatment plant had been built, tested and set into operation by the original contractors who, having completed their work, simply left the site for the new owners to operate. Unfortunately, they had very little or no idea at all how to do so and simply hired Operatives and Craftsmen without a basic understanding of wastewater treatment. No wonder they had problems occasionally and engaged Berli-Jucker/Thames Water to do it for them!

When I returned to the settlement tank, I discovered that SHIT was indeed happening at that very moment. One man was standing on the floor of the half-empty tank and another was climbing barefoot down a rickety old bamboo ladder to join him. Both men were wearing shorts. Their intention was to see what was wrong with the scraper blade, laudable perhaps but rather foolish under the circumstances. I told them to come out quick and wait for the sludge to be removed first. They would probably get some sort of skin infection and be very unwell! Unfortunately, I was unable to speak a word of Thai at that time and they had no idea what I was talking about so just smiled happily and got themselves liberally coated with sludge up to their waists with plenty of splodges of it over the rest of their bodies, including their faces and hair. In desperation, I went to find my driver whose knowledge of English would be beneficial and got him to speak to the men.

"Oh, don't worry Mr David," he said, "they say they're OK because they can hose it off when they come out!"

I asked him to explain what they were standing in but of course, had to explain it to him first. There was a look of horror on his face when he realised what sludge comprised at a sewage works and it took a matter of seconds for him to persuade the two Operatives to get out of the tank and have a jolly good wash! It so happened that they both subsequently developed a nasty looking skin rash on their legs and private parts, which surely deterred them, and undoubtedly all the other employees, from getting smothered in it again. Fortunately, some locally produced skin cream soon put the rash to flight.

Later the tank was emptied by the excavator, the scraper blade subsequently sorted out and the tank put back into service the following day. The other settlement tanks were also sorted after a few days and the treatment plant was able to run properly, although it took a great deal of effort on my part to show the Operatives what they had to do. Fortunately, I was provided with assistance in this task by a truly bilingual young engineer who also worked for the company.

It was gratifying too that Ernie, upon my advice, soon equipped all the operational staff with decent wellington boots, cotton overalls and waterproof gloves for working in dirty conditions. They had never been issued with anything of that nature before. Health and safety at work was, and to a very large extent still is, quite low on the priority lists in Thailand.

Men standing barefoot in septic raw sludge

A very inexperienced driver.

Towards the end of this, my first trip to Thailand, the car had a puncture on the way back to the office. My driver pulled into a petrol station, got out of the car and began talking to one of the pump attendants. I hadn't realised there was a puncture and wondered what the stop was in aid of. After about ten minutes my driver came back to the car and told me we would be delayed for some time.

"Why?" I asked, "What's the problem?" He told me it was a broken wheel so I got out to look. The tyre was fairly flat but nothing else.

"Can't you pump it up?" I asked. When told the air pump was unserviceable, I suggested he simply change the wheel. I wanted to get back to my hotel because Ernie and I were going out for the evening.

"No tools at this place," he said, "We have to wait for help!" With that, I opened the boot of the car, removed the jack and spanner that were clearly visible, jacked up the car and changed the wheel. It took me about six minutes but all the while, the driver and pump attendant stood watching with their mouths agape. I put the tools back in the car and told my driver, "Get your bloody finger out and drive me to the Grand Pacific Hotel P.D.Q.!"

On the way home, I told him that he'd better learn how to change a wheel on the car without delay, otherwise, Mr Ernie would surely be looking for another driver!

I never said anything to Ernie about the wheel change but maybe what I said to the driver was prophetic on my part, for on my next trip to Thailand a few months later, I was told that the young man had been killed in a road accident and there was a different driver to take me around. It was sad news indeed because he had only been married a few weeks before the accident…

*****

Other consultancy work.

Apart from the occasional trip to Thailand for Thames Water, there was other work in many places throughout the United Kingdom and on two occasions in Hong Kong. Essentially these jobs involved the start-up and commissioning of new treatment plants and in most cases, everything was well organised by the main contractors and their design consultants. Most of my own contracts lasted for two or three months and took me to the North of Scotland, the North, South and Midlands of England and on a few occasions even to treatment works within Thames Water. It was especially rewarding to supervise some installation work in the aeration lanes at Rye Meads where I had been Manager for a few years. The two trips to Hong Kong were also most rewarding, especially when the Chinese contractor asked me to stay on after finishing my work and to work for them for a couple of months. It was financially attractive too!

New primary settlement tank floating at Littlehampton.

One of the jobs I did in a consultancy capacity was as Commissioning Manager at a new sewage treatment works for the town of Littlehampton in

Sussex. This plant was built on a brand-new site and was virtually completed before the sewage flow was diverted into it so commissioning was a very straightforward exercise. The workload, however, was quite intense because all the liquid treatment sections were brought online at the same time, from the inlet screens to the final effluent tanks. All the machinery was test run and adjusted as appropriate with the tanks filled with clean water so on the start-up day it was only a question of opening the appropriate valves and switching on the inlet feed pumps and the various other machinery to put the treatment works into operation.

The anaerobic digesters were still in need of a few minor jobs to be completed but they were able to receive raw sludge ready to get the digestion process started.

On the day I arrived to start work at Littlehampton, I met a young man who was the Mechanical Installation Engineer for the site. This young man was an extremely rude individual and clearly thought he was an expert in every aspect of wastewater treatment. He told me there was no need for me to have been appointed to do the commissioning of the process because he was quite capable of doing it all himself. Furthermore, as he had supervised all the mechanical installation, he knew the plant inside and out, while I would probably take weeks to find my way around it. I was moved to tell him that I was running sewage treatment works far bigger and much more complicated than the Littlehampton plant probably before his mother and father were born and most certainly before they had left school. The young man just scoffed at that and told me that he wouldn't be offering me any help during the commissioning.

I made the site Senior Engineer aware of the young man's attitude and pointed out that there had better not be any strife caused by this individual deliberately causing problems for me or I would take the matter to the highest echelons of the company. The Senior Engineer promised to have a word with the swollen-headed young fool but whether or not he did so, I have no idea.

The commissioning proceeded well enough until there was a problem desludging one of the primary settlement tanks. It became quite clear that the sludge withdrawal pipe was blocked and it was suspected to be due to an empty sack having blown into the tank and sunk. There were large numbers of these woven plastic sacks on the site, usually left in piles of a dozen or so with something placed on them to stop them blowing about the site. What they may have contained I had no idea but somebody must have required them or wanted to return them to some supplier because otherwise they would have been collected up and disposed of. Many of them did blow around the site and were frequently retrieved from the operational tanks but one or two of them had probably sunk in the primary tank before they were retrieved and subsequently were drawn into the desludging pipe in the central well of the structure. Attempts were made to clear the blockage by the use of a hook on a long pole but although the operative said he could feel a sack or something in the tank there was no possibility of removing it that way. The young mechanical engineer declared that it would be very easy to clear the blockage by simply reversing the Mono E.H.R sludge withdrawal pump to pressurise the pipeline and force the blockage out into the tank. I told him it would not be possible because the pump stator would be severely damaged but he nevertheless surreptitiously changed the electrical phases over on the pump's drive motor and tried his theory. Of course, the pump was badly damaged after running dry for about twenty minutes and subsequently required a new stator to be fitted. The crafty young fool, however, re-aligned the phases on the drive motor to hide his actions but the electrician who originally wired it up was able to see what had been done and reported it to the Senior Engineer.

The next idea put across was that the tank should simply be emptied, hosed out as necessary and then cleared of whatever was causing the blockage. It was pointed out by a number of people, including myself, that the primary settlement tanks had no anti-floatation valves in them. During their construction, the ground was continuously dewatered with well-point equipment which was not stopped until the tanks were completed and eventually filled with water. I am not a civil engineer so I do not understand the reason for not installing anti-floatation valves in these tanks but I was quite certain there would be a risk of them floating if they were emptied whilst the water table was high. However, my opinion, which was shared by several others, was pooh-poohed by the fool and when everybody else had left work that evening, he had a six-inch pump rigged up to empty the contents of the blocked tank into its neighbour.

As had been predicted SHIT happened! All was revealed when people arrived for work the following morning. The tank could be seen lying very slightly askew but it wasn't simply a case of the structure floating. Indeed the settlement tank, no doubt having cost several hundred thousand pounds for the reinforced concrete alone, had cracked right across its base and up both sides. The crack had opened to almost an inch in places and was going to cost a great deal of time, effort and money to repair. Groundwater covered the base of the tank but it was possible to see the reason for the blockage of the sludge withdrawal pipe and it was clearly caused by sacking that must have been blown in from the site.

For me, this was the last straw. Having worked at the treatment plant for no more than six weeks, I decided to leave. There was work readily available elsewhere and my employment agency was quite willing to arrange an interview for me in Leeds, where I subsequently worked for several months before going to Egypt. It transpired that there were two or three people at Littlehampton who lost their jobs over this fiasco and I hoped that one of them might be the rude, swollen-headed young man who thought he knew everything!

*****

Chapter 11
From Leeds to Cairo

My contract in Leeds was to commission a new sludge dewatering facility at the city's main sewage treatment works. In addition to the dewatering facility, was a German-built sludge incinerator plant for disposal of the dried sludge cake. This ultimately reduced the sludge, which had hitherto been disposed of at sea I believe, to fine ash that would be used in certain concrete products. One of the jobs I was asked to do, was to inspect the welded seams on the stainless-steel exhaust chimney from the sludge incinerator. The engineer who should have made the inspection suffered from vertigo apparently and therefore refused to get into the access cradle to make the inspection, much of which was many metres from the ground. Furthermore, it was a windy, wet day and nobody else wanted to do the inspection either. This gave the German engineer from the installation company an opportunity to deride the Englanders for being afraid of the weather so I was only too pleased to do the job. It was, however, most unpleasant getting cold and wet in a restricted cradle, especially with an irate German as company who began to object to my comments that the welding was little better than duck-shit. Why on earth the welded sections couldn't have been inspected before the chimney was erected, I have no idea!

Thankfully, my mobile telephone rang and I received a request from Thames Water International to take a job as Commissioning Manager on the largest sewage treatment plant in the world at Gabal el Asfar in Cairo, Egypt. The thought of being warm and dry overcame all other considerations at that moment, so I accepted without question. Four days later, I was in Cairo ready to begin work with a large Italian joint venture organisation known as ANSCO, a combination of Ansaldo and Condotti – two large Italian companies.

I believe the exhaust chimney was dismantled and the duck-shit welding replaced by good standard work at a factory in Leeds! That must have made the German engineer even more irate!

Gabal el Asfar

The term means Yellow Mountain and refers to a huge sand dune just outside Cairo. The sand dune moves slowly in one direction for half the year as the wind blows the sand from one side of it, over the peak and then down the other side. The process is reversed for the other half of the year so Gabal el Asfar remains more or less in the same place. The surrounding district carries the same name and so does the enormous sewage treatment works built there. This works was, and possibly still is, the largest such treatment plant in the world, designed to serve a population of 6.3 million people at that time. The project had been in progress for nearly seven years and was nearing its commissioning phase when I arrived there to work. Nevertheless, there was still an enormous amount of construction to be finished before the treatment works was completed.

Little did I know at the time of my arrival in Cairo that Gabal el Asfar had already been and would continue to be the scene of dreadful SHIT happenings, some of them the worst I have ever encountered!

*****

Soldier sticking a bayonet up his nose in a lookout tower in Cairo

My colleague Marcello and I were trying to find a particular pumping station on the outskirts of Cairo that was the British built version of the main inlet pumping station at Gabal el Asfar. This station was just to lift the wastewater sufficiently to give it adequate fall down to the main inlet of the treatment plant because the land in that area is completely flat. We wanted to see what it was like, what drive motors and gearboxes had been installed on the screw pumps etc. and to see how the design and operation of it compared with the Italian built system at the treatment plant. We were aware that this pumping station, and indeed all the others on the British built catchment system, had been completed for a very long time and that the British contractor was anxious to get the system operational and handed over to the Egyptians but had to wait for the completion of the inlet works at Gabal el Asfar, which was still a couple of months off.

Fortunately, Marcello spoke quite good Arabic and was able to ask local people for directions but nobody in that part of Cairo had the faintest idea where the pumping station was or, for that matter, what on earth it could be either. The directions given by the Italian management were sketchy indeed because none of them had ever been to see the station anyway so we soon became lost. Eventually, however, Marcello spoke to an Egyptian who told us there was a new government structure nearby and directed us to it; perhaps it was the pumping station.

Most outdoor government structures were built in the same fashion in Cairo at that time, with a two-metre high concrete block wall around them and guard towers at strategic points within the walled area. Indeed, Gabal el Asfar treatment works was built in the same way but as yet the guard towers were incomplete and, of course, there were no guards manning them. The towers were probably four metres high and reminded me of the old type of gas-fired streetlamps in some urban areas of London, though of course much bigger. They had a central pillar, in this case, made of concrete rather than cast iron like the streetlamps, with a steel access ladder up to the observation box. The observation box comprised a concrete base with four glass sides sloping outwards to the top. One of the glass sides was also the access door. Atop the glass sides was a round steel cover that extended well beyond the glazed area to afford shade to the occupying soldier/guard, who also had a high stool to sit on while on duty in the tower. I don't know if there was any cooling system in these towers but without one the inside of the glass box must have been unbelievably hot during the daytime; temperatures in summer frequently exceed 40°C in the shade.

It transpired that this government structure was not the pumping station we were looking for and the access gates were closed anyway. There was, however, a guard/observation tower near the gates with a soldier inside. He was seated and was armed with an automatic rifle and, believe it or not, a fixed bayonet but appeared to be dozing with his head slumped slightly forward. Marcello decided to ask the soldier if he knew where the pumping station was and so he called to him in Arabic. There was absolutely no response, because for sure the man was sleeping but when we both yelled very loudly, "Wake up!" in English from me and its equivalent in Arabic from Marcello, the soldier awoke with a start.

Unfortunately for the poor lad, SHIT happened for him and subsequently, very nearly for us too!

As the soldier awoke, he nodded forwards and the point of his bayonet went up his nose, causing a great spurt of blood and no doubt a deal of pain, which elicited a piercing scream from the man. Marcello said something in Arabic, which he later claimed was the equivalent of, "Oh sorry, are you all right?" but the soldier's reaction was to yell obscenities to us, open the glass door of his tower and shin down the ladder very rapidly, rifle in hand. We decided to make ourselves scarce and, jumping into the car, drove off as quickly as possible before he could open the gate and shoot at us (or worse stick his bayonet up our backsides)! Naturally, we howled with laughter once we reached a safe distance from the place but we still had no idea where the pumping station could be.

I felt rather sorry for the soldier but he probably soon recovered and I have no doubt he would be more careful about nodding off again whilst on duty with a fixed bayonet so close to his face.

*****

Buffalo cow poos into my car.

Eventually, we managed to find somebody who knew where the British built pumping station was and we were directed to the right place. I was driving the car, a Korean-built SsangYong Musso, and had opened all the windows to get some fresh air into it but, when I stopped outside the pumping station, I just switched off the engine and left the windows open. Marcello reminded me to close them all because of likely theft in the back streets of the city and I was in the process of fishing the keys out of my pocket again when he became anxious. "Quick, quick!" he yelled, "Look what's coming!"

Coming towards us, on the opposite side of this narrow street, was an ancient tractor towing a huge trailer with some enormous cattle on board. The cattle were, in fact, two female buffaloes that were extremely fat and undoubtedly pregnant. They were standing side by side, one facing the middle of the road and the other facing the opposite way. The latter was very restless and was kicking lots of farmyard muck off the trailer onto the road and it was extremely likely to hit the car. Frantically I got the keys out of my pocket, shoved the ignition key in and turned it to power the windows. First, the rear window was closed and Marcello had closed the two on the passenger side but the driver's window would not close. Then I realised that it wasn't just farmyard muck that was flying out from the old trailer. SHIT was happening quite literally!

The restless buffalo cow was emptying her bowels too and had a range of a metre or more! Furiously I began closing the driver's window manually with the handle but was not quite quick enough. A stream of foul-smelling, almost liquid buffalo excrement hit the windscreen from the outside, the half-closed window from the outside and, through the gap, hit me, the steering wheel, the dashboard and the windscreen from the inside! The rear of the car was liberally coated too! When the trailer and its obscene load had passed, I leapt from the car to see Marcello absolutely convulsed with laughter, as were several passers-by. In the end, I had to laugh as well!

This disgusting episode had taken just a few seconds to unfold but the clean-up took probably half an hour to achieve. Fortunately, there was a convenient water supply at the pumping station where the car could be hosed down and its interior washed clean of buffalo poo. More importantly, there was a toilet and washbasin facility where I was able to clean the mess from my arm and my hair. The Egyptian caretaker staff at the pumping station were most helpful and provided soap and a towel but they were almost unable to speak because of their giggling.

Having established that the pumping station was very similar indeed to the Italian-built inlet station and that it was more than ready for operation, we left to return to the Gabal el Asfar plant. It was around lunchtime so we decided to stop for a bite to eat at, of all places, a Wendy Burger restaurant, where we both ordered a hamburger and a fizzy drink. One meal was delivered to the table within two minutes but the other one, we were told, would take another ten minutes or so. We didn't bother to ask why. Marcello, being a gentleman at heart, invited me to eat first because of the strife I had already suffered that day so I got stuck into the food. It tasted all right but the hamburger appeared to have a weird texture and I put that down to the fact that I rarely eat such food and, furthermore. it was probably made in Egypt and therefore had different ingredients from a British or American one. Little did I realise that it was probably due to the fact that it had been prepared the previous day and had sat without refrigeration for many hours before being shoved in a microwave to heat up! This revelation was made to me by the doctor I was obliged to see that evening.

Late in the afternoon, I became nauseous and had considerable griping stomach pains. My work colleagues suggested I should go to see the site's resident doctor because I was looking very pale and they were concerned for my well-being. The resident doctor at Gabal el Asfar had a small surgery housed in a converted 40-foot sea container. His purpose on site was to treat minor injuries incurred by the workforce, such as cuts and abrasions, foreign bodies in the eyes, sprains and bruises etc. and he was well equipped to do just that kind of work but probably not set up to treat what was very likely to be violent food poisoning. Somebody else suggested I should go home to bed and I needed very little encouragement to do so. At the time, I was still living at the Swiss Hotel near the airport and as I walked through the reception lounge the duty manager asked me if I was all right.

"You look very pale, Mister," he said, "Do you need a doctor?"

I told him I did and he said he would call one and send him to my room. "You go and lie down now and don't lock your door," said the duty manager.

About half an hour later, there was a knock on my door.

"It's the doctor 'ere, can I come in?" said a deep reassuring voice.

"O.K.," was my somewhat feeble reply as another stomach cramp twisted my inside. A tall, smart man entered the room carrying his medical bag.

"What's up, then?" he asked.

"I think I've eaten something that was bad," I replied.

"Got the shits?" asked the doctor, "Any pains in the belly?"

"I've got stomach cramps and feel sick but no toilet problems yet," was my answer.

"O.K. then, let's have a look at yer," as he put the stethoscope to his ears. "Chest sounds all right," he said and then pressed my stomach area, which made me wince a little. He then placed the stethoscope on my stomach and exclaimed, "Wooh you've definitely got something festering away in there boy, what was it you ate?" I told him it was a hamburger with chips and salad at the Wendy Burger restaurant.

"Gawd you never want to eat there boy, it's not always fresh food. They keep it 'anging about for days sometimes! It's definitely food poisoning, I'll write a prescription for some pills and medicine. Don't worry about it, the 'otel staff'll pick it up for yer. Drink plenty o' water, don't starve yerself but don't eat much OK? You'll be all right in a couple o' days. Just ask the 'otel to bring you a little plate o' mashed taters if you need something, they're pretty good at that 'ere."

At this point, I just had to ask the doctor a question.

"Where do you come from mate?"

"Egypt of course," was the immediate reply.

"Not with that accent you don't, you're almost a cockney."

"Oh right," said the doctor, "I guess you're from London too then. I worked for twenty-five years there at Guy's Hospital, Whipp's Cross and North Middlesex. Loved it but came back 'ere to set up on me own. All right then, that'll cost yer sixty-seven pounds, that's L.E.*o' course, not quid. The prescription'll be extra but the 'otel'll put that on yer bill." I gave him the money and with that, the doctor left.

I got the medicine within an hour and sure enough two days later all the stomach cramps, sickness and toilet problems had gone and I was once again as fit as a fiddle. The hotel's mashed potatoes were very nicely done but after a day with nothing else to eat, I didn't fancy them anymore. As for Wendy Burger, I have never been into one of their restaurants again and have only been to any of the other hamburger places a couple of times since. Ugh!

*****

Starting flow to new inlet chamber at Gabal el Asfar

As soon as the new Inlet Pumping Station was able to pump the flow, it was agreed that the British contractors who had built the trunk sewers and upstream pumping stations should start up and commission their new system. Although our new pumps had been test-run and the gearbox cooling units had been tested, the pumping station was a long way from being completed. There were no safety handrails beside the ten huge Archimedean screw pumps and no covers to shield the pumps from the fierce Egyptian sun. Furthermore, there were no walkways over the pump inlet chambers so the pumping station was an extremely unsafe place to work. Nevertheless, the Consultants' Resident Engineers and the Italian Project Managers all agreed that the pumping station could begin operating forthwith, despite my pleas for at least the safety railings and walkways to be installed first.

Bearing in mind the several fatalities that had occurred at the site over previous years, it showed a distinct lack of care and concern on their part and, in my opinion, a significant lack of professionalism. On the appointed day, however, sewage started to flow into the treatment plant's huge inlet chamber, where two of the enormous inlet penstocks had already been partially opened. It fell to me to organise the Egyptian operators, for whom I now had responsibility, to fully open these penstocks manually with hand-wheels that were meant for use elsewhere because the proper ones had not been fitted and powered units were never included in the design.

Once the penstocks were opened sufficiently, by a six-man crew feverishly working in relays to turn the hand-wheels, it was observed that a large amount of bedding, i.e. sheets, blankets, pillows and bedrolls had been held up behind the penstocks and suddenly released into the rapidly filling inlet chamber. There was even a small interior sprung mattress and several large pieces of wood but where had all that stuff come from? The answer was the sewer itself! Apparently, the new pipeline, which is huge, had been used by many families as a place to live and could be accessed at several man-entry points along its length. Clearly, some of them didn't remove their bedding in time for the tidal wave of Cairo sewage that would have washed it all away. My problem was to get these large objects removed from the inlet chamber before they were swept into the main pumping station but fortunately this proved to be a relatively simple task. It was undertaken by a few men with grappling hooks on ropes. The real fear, of course, was that some of the people living in the pipeline might not have got out in time but we never heard of anyone being lost or injured.

After a further frantic effort with the wrong hand-wheels the huge feeder penstocks to the main pumping station were also opened, this time by an eight-man crew working in relays, the seventh and eighth men being myself and my Assistant Manager, also named David, both sweating profusely at the effort required. Fortunately, the feed penstocks to the individual Archimedean screw pumps were powered and could, therefore, be opened or closed in just a few minutes by the press of a button. With just four or five pumps running, all the sewage flow, about half the design load to the new plant. was being comfortably handled.

The treatment plant, however, was still a very long way from being operational, so this large volume of filthy water was diverted directly into the bypass channel and thence to the final effluent channel connecting with the River Nile. This channel was partially filled with good clean water, presumably having backed up from the river, which was at its highest level at that time of the year. There were a few big fish seen in it occasionally and sometimes they were caught by the site workers for food. Everybody assumed that this SHIT happening would see the last of the fish in the final channel and probably significant pollution in the River Nile but such did not turn out to be the case. In fact, after no more than a few days there were plenty of fish in the final effluent channel, presumably attracted by a new source of food. Many were being caught and eaten by the site workers, although how anyone could eat fish taken from untreated Cairo sewage is difficult to imagine, but I guess if people are poor enough, they will eat any food that's available and some of those people were very poor indeed!

Operating the new inlet pumping station was quite straightforward but it still remained a very hazardous area to work in. My constant badgering of the Resident Engineers to get the contractors to install the safety rails, walkways, etc. fell on deaf ears but eventually, things did start to happen. A huge pile of hand railing and support stanchions arrived on site; work began on the stairways next to the screw pumps and the walkways over their inlet chambers but this gave rise to the most dreadful SHIT happening I have ever experienced in my life.

*****

Death on a screw pump

Work was progressing slowly on the installation of safety hand railing at the inlet pumping station and with the help of my Assistant Manager Dave, I had put together a 'Permit to Work' system for the Arab Contractors that were doing the work. They were obliged to inform me when they were to carry out the work so that the pumps could be shut off whilst they were installing the hand railing alongside them and would sign off when they finished for the day. This permit system was based on that in operation within Thames Water, where it was very effective. The Chief Resident Engineer had been informed and a copy of the Permit to Work system was placed upon his desk a week before the work started but he had never commented upon it. At the same time as the hand railing was being installed, sun covers were being installed over the screw pumps. This was to prevent these very long structures from distorting in the heat of the day but they also provided additional safety protection by shrouding what were potentially lethal machines.

The pumps were nearly 20 metres long and comprised a 3.1-metre diameter, triple threaded screw, supported by a single bearing at the bottom and driven by a huge electric motor and gearbox at the top end. The massive bottom bearing was pressure-lubricated by a total-loss greasing system. Each of these ten pumps, rotating at only 60 RPM, would lift nearly 2 cubic metres of sewage per second from their inlet chamber to the treatment works feed channel. The design allowed for a maximum of eight pumps to run on duty with two remaining as standby, so flow rates could reach the equivalent of nearly 1.4 million cubic metres per day (nearly 310 million imperial gallons), by any standards a vast volume of sewage.

Once all the hand railing and sun covers had been fitted it was relatively safe for operations personnel to work around these enormous machines and was something of a relief to most of us. There was just one major piece of safety work left to do, which was to install the walkways over the individual pump inlet chambers to enable their huge, powered-penstocks to be safely accessed. Hitherto, access to these penstocks had been somewhat precarious because two very large sheets of shuttering plywood had to be used, one over the other, to be strong enough, whilst bridging the inlet chamber, to support the weight of a man. Dave and I were forever badgering our staff to make sure these plywood bridges were firmly placed before trusting their weight upon them but I suspect there were occasions when pure luck had preserved their lives rather than heeding their instructions.

As each one of the walkways were installed the Permit to Work called for the foreman to provide me with a method statement. The inlet penstock would be closed and the pump then shut off before work started. Everything was signed off and the installation began. Two steel 'I' beams were bolted into slots in the concrete walls and grouted in; steel chequer plates were then bolted into place on top of the beams and the chambers were very neatly and safely covered.

It took a couple of days to fix up eight of the inlet chambers but the two end ones, N°1 and N°10, could not be completed for a little time. This was because the end walls had no pre-formed openings to fit the 'I' beams so they had to be modified with a welded plate that could be bolted vertically to the outer wall with chemical anchor bolts. After a couple of days all was ready; a Permit to Work was duly signed off and the N°1 pump and inlet penstock were inspected, ready for the work to proceed safely. The N°10 pump, however, was in operation because its bottom bearing greasing system had been overhauled that morning and it was being run in for a few hours. The pump next to it was also having its bearing seen to so it was not in operation. I therefore told the Arab Contractors' foreman to complete the N°1 installation first and then get a second Permit to Work for N°10 pump but unfortunately, that was never relayed to the workmen doing the job and as a result, the worst-imaginable SHIT happening occurred.

After lunch that day, an inspection was made of the N°1 installation and all was seen to have been completed. The contractor's workmen were not to be seen, presumably not yet back from lunch, so I stood at the high level of the pumping station waiting for the foreman and watching the vast volume of sewage discharging from the four operating screw pumps, which still included N°10. Suddenly, a strange, muted sound, as if a baby was crying, was coming from the N°10 discharge channel. The sound was getting louder but was difficult to identify because of the overall noise from this massive pumping station with its huge motors and gearboxes and the noise of the cascading waters. Then the shape of a man burst from the discharge into the main feed channel, a man wailing very loudly and surrounded by red sewage. One of his legs was at a very strange angle to the rest of his body as he splashed into the channel and was carried down to the bypass.

Shocked, I ran through the pumping station, down the stairs by the screw pumps and saw panic-stricken Egyptians running about all over the place. Yelling at a couple of my own staff I told them to go to the bypass channel as the man was being washed around it. "Quick, get him out of the channel!" I screamed, which amazingly they did with the aid of a grappling hook on a rope. As they pulled him out, I could see this young man, now hardly making a sound, had his left leg almost completely severed at the thigh and was missing his right hand and wrist; there was blood everywhere. The Egyptians, wildly panicking and volatile were mostly running around like headless chickens, not knowing what to do but just then a Datsun pick-up truck came past the scene so, yelling at full voice, which happens to be very loud in my case, I called him to stop and come over, which to his credit he did without questioning why.

"Now get this man on the truck!" I told them, "And you (to the driver) get him to the hospital as quick as you can! You two (to my own staff) go with him! Now! Now!" They did exactly what I said.

"Christ, what a mess," I muttered to myself a few moments later, as a lighted cigarette was placed between my lips by one of the biggest men I have ever known, a Nubian fellow who was just over seven feet tall and was one of the mechanics working on the bearing greasers. As I took a huge drag on the powerful Egyptian cigarette, he told me what had happened.

"Mr David," he said, "these men passing me with the steel. I trying to stop them because the pump running but they ignoring me and the first one standing on plywood and it fall down. The second one go in too but I pull him out. He sitting down there. The two more run away."

Walking down to the rescued man, we saw that he was in a state of tremendous shock and could barely speak but when he had calmed down a little he explained, via the Nubian giant as interpreter, what had happened.

There were four men to install the walkways and they were told by the foreman to start on N°10 straight after lunch, the four of them picked up the heavy beam, the first had it on his right shoulder, the second on his left, the third on his right etc. They walked past the Nubian fellow who was still working on the greaser of the adjacent pump's bearing but when he told them to wait, the front two men were already standing on the plywood bridge, which had obviously moved, and they fell into the chamber with the plywood and the beam. The poor lad at the front was instantly washed up the pump and undoubtedly hit by the leading edges of at least two of the three spirals, causing the horrendous injuries. The second, our rescued man, was able to hang on to the heavy beam because it was on his left shoulder, closest to the pump and therefore affording him some protection from the powerful wash of the water. He was then fished out quite literally by the Nubian giant leaning over the dividing wall and grabbing him by his clothing. The following day when I saw this young man, he was covered in boils resulting from the shock but was sent off-site by someone and I never saw him again. The third and fourth men carrying the beam fled the site and, so far, as I know, never returned. Nor for that matter did the Arab Contractors' foreman!

Having pieced together, as best as I could, the train of events, I made my way back to the office buildings to talk to the Italian managers, after first having realised that pump N°10 was still running with a steel beam across its inlet and two sheets of shuttering plywood that it was slowly chewing to pieces. The pump was shut down, its inlet penstock closed and pump N°9 started in its place.

It was probably well over an hour after the event that I got back to the offices and the first person I saw was the site's resident doctor who was washing the inside of his car with a bucket of soapy water and a sponge. The car was a Renault Floride, an elderly but smart little two-door sporty saloon and clearly very messy

165

inside. What's more, the mess being sloshed out of it was obviously blood and it looked more as if he was sluicing out a butcher's shop. The moment he saw me, the doctor, eyes blazing and looking very wild indeed, stomped towards me waving the bloody sponge in his hand and yelling at full voice.

"Why did you tell them to bring that man to me? I couldn't help him! Look at my car, it's nearly ruined!"

"I told them to take him to the HOSPITAL man, what the hell did they come here for?" was my immediate full-throttle reply.

"Because the pick-up truck isn't licensed for use on the road you damned fool, it's only a site truck! They couldn't take him to the hospital in case they were seen by the police so they brought him here and I had to take him in my car! MY CAR! Just look at it!" he screamed.

"F**K YOUR CAR MATE!" I bellowed. "CALL ME A DAMNED FOOL AGAIN AND YOU'LL BE WEARING THE BLOODY THING! OK?" as the pent-up trauma of the past couple of hours was released.

"More important than your car, how is the young man?" I asked with a little more restraint.

"Dead, of course!" came the sullen reply. "His leg was almost off and a hand was missing. There was nothing they could do for him after losing all that blood!"

"Could they have saved him if they'd gone straight to the hospital instead of fussing over a bit of paper?" I asked. "No policeman would have stopped them over such a triviality anyway!"

"No chance at all!" said the doctor, "The boy was too far gone! Look, I'm sorry about losing my temper, it was a shock for me too you know."

"Yes, I understand, doctor," I replied and offered to help him clean his pride and joy Renault Floride. Thankfully, he declined the offer.

When I reached the Project Director's office, the Italian managers were already discussing the accident. They didn't yet know the full details or the fact that the young man had died but when I filled in the gaps for them they did not appear to be particularly concerned. "There have been many fatalities on this job Mr David." I was told!

The following day, however, brought the B.P.B.C. syndrome to the fore because the Chief Resident Engineer called a meeting to discuss the matter.

The Chief Resident Engineer was something of an enigma in my opinion. To me, he was rarely available in his office and even more rarely seen outside it.

Other members of the Resident Engineers team never seemed to know where he was when I tried to discuss anything with him but it was well known that he went horse riding on Saturdays and Sundays and, I believe, played golf quite a lot too. (Everybody else on-site worked a six-day week with their only day off being Friday, the Islamic Sabbath).

The Chief Resident Engineer opened the meeting and firstly criticised the Italians for being late with the completion of the Inlet Pumping Station and they all made their excuses. Then it was the turn of the Arab Contractors for not instructing their workforce in matters of safety and similar B.P.B.C. excuses were trailed out. The final bit of venom, however, clearly for his own B.P.B.C. was reserved for me.

"You were responsible for operating the pumping station," he said snootily, "Why was there no Permit to Work system in place?"

Interestingly, there had never been a Permit to Work system of any kind at the site before Dave and I put ours together.

"There was and there is a Permit to Work system in place and I have signed method statements and sign off sheets in the same style as those used in Thames Water," was my acid reply.

"So, why haven't I seen this Permit to Work system?" he sneered, "Why have you kept it a secret from me? I am the Chief Resident Engineer and should have known about it. What's your answer to that then Mr Thames Water?"

Remaining calm, I reminded him that I had mentioned it to him several weeks beforehand that a Permit to Work system would be put together and also pointed out that it had been placed on the top of his almost overflowing in-tray before the hand-railing etc. had even been delivered to site. I asked him why he had not commented upon it as requested and then, in a similarly sneering manner, asked if he had actually looked in his in-tray during the past few weeks. Without giving him a chance to respond, I turned to the whole gathering and informed them that, in my opinion, everybody around the table was in some way responsible for the young man's tragic death. I started with the Italian Project Management, saying:

"If you people had concentrated on getting the Inlet Pumping Station ready for safe operation it wouldn't have been necessary for construction personnel to be working on a live station in the first place."

Then without pause, I addressed the Arab Contractors' representative:

"If you people had properly instructed your workforce in safety matters and your foreman had complied with the Permit to Work the accident wouldn't have happened. After all, the N°1 pump's walkway was completed safely by the same bunch of people on the same day!"

A screw pump similar to that which caused the young man's fatal injuries

Then turning to the Chief Resident Engineer and also the Italian Project Management I pointed out very forcefully that if they had listened to me when I almost begged them to delay operation of the pumping station until it was properly safe to do so, any accidents would have been avoided. Finally, and before the Chief Resident Engineer could respond, I admitted that I too should take some responsibility for the tragedy, telling them that if I had refused to operate the pumping station before it was made safe there would have been no chance of anybody being hurt and, looking him straight in the eyes added;

"Before you ask why I didn't refuse, it was because, as YOU well know, I would have been on the next plane back to England because SOMEONE would have informed Thames Water that I was holding up the job!"

With that, I reminded the whole group that they should learn from this tragic event and make sure nothing like it ever happened again. There was not a single comment as I stood up and left the meeting. Later on, however, as we were at lunch in the canteen, one of the Italian managers said quietly;

"I was impressed with what you said at the meeting this morning Mr David. You were quite right! We all need to learn from this tragedy. Too many lives have been lost on this site." That made me feel much better!

Apparently, there was some compensation paid to the young man's parents for the loss of their son but I believe it was a quite paltry figure. A poor man's life, wherever he may be, is always regarded as cheap!

*****

Driving through a sewage spill in Cairo and soaking passengers in a bus.

My drive from the Swiss Hotel to work each morning took me through a very busy street in Cairo. The driving style in Egypt at that time was, like many other countries, extremely bad and was based on the idea of 'me first, me first and to Hell with everybody else!' In order to get to work on time, it was necessary to adopt the same attitude to driving as the rest, though I didn't go to the extremes of driving along the footpath or ignoring the traffic lights as many others did, especially the bus drivers!

One morning, after negotiating a particularly bad traffic snarl-up, it was possible to put my foot down a little bit as the road cleared. In front of me was a private bus that was hogging the outside lane, so I decided to overtake it on the inside lane. Almost immediately, the bus changed lanes and forced me to brake sharply to avoid a collision so now, somewhat enraged, I slewed the car back to overtake on the outside lane. What I hadn't realised was that the bus driver could clearly see well ahead of me and had changed lanes because he could see the outside lane was flooded to a depth of several inches just a short distance ahead. Nevertheless, I was committed to overtaking the bus and was accelerating hard but before completing the manoeuvre I hit the flooded section of the road. SHIT happened immediately!

The SsangYong hit the flood when level with the middle of the bus and a huge wave of water shot up the side of it and continued to do so until the bus had been overtaken. Only by a glance in the side mirror and catching sight of the sopping wet driver gesticulating wildly did I realise that all the windows of the bus were fully open. Furthermore, from the evil stench that had arisen, it was clear that the flood was not coming from a burst water main but probably from a blocked sewer. For sure there could be trouble ahead!

The SsangYong was not a particularly nimble vehicle and clearly, the bus was capable of quite a good turn of speed. Consequently, every quick glance in my driving mirror showed its radiator getting closer and closer until, in fear of being literally shoved off the road, I signalled and pulled over to the kerb, taking the precaution of checking that all the doors and windows were well and truly locked. The bus skidded to a halt at an angle across the front of the SsangYong, presumably to forestall any escape on my part, so naturally, I selected reverse gear and was ready to make a hasty retreat if necessary. The appearance of the bus driver and about a dozen extremely irate passengers assured me that retreat may well be the only way to avoid a good beating, which is something an Egyptian mob is very likely to resort to! Raising the palms of my hands as a recognised gesture of submission in that part of the world and mouthing the word sorry with my best attempt at a pitiful, apologetic face, seemed to calm them down somewhat and just then one of the men pointed at me whilst yelling something to the others. With that, they all got back on the bus and it drove off. I followed it at a respectful distance until, to my amazement, it turned into the Gabal el Asfar treatment works. These men were part of the construction workforce and, although I only vaguely recognised one of them, they all clearly recognised me. I thought it prudent, therefore, to get out of the car and offer them my apologies, genuine actually, for accidentally soaking them with foul water. Many of them could speak some English, the number of Egyptians that can has never ceased to amaze me, and all said they accepted that it was not done deliberately; a couple of them shook hands with me to prove it. Thereafter I saw some of these men quite often at the site and was frequently offered a cigarette by them, though sometimes only in exchange for one of my own Dunhill Internationals, and on one occasion was even invited to share their packed lunch with a group of them. I politely declined, however, pretending I had already eaten mine at the Europeans' canteen. Theirs looked quite unpalatable to me!

Although seemingly a very volatile people and at times remarkably unpredictable, I nevertheless grew to like the Egyptians I lived among and worked with in Cairo. Above all, they seem to have a good sense of humour and we shared many a good laugh together.

*****

Man shot in the backside.

Much of the land used for the construction of this enormous treatment works had once been used for agriculture. There were certainly some extensive date groves just outside the perimeter of the site and groups of teenage children were frequently to be seen herding sheep and goats across the site to pasture. I was informed that one of the dispossessed farmers, who most likely had been compensated by the Egyptian Government, was actually the leader of the site security who controlled the Official access/egress point to Gabal el Asfar, which was via an asphalt road built for heavy construction traffic. This man, probably about sixty years old, was frequently to be seen at the site entrance gate where we entered each morning and left each evening. He was an affable character, always dressed in a grey galabeya* with a white turban covering his head and, had he worn an army snake-buckle belt around the turban, would have made a passable double for the Indian bearer in the TV comedy series 'It Ain't Half Hot Mum'.* One day he spoke to Dave and me in Italian but we did not understand him and I informed him we were English. Subsequently, every time either of us drove past him at the gate he would stand to attention, salute and yell, "Sir!" Most people had a good chuckle at that.

His attitude was rather different, however, when Dave and I decided to go into work on a special holiday. I cannot recall what the holiday signified to the Islamic world but it was obviously important to the Egyptian people and nobody went to work on that day. Dave and I decided it would be useful for getting our Health & Safety documents up to scratch because there would be no disturbance from the Italians who normally would have been working in adjacent site offices and it would be nice and quiet for us to work for a few hours. We could easily get the documents finished without any great effort, so I picked Dave up at his flat and drove along almost deserted roads to the site. Of course, the entrance gate was closed so I sounded the horn a few times to attract attention from the gatekeeper, all to no avail. After a while, I decided to just blare the horn continuously in the hope that someone would hear it and take notice. It worked but unfortunately, there was a minor SHIT happening as well.

The entrance gate burst open and out came the old Security Leader followed by two or three other Egyptian men. They were all yelling and gesticulating wildly, obviously telling us to clear off. I got out of the car to explain what Dave and I wanted but the old man did not recognise me at all. He and his entourage were clearly off their heads, not with alcohol I'm sure but probably with the local inhalant known as 'Bango'. As I approached the man, he suddenly hoisted up his galabeya and drew an ancient Webley pistol on a lanyard and proceeded to wave it in my general direction, uttering strange guttural oaths at the same time. When he cocked the piece, I decided it was time to disappear as quickly as possible and fled to the car, whacked it into reverse and roared away from the old fool as if our lives depended upon it, which they may well have done! So Dave and I decided to go home again and do the Health & Safety documents some other time like most sensible people would have done too! After the holiday I went to work as normal and received the smart welcome and salute from the old security man so I was even more certain that he had been spaced out on the previous day.

A while later, both Dave and I were looking around a new construction area where sludge storage bays were being built. A bunch of children came across the site driving brown sheep, a couple of draft buffaloes and a few goats. Leading this procession was a girl of about fourteen on a donkey. She was clothed in the Islamic style with her hair covered by a scarf etc. but as she passed us, she deliberately hoisted up her robes to show off her thighs. Furthermore, she turned to Dave and me and smiled in a rather provocative manner while simulating kisses to us. I clearly remember Dave's remark in reaction to the young girl's gestures.

"Not on your life mate, I don't want my old fella lopped off with a scimitar!" and we both howled with laughter.

It seems, however, that other men on the site may have had different ideas because a week or two later the news came around that an Egyptian man from Upper Egypt* had been shot in the backside from close range by none other than the Security Leader for, allegedly, interfering with the same young girl who just happened to be the old man's granddaughter. It transpired that the culprit had half his right buttock blown off by the said ancient Webley pistol and was hospitalised immediately, never to return to the site.

There was no talk of police being called and we never discovered what, if any, chastisement the teenage girl subsequently suffered but for sure nobody, especially Dave and me, wanted to fall foul of the old security leader again. I often wonder what might have happened if we had tried to remonstrate with him when he wouldn't let us into the site to work on the holiday. We may well have been staggering about with only half a bum each! Crikey, what a thought!

*****

Death of concrete lorry cleaner at Gabal el Asfar

As was to be expected in a place where a poor man's life is considered almost valueless by the fabulously rich, no lesson was learnt from the death of the young man who fell into the inlet chamber of the screw pump. Within just a few days the incident was forgotten by everybody except those who witnessed the tragedy. In fact, the only time it was ever mentioned again to me was when the onsite doctor called me over to show me his car. The interior of the little Renault Floride had been completely renovated, to such an extent that it looked brand new. He was very proud of his little car again and I'm quite sure would never allow an injured man anywhere near it in future!

Construction continued on the site with further pumping stations being completed and large concrete access stairways being built up to them, because they were well above ground level. The concrete was mixed on site; a huge American-built mixer lorry, having been loaded with the sand, stone, cement and water at a modern silo, trundled around the site for as much as two or three kilometres to the point of construction, by which time the concrete was mixed and ready for pouring. Off-loading of the vehicle, however, could be quite a slow process because, if the point of pour could not be readily accessed by the mixer's delivery chute, there was no way of getting the concrete into the shuttering other than by manual labour. Nowhere on this enormous construction site did I ever see a wheelbarrow used to hump liquid concrete, nor did I ever see a concrete pump that the mixer could be rapidly emptied with. Instead, concrete was shifted from the lorry by twenty or so labourers, each equipped with a tightly woven basket to carry no more than 25kg of the mix on their heads. They had to fill the basket from the mixer's chute, lift it onto their heads and walk as quickly as possible up to the point of pour, empty the basket and get back to the vehicle at

173

the double to collect the next load. Apparently, the cumulative effect of the slow offloading was to cause a bit of concrete to go off and remain in the vehicle each time. This eventually caused the inside of the mixer drum to become fouled and the mixing paddles to lose their efficiency, resulting in very poor mixing. To overcome this problem a man was put into the mixing drum to break up the accumulated concrete with a pneumatic jackhammer and clean up the mixing paddles. That must have been the most un-enviable job imaginable. It would have been absolutely deafening within the mixer, unbearably hot and, to say the least, extremely hazardous and exhausting work but nevertheless, one unfortunate young Egyptian duly climbed into the machine and started bashing away with the jackhammer. Of course, SHIT happened and once again ended in tragedy!

Fortunately for me, I did not witness this event but only heard about it later in the canteen where it was being discussed by some of the Italian managers. Apparently, somebody decided a jackhammer could not be used effectively at the horizontal because it was too heavy so it needed to be used vertically downwards in the mixer drum, therefore the drum would need to be turned every so often to get access to it all at the vertical. Possibly that was sound thinking but, what was not, was the decision to rotate the drum while the man was still inside it. Allegedly, as soon as the jackhammer was stopped for a moment it was assumed the drum should be rotated a little to expose a bit more of it to the vertical and make things easier for the worker inside. The lorry was therefore started and the mixer-drum drive engaged, the net result being that it rotated very quickly because the lorry's engine was revving fast; it was not the regular driver who had started it up. The young man inside was revolved with the jackhammer, the lumps of recently broken concrete and of course at least one exposed mixing paddle. Nobody knew for how long but it was guessed at about ten to fifteen seconds and may, therefore, have been for as few as eight revolutions but it was sufficient to batter the poor chap to death and smash his face into an unrecognisable mess. A most dreadful thing to happen!

As ever, several of the Egyptian workers fled the site as soon as they realised there had been a fatality and the B.P.B.C. syndrome came to the fore. However, the most sickening thing about this tragedy was that many people, Egyptian, Italian and even one of the few Englishmen on the site, seemed to think it was very funny. The words, "Hey, did you hear about that twit getting battered to death in the concrete mixer? What a hoot, it could only happen in Egypt!" were actually spoken to me with a chuckle or two thrown in.

My unprintable reply was extremely venomous and the man responsible did not speak to me again. Fortunately, he returned to England a few days later and never came back to Gabal el Asfar.

*****

Boy dies getting water.

There was an enormous syphon to feed the mixed liquors into the final separating tanks. The syphon discharged into the centre of a circular distribution chamber, the floor of which sloped conically up to a circular wall in which were installed adjustable weirs. Each weir discharged into a smaller syphon chamber feeding to the centre of its individual final separating tank. The adjustable weirs were still being fitted and their frameworks grouted into the structural concrete.

The main syphon had already been tested for leakage and the huge pipework had been left filled with water, the level of which had fallen considerably by evaporation over a period of a few weeks. It was nevertheless a convenient source of clean water for the construction workers to knock up their grout and bagging-mix when smooth-finishing the concrete. They would send their boy helpers to collect water from the centre of the cone by dropping a bucket on a line into the syphon. Unfortunately, however, it was becoming increasingly difficult to collect the water due to its level dropping and one boy's line was now too short for him to readily fill his bucket. He would have had to kneel on the edge of the concrete and reach down to get the water. SHIT happened with yet another tragedy!

There was nothing for the boy to hold on to and the sloping floor of the cone probably caused him to over-balance and fall into the syphon. Nobody heard him call out and he was not missed for some time.

When, however, he was missed and was subsequently seen floating face down in the water the construction workers were reluctant to try to get him out because (allegedly) none of them could swim. One of my maintenance electricians happened to be passing nearby and climbed the scaffolding to see what all the fuss was about at the syphon. This fellow was one of those that had fished the dying man out of the bypass channel some months earlier and was considerably less volatile than most of the other Egyptians. Furthermore, he could swim and he lost no time in jumping into the syphon to help the stricken boy but it was all to no avail as the lad had drowned. Nevertheless, he did try resuscitation procedures when eventually a group of men hauled them both out, though he probably knew it was a waste of time.

Later on the same day, incredibly, there was another fatality involving one of these young boys elsewhere on the site, at the new final effluent channel. This was a concrete channel of around three metres depth, some of which was below ground level and some of which was eventually to be supported by an embankment. At the time the top of the sidewalls on this section were nearly two metres above ground on one side and three metres above concrete on the other. There was about a half metre of water in the channel, probably to protect the new concrete base from the fierce Egyptian sun. Apparently, a group of these youngsters walked along the channel wall as a short cut to their next point of work but one of them tripped and fell headfirst into the channel. There were, of course, no handrails. Had the water been deeper it might have cushioned his fall but unfortunately, he was knocked completely unconscious and laid for several minutes face down in the shallow water before his companions were able to get him out. He was dead when they finally reached him, either from serious head injuries or possibly from drowning. The latter was the reason given officially but as usual, very few people seemed to care anyway. Although I was not a witness to either event, I shall always remember that day's sad and unnecessary waste of two young lives……

*****

Boys collecting rocks from new pumping well.

I was informed that the new primary sludge pumping station was completed and ready for testing, though there was no sludge to pump at this stage. Incredibly, two of the Italian Managers asked me to help in supervising the testing for them as they were uncertain how to do it without sludge! My simple suggestion that they always ought to test-run such pumps on water first, seemed to put me in the class of a genius in their eyes. Amazing! Anyway, it was agreed that I would produce a method statement for them and submit it to the Chief Resident Engineer for approval. This included a preliminary inspection of the new pumping well to ensure it was completely clean and free from any construction equipment or materials. Needless to say, there was no approval from the Chief Resident Engineer but one of his assistants agreed with it, signed it off and then probably forgot all about it.

I went to inspect the new pumping station and discovered from a quick glance that the pumping well was littered with bits of wood, lumps of concrete and rocks, many plastic bags and all sorts of other trash. Clearly, nobody had given any thought to cleaning it out before test running the pumps. The Italians immediately instructed the contractors to get the well cleaned out to my satisfaction and announced smugly that it would be done without delay. Sure enough, within twenty minutes a group of youngsters began climbing into the pumping well, which was at least eight metres deep and surrounded on three sides by hand-railing of more than a metre height. These youngsters (boys of around thirteen or fourteen years old) were provided with nothing whatsoever to do the job; they had no ladders, no ropes and no collection containers for the rubbish. All they had were their flip-flop sandals and their galabeyas! They all managed to climb down to the bottom of the pumping well by removing their sandals and monkey climbing down a nine-inch diameter plastic vent pipe clamped to the rear wall, (i.e. by gripping the pipe with their hands and pressing their bare feet against the concrete wall they effectively walked backwards down to the floor of the well.) I was quite horrified to see them do this and was certain that sooner or later one would fall and have a serious accident. Far worse was to see these boys pick up rocks or chunks of concrete, place them in the skirts of their galabeyas, which they would then hold in their teeth, and monkey climb back up the pipe to deposit the rubbish beside the pumping station. Older and bigger men would never have been able to do this kind of acrobatics unless they were super-fit stuntmen but these people were effectively children. I told them to stop and hastened to the Resident Engineers' office to report what was happening before somebody was seriously injured.

The response from the particular Resident Engineer I spoke with was quite astonishing, particularly after the recent tragedies on the site. I was politely told, "Ignore what's happening because these people are so poor that their children have to work to help feed their families. If they are prevented from doing the job because of your perceived dangers they won't be paid and will probably have no food tonight. What would you rather see, kids sent home with nothing or kids getting a chance to eat?"

My reply was to tell him that I would rather see all these young boys go home in one piece than to see some of them dead or seriously injured just because the Resident Engineers on the site were not prepared to do their job properly. Furthermore, though I knew that much of the manual workforce was indeed made up from very poor folk I did not believe that children needed to risk their lives and limbs in that way just to secure a meal that night. Finally, I reminded him that he or any other member of the Resident Engineers group had better not dare to hint at negligence on my part if there was indeed an accident! Not surprisingly, when I returned to the new pumping station, I found that SHIT had happened.

One of the boys had fallen from the vent pipe and had landed on another lad who was bending to pick up trash. Fortunately, although both were hurt, neither sustained a serious injury because the faller had been only a couple of metres from the floor when he dropped. The others were unable to get them out of the well without lifting equipment so they had been provided with a couple of ropes by their employer. These were subsequently augmented with a plastic bucket and a sack to remove the debris from the pumping well but the access and egress were still achieved by monkey climbing on the vent pipe or on a rope. Later my very damning report on the matter was sent to the Italian Project Manager with a copy to the Chief Resident Engineer but neither of them responded. It was gratifying, however, that the next time I saw those young boys entering pumping wells and concrete tanks, I found they were using good ropes, containers for lifting the construction debris etc. and a couple of decent extension ladders so perhaps my words had not fallen on completely deaf ears after all.

*****

Starting flow down a cleaned-out pipeline as Timossi watched.

During the commissioning of completed stages at Gabal el Asfar it was nearly always the case that pipelines, channels, chambers etc. had not been cleaned out before flows were allowed into them. Most of the time it was just a messy nuisance but at others, it caused serious problems and could be hazardous to the health and safety of personnel involved. There had been occasions when pumps and other machinery had been blocked or damaged and I thought it was high time to formally complain about it to the Resident Engineers. It was, after all, their job to ensure the plant was ready for commissioning, not mine, so I wrote a stern memo to them on the subject. Their reaction was slow in coming because the memo sat in the Chief Resident Engineer's in-tray for a week or more before being handed down to one of his staff to deal with. The reply I received pointed out that the Arab Contractors were responsible for cleaning up under the instructions of ANSCO's Italian Management but they also sent a copy of the correspondence to the Senior Italian Manager, who passed it to his deputy, a pleasant fellow named Timossi, who came to my office to discuss the matter personally. He said the Italians always instructed the Arab Contractors' people to clean up so it was to them I should be complaining. I pointed out, however, that the role of the Resident Engineers was to make sure the work was done to specification.

"By getting off their lazy arses and making a proper inspection!" I said. "If the work is incomplete their job should be to INSTRUCT ANSCO to MAKE the Arab Contractors go back and do it properly! Christ, with idle buggers like that in charge it's a small wonder we lost the Empire!" Timossi's reply showed his hurt feelings somewhat.

"Mr David, please not call me idle. I am work hard here!"

"No Timossi," I assured him, "I don't mean you old chap, I mean those Resident Engineer Brits! Anyway, you lot never had an Empire!"

Timossi promised to make sure the Arab Contractors did a proper clean up job the next time and pointed out that the first of the new grit channels would be ready to receive flow on the following day. He would personally inspect everything to make sure it was perfectly clean for Mr David and his very fussy Egyptian Operatives to take over. The sarcasm was not lost on me!

That evening, my friend Marcello and I were having our late meal together. He told me that Timossi had asked him if there was anything bothering me outside of work because he thought I was grumpy and belligerent. Marcello, being the eternal playboy, had told his boss that I was always grumpy and belligerent, that's why I had been sent to Egypt in the first place. I thanked him kindly for the defamation of my character and told him, though not in these precise words, to have an affair with a tarantula, to which he replied that he would love to because he really fancied females with long legs and spiders had plenty of them. Of course, we had a good laugh and polished off another couple of Egyptian 'Stella' beers. Then Marcello told me that Timossi had also muttered something about me being upset about the Empire but didn't understand what it was all about, so I had to explain about the idle Resident Engineers who never did proper inspections etc. plus my remark about losing the British Empire and Italy not having one to lose.

"Well you should understand," said Marcello, "Timossi's English is not always good enough to catch your crude London accent. In fact, the ANSCO people are at a disadvantage all the time here. Everything in this contract has to be done in English because Egyptians don't speak Italian and the Italians don't speak Egyptian Arabic. There's always going to be misunderstandings between different groups of people because nobody's English is perfect. That's why the Resident Engineers hardly speak to anyone." That made sense to me and it helped to explain probably why a lot of things had gone wrong on this project in the past.

The following day everybody had gathered at the new grit removal plant, which comprised a number of huge constant-velocity channels, each with a travelling suction machine for the removal of grit that settled to the bottom. They were of similar design to the grit separating channels at many of the treatment plants I was familiar with in England but many times bigger. This was, after all, the largest sewage treatment works on the planet at that time and Egypt does have an awful lot of sand and grit!

The first channel was as clean and tidy as it could possibly be. Timossi came over to me and sarcastically said, "Well Mr David, is this good enough for the Empire?"

When assured that it was good enough for me and assured by one of the Resident Engineers present that it was good enough for Royalty, he asked for the powered penstock to be opened and let the first flush of Cairo sewage through the new unit. SHIT happened!

The first surge of water brought with it many pieces of wood that had been scaffolding at some time, several pieces of shuttering plywood, empty paint tins, lots of rags, paper and cardboard, several flip-flop sandals, a number of old buckets and a filthy old mattress. Timossi just stood there with his mouth open and I was moved to say to him, "No wonder you Italians never had an Empire! Let's face it, mate you couldn't organise a piss-up in a brewery!"

The Resident Engineer present hooted with laughter and commented that someone hadn't done his job properly. What an opportunity! I turned on him and snarled, "YES, AND THAT WAS YOU! That pipeline should have been checked out from the screen to the penstock by the Resident Engineering section.

That's why I complained to you lot in the first place. You're no more use than a pork pie is to a starving Jew!" With that, I went back to my office to compile my monthly report to Thames Water in UK, while the new grit channel was drained and cleaned out again, this time together with the screen chamber and pipeline that fed to it.

At 12.30 pm, I made my way to the Italian canteen as usual to have lunch. Timossi was sitting opposite me and asked if I was all right.

"Yes, of course, I am Timossi," I said. "These things are all just a part of everyday life. No hard feelings."

We settled down to have lunch in a cordial atmosphere. Then another of the Italian managers, a fellow named Genoletti passed a comment.

"Meester David," he said, "Whata you needa is a holidaya to makea you feela better. I'ma going homa nexta weeka for holidaya."

I asked him where his home was.

"Ina Taranto," came the reply.

"Oh, down at the heel of Italy," I said.

"Yes, that'sa righta. Howa you knowa dat?"

"Well Genoletti," I replied, "in November 1940 we sank half your navy there. I learnt about it in history lessons!"

Whereupon Marcello, seated next to me at the table, yelled in English to Timossi, "SO THAT'S WHY WE NEVER HAD AN EMPIRE. THE BLOODY ENGLISH WRECKED OUR NAVY. THE BASTARDS!"

Some words were undoubtedly lost on a few people but everyone roared with laughter at Marcello's remark. Timossi turned to the Finance and Admin Manager, a man with a surprising likeness to Mussolini, saying, "Hey, Torkio, open that bottle of grappa! Let's all have a drink with Meester David. He's one of us!" It was marvellous. I felt like a king!

It never ceased to amaze me that the Italians never addressed each other by their Christian names nor used the term Mr except when they were talking to me. They all knew my surname but pronounced it Marapoli, which certainly never bothered me, but they always called me Mr David. My assistant and colleague, Dave Banner, was always addressed by his surname only, by everyone except Marcello. I never knew why!

*****

181

Sludge oil well.

Finally, the day arrived when the new Digested Sludge pumping station would be operated in anger. The pumping well was more than half full and the level was still slowly rising as the sludge was being drained down from the operational digesters. It was decided to operate each pump for ten minutes at a time to ensure they were all tested equally whilst pumping this slightly viscous fluid containing around two per cent solids. They were all supposed to have been tested with water beforehand as part of the general testing procedure for the new equipment. The pumping main stretched quite some distance to a large, raised holding tank, from which it would be fed to the dewatering plant containing a large number of filter-belt presses. There it would be mechanically dewatered and converted into a cake for subsequent use as a soil conditioner. Dave, my Assistant Manager, was stationed at the top of the holding tank to see the sludge arrive and ensure there was no rubbish or construction materials flushed out of the pipe. He would let me know when the sludge arrived at the holding tank.

The first pump ran up to speed and recorded the correct amperage, rpm, etc. and the level in the pumping well began to fall. All seemed to be OK. The well level, however, was not dropping very quickly so it was decided to start up a second pump. Again all seemed to be OK and the pumping well level began to fall rather more quickly. I called Dave to find out if the sludge had arrived yet at the holding tank but the moment he answered the phone, SHIT happened, quite literally.

A sudden spout of black liquid erupted from the desert sand about halfway along the delivery pipeline. The spout grew larger and looked for all the world like a freshly drilled oil well. The pumps were quickly stopped and the feed to the pumping well was shut off. Amid howls of laughter, I drove with a couple of the Plant Operatives to the spot, taking care not to get too close lest the old SsangYong should sink into the saturated sand. There was in fact already a substantial hole in the ground and the sludge was rapidly soaking away, no doubt washing a considerable amount of sand into the pipeline. The Italian Project Manager was informed of the pipeline failure but he dismissed the problem as being shoddy workmanship by the construction contractor who had probably not made the pipe-joint properly at that point.

The following day the pipeline was excavated, only to reveal that there was nothing wrong with the pipe-joint because there was no pipe to join at that point.

There were actually two lengths of pipe missing, although nobody could offer any reason why this should be so. It was claimed that the pipeline had been pressure-tested right up to the holding tank and the Italians had allegedly test run all the sludge pumps on water and delivered it to the holding tank. Clearly, both matters were a tissue of lies and one was forced to wonder how many other tests had been falsified on that massive construction site.

Needless to say, the two pipe-ends did not line up properly and required quite a lot of excavation and realignment to get the two missing lengths into place. Subsequently the Resident Engineers were noticeably present when pressure testing was carried out.

*****

I met President Mubarak

Gabal el Asfar Sewage Treatment Works, named after the great Yellow Mountain sand dune to the Northeast of Cairo was something for any country to be proud of. It was fairly conventional in its design, ordinarily built without any fancy new construction systems but, most remarkably, it was the largest sewage treatment works on Earth at the time. Furthermore, it was in Egypt and was built to serve one of the world's greatest ancient cities, namely Cairo. Egypt was known as a Third World Country yet it contained monumental relics of advanced civilisations that were all-powerful when most of humanity was still scratching about with stone implements and clubs. Egyptian sewerage and sewage treatment systems were generally far more advanced than in certain other, so-called First World Countries where I subsequently worked.

As the various sections of Gabal el Asfar began to go into service the Egyptian Government made plans for a Grand Opening Ceremony to be performed by the then President, Hosni Mubarak. The plans included: who would be on site, who the President would meet, how he would be protected, what he would be shown and where the Official Commemoration Plaque would be unveiled. Consultations went on for weeks between various Government Officials and people from the different organisations involved in the plant's construction and commissioning. There would also be people invited from the Country's trading partners and of course the news media.

I was obliged to speak with a number of Government officials about what the President would be shown and was asked by another Mubarak, a distant relative of the President, to suggest something that the news media could show off as well. I suggested that after the unveiling ceremony, Mr Mubarak could be shown a sample bottle containing crude sewage and have it explained that this was what the treatment plant was there for. Meanwhile, the TV cameras and others would be following my chemist who had recently arrived from Thames Water in England to do some basic analysis. He would take a sample of the treated effluent from the adjacent channel so the President and the media could make a comparison of the two bottles, i.e. the dirty water coming in and the clean, treated water going out. This was considered to be a brilliant idea and I was well pleased. I was also told that there must be no ordinary Egyptians present when the President performed the ceremonial opening so I should tell all the operatives and craftsmen to take the day off. I didn't know if they were going to be paid or not! I pointed out, however, that a massive plant of this nature required constant attendance and that operatives were on shift throughout the day. Therefore, the shift operating at the time of the visit would have to be there to ensure the plant continued to work properly while the President, and the news media too, were on site. This was agreed but I was told that I would have to present every shift operative's and every craftsman's name and identity card number to the President's bodyguard commander before the Opening Ceremony. They certainly didn't trust their own people in those days!

There came the day of the Grand Opening of the world's largest sewage treatment works, designed to serve a population of 6.3 million people. From 7.00 am until the President had finally left the site at 12.00 noon, a helicopter gun-ship clattered round and round the treatment works with a squaddie sitting by the open side door of the aircraft behind a fearsome-looking heavy machine gun or cannon, clearly waiting for something or someone to shoot at. A couple of hours later two army lorries appeared on the site with the flag of Egypt flying conspicuously from each one. They were bulled-up and polished smarter than any other army vehicles I had ever seen and were full of equally bulled-up soldiers, every one of whom was fully armed with pistol, rifle and bayonet. In a jeep, leading the group was a young officer who leapt from the vehicle and barked a few orders. The soldiers quickly got into their allotted positions along the approach road to the unveiling site; there were fifty of them and they were all big, powerful-looking, young men. The officer went to each one, in turn, checked his weapons and issued him with a few rounds of ammunition for each piece, which the soldier loaded into his guns while the officer watched him like a hawk. When all were armed, the drivers removed the ammunition boxes and drove the vehicles out of sight while the officer stood all the guards to attention, told them to fix bayonets and ordered them to swear their oath of allegiance to the President. (That bit was explained to me by Marcello, who was also watching the proceedings). They were then stood at ease, though in the blazing Egyptian sun, to await the President's arrival. The young officer then approached us and asked, in impeccable English, "Which one is Mr David please?"

He wanted the list of names and identity card numbers of the shift operatives and craftsmen on site, which I duly gave him, and he asked if they had been told to keep out of site when the President arrived. I confirmed that they had been so told and enquired the reason for it.

"Purely for security, sir," was the reply.

I presumed, quite rightly as it transpired, that everyone apart from the Presidential Guards, was regarded as a potential assassin. The young man then stood chatting pleasantly with me for about ten minutes until the Presidential cavalcade was spotted entering the site. He then became a snarling automaton, barking orders at his troops, who all snapped to attention every bit as smartly as the Buckingham Palace Guards and at the precise moment presented arms to the great man. Everybody else had been requested to stand in their allocated places, mine being right opposite where the Presidential car would stop.

The large cavalcade comprised a Mercedes limousine leading a large American boxed-in pick-up with a 20mm cannon poking through the side window, followed by another Mercedes limousine and another boxed-in pick-up with a 20mm cannon poking through the opposite side's window; bringing up the rear were four troop-carrying lorries full of soldiers, the fourth one towing a small artillery piece as well. The limousines were obviously heavily armoured and from the way they appeared to ride, I would estimate their weight to have been at least three or four tons each. Perhaps they were expecting an attack by the Israelis!

Officials quickly alighted from the lead limousine and from the bulges in their inside pockets it was quite obvious these big men were armed too. One of them walked to the door of the second limousine and opened it. Out stepped an aide followed by the shorter figure of President Mubarak himself. At that moment, I glanced at the first pick-up and noticed the 20mm cannon appeared to be aimed straight at my head. It occurred to me that I had better not even sneeze!

The President looked at me then muttered something to his aide, who bent over and whispered a reply. Now smiling broadly and with his hand outstretched he walked up to me and clasped my hand with a firm, genuine grip of greeting. "Good day Mr...Marp...pole," he said with slight difficulty, "Thank you for coming to my country. You have done a grand job!"

"Thank you Mr President," I replied, "it is a pleasure to meet you!"

He moved on to the next person, muttered to his aide again and once more received a slowly whispered reply.

"Good day Mr...Russo...lillo. Thank you for coming to my country. You have done a grand job!"

"Thank you Meester Preseedent," my Italian colleague replied, "eet ees a pleasure to meet you!"

This parrot-like conversation was repeated with varying degrees of Anglo/Italian accent about ten times and was rather amusing. Doubtless, the President had rehearsed what he would say and clearly the Italian people had taken their cue from me. That probably explained why they wanted me to be the first in the line. It did, nevertheless, show that Hosni Mubarak, at that time a leading player on the world's political stage, had at least the courtesy to find out the name of whomever he was meeting so that he could address them properly. I admired him for that.

When all had been met, the plaque unveiled and the Presidential speech spoken, the demonstration was made to show the difference between the incoming sewage and the outgoing final effluent. There was a great deal of pride and satisfaction shown by the Egyptian news media people, especially toward their counterparts from the countries of Egypt's trading partners. When the show was over there was a great deal of Chianti and grappa consumed in the Italian canteen. I thoroughly enjoyed it.

Newspaper clip of President Hosni Mubarak officially opening the new plant at Gabal el Asfar

Source: Al Akhbar

It was, however, to be my last bit of enjoyment in Egypt because just a few weeks later SHIT happened in a very unpleasant way. It was perpetrated by certain individuals for whom I have subsequently felt nothing but utter contempt.

Without my being informed, another operations manager was sent out to Egypt. This character was one I considered for many years to be of very poor work ethic, a born liar and somebody that was so far up the boss's rectum only the soles of his shoes were visible and they were brown too! The boss, in this case, had at one time been my senior manager and was an individual almost universally disliked for his rudeness and incompetence. It was he, along with a couple of similar people in Thames Water's Senior Management structure that had changed the wastewater organisation to make a number of my colleagues and I redundant. Remarkably we were nearly all taken back on as consultants when things subsequently went downhill and this was the reason for my being asked to work for the International Section. However, the same senior manager had now been transferred to Thames Water International and clearly did not want me in his organisation. The International Secretary, a lady by the name of Etheldreda, came out to Egypt specially to tell me that I was to be given a month's notice forthwith and that furthermore the month's fees would be paid instantly so I was free to go that day. I was absolutely disgusted with the treatment I had received and the fact that no reason was given for the cancellation of my contract. The contract was written in such a way, however, that it was not a requirement to do so.

The Italian Management of ANSCO was, to a man, also disgusted with my treatment and a letter of protest was written to Thames Water International but all to no avail.

I left Egypt a few days later and went for a short trip to Bangkok in search of work. Rather surprisingly I met an ex-colleague from Thames Water International in a bar there. He was aware that I had been pushed out and also knew why but would not disclose the reason for fear of also being pushed out.

After a year or so I heard from my old friend Marcello that the Operations Manager they sent to Egypt to pick up the reins of my job had died. Apparently, he had not turned up for work for several days and could not be contacted by telephone so police were called to his flat. He was found dead in bed, having expired from natural causes. I was unmoved by the news. Similarly, a few years later, I was completely unfazed by the news that Thames Water International had been closed down. By then I was working very happily for a Thai company in Bangkok.

*****

Chapter 12

From Cairo to
Bangkok and Beyond

I return to UK for a spell.

On return from Cairo, I began to search for project work through various agencies. At that time there was a fair amount of activity in the wastewater treatment industry due to changes in the law and new requirements for effluent standards. Work in commissioning of new plant was not difficult to find and for several months I was employed with a sizeable company doing work for the North of Scotland Water Authority in the area of Aberdeen. Two of the sewage works serving the city were being completely refurbished but there were occasions when the standard of construction left something to be desired. Indeed on one occasion, I was obliged to point out to one of the customer's engineers that the new inlet flume was not properly made and therefore was providing erroneous readings for the incoming flow. I had already pointed out the errors to the construction company but they chose to ignore it. Actually, I was told that my job was simply to commission the new works and therefore mind my own business about engineering errors.

Unfortunately, the customer's engineer blurted out what I had subsequently revealed to him and when I returned from a short holiday, I was told I no longer had a job, this despite the fact that just a week or two earlier my contract had been extended for a further six months. I started legal action against the contractor but as it happened there was an alternative offer of work in Thailand for a Thai Company known as Utility Business Alliance. I accepted it and went to work in Bangkok for several years. It was the happiest time of my working career, even though there were occasional SHIT happenings.

****

Snake in screenings bin at Nong Khaem (BMA3)

Next door to the wastewater treatment plant at Nong Khaem was the refuse disposal depot for that area. Huge quantities of refuse were brought in by the collection vehicles and it was sorted in a large building close to the boundary wall of the treatment plant. Metals, wood, plastics etc. were gathered into huge piles and subsequently loaded onto differently articulated-lorries for transportation to the various recycling plants. There was also a great deal of kitchen waste brought in with the trash and this, though also removed elsewhere for ultimate disposal, seemed to litter the whole site for long periods and undoubtedly encouraged rodents of all kinds. In their wake came hordes of dogs, which bred prolifically on the wastewater treatment plant site too, and naturally quite a lot of snakes. It was not uncommon, therefore, to see the occasional snake on our site during normal working hours and even the occasional large monitor lizard ambling along the site roads. Generally speaking, probably because our site was quite tidy and the grass was kept mown short, snakes were rarely encountered close to and never within buildings except for the inlet works, which was partially below ground level. They could occasionally get in via the access doors which were frequently left open by the operatives. Sometimes, they would get washed through the sewers into the inlet pumping well, especially during heavy rainfall, and some could actually climb up the lifting chains on the large submersible pumps and get loose in the building.

One day the works supervisor, told me she had seen a small python draped over the concrete lintel of an access door just as she was about to exit the building, whereupon she panicked and fled back to the inlet chamber where operatives were working on the screens. Apparently, they quickly disposed of the creature and she left the building just a little bit shaken. A few days later, however, this lady was once again confronted by a small snake which was coiled up inside an electrical control box she had opened. This was actually a very young cobra, under certain circumstances just as dangerous as a large, fully grown one but on this occasion, she did not panic. Indeed she killed it by poking it out of the box with a stick and then stamping on it as soon as it hit the ground. Sensibly, she was wearing her newly provided safety footwear at the time but thereafter was petrified lest the mother might be lurking nearby! On another occasion, the same lady asked me to accompany her to the inlet works building because there was a big snake draped along some electrical conduit nearby the pumping well. This certainly was a much larger serpent than any I had seen at Nong Khaem so far, being probably five feet long and as thick as my arm at the middle of its body. How it managed to climb onto the electrical conduit I could hardly imagine, let alone how it managed to simply lie there motionless for several hours with only an occasional flickering of its forked tongue to show that it was actually alive. I recognised it as a reticulated python, from my book entitled 'Snakes and Other Reptiles of Thailand and South-East Asia', and even though it was probably harmless we decided this beast was too big for amateurs to deal with and therefore sent for a professional snake handler to remove it. After it was removed it occurred to me that it would probably end up as somebody's show-off dinner in some expensive Chinese restaurant and I felt some remorse about that.

Thereafter everyone entering the inlet works had an eye out for snakes, especially anyone like me who was not used to seeing the things and had no knowledge of how to deal with them. I always looked around carefully as I entered the building, above the entrance door, around the electrical conduits, on the stairs, around the pipework, on the pump lifting chains and in the pumping well, where on one occasion, following a rainstorm, I saw three snakes, one of which was a sizeable dark brown cobra and the others were small green snakes that I presumed to be some kind of pit vipers. There was a good deal of floating trash in the pumping well that had been flushed through or over the screens by the high flows so the operatives lowered the fine mesh trash basket to collect it, together with the serpents, from the surface of the water. Almost as soon as the basket began to submerge all three snakes swam towards it and were easily captured. It was quickly hauled back up and deposited on the concrete floor surrounding the pumping well and as each snake made its way over the sides of the basket its head was chopped off by an operative wielding a long-handled mattock. The cobra was actually just under a metre long and the other two were less than half that length but certainly were venomous white-lipped vipers. The operatives seemed to be quite unconcerned that venomous serpents came into the building and through the sewers and were always ready to deal with them. They warned me to be very careful to keep away from these creatures and not to touch the severed heads until they had been dead for at least half an hour. I didn't really need any further warnings; I can only be comfortable near snakes when they are separated from me by a thick layer of plate glass making up a display case from which they cannot escape, like you would find in a zoo!

After the first year of operations at Nong Khaem, it was extremely rare to see a snake on the site or in the inlet works, possibly because efforts had been made to control the rodent population at the refuse collection site and at the local street markets so the problem seemed to have disappeared. Nevertheless, one day I went into the inlet works alone and SHIT happened once again!

There had been some adjustments made to the screen rakes because a great deal of the trash had been dropping back into the inlet chamber and causing frequent malfunction of the machinery. The screens were running as I approached them and they appeared to be working correctly, the trash being dropped cleanly into the receiving bins. Looking at the front of the screens I could see no accumulations of trash so presumed everything was now satisfactory. The bins were very large and stood on a raised plinth so were too high even for me at 6ft 3inches tall to look into them without the aid of a stepladder. There was a small one there that was used by the operatives but I was afraid to use it because it looked too flimsy to take my weight of 110kg, so instead I stood tiptoed on the plinth and hauled myself up on the edge of a bin to peer quickly over the side and see what trash had been collected. This brought me face to face with another serpent, a rather fat one of dark colour with strange zigzag markings on it. We faced each other for what must only have been a fraction of a second before my fingers dropped off the side of the bin and I fled the scene! The type of snake remains unknown to me; it appears not to feature in my little reference book so it might even have been harmless but I did not wait around to find out! Having warned the operatives and other staff about the danger I resolved not to go back to the inlet works building unaccompanied and insisted that everyone else should follow the same rule. The bins were removed and emptied later that day but I heard no report of the snake being killed or even seen so presumed it to have hidden in the trash and been dumped at the refuse collection site or to have slipped back into the inlet well to either escape into the sewer or be drawn up one of the pumps and macerated. Maybe it just hid in a dark corner for a while and made its way out through an open door to prey on the hordes of puppy dogs on the site. Nobody knows!

*****

Green snake under the supervisor's car at BMA3

At the Nong Khaem plant, there was a parking shade nearby the office building with sufficient space for a dozen cars so all the supervisory and office staff had a parking space there. It was only 10 metres from the boundary wall between the treatment plant and the refuse collection site.

One day I walked to my car and on reaching the end of the parking shade saw a green ribbon, apparently hanging from the back of the car belonging to one of my supervisors. The ribbon was fluttering in the breeze but in rather an odd way; it was the end apparently fixed to the car that was fluttering while the end on the road surface was not moving. "How odd," I thought, but getting closer to my vehicle, which was adjacent to the one with the ribbon, was able to see that it wasn't a ribbon at all but a long, green snake with its flat-sided body largely reared up and supported by a relatively small part of it on the road. The snake appeared to be looking at its own reflection in the back window of the car and was moving its head from side to side with its mouth open. Not knowing whether or not this serpent was dangerous I approached my vehicle with caution but on seeing me the creature moved very rapidly; it dropped immediately to ground level and disappeared beneath the supervisor's car. As it did not reappear and was not visible from a quick glance under the car, I presumed it to have taken refuge around the driveshaft or the differential. It would be better to warn the vehicle's owner of this lest there should be a nasty SHIT happening later!

The supervisor came quickly with several others to shoo the invading serpent from his car but nobody was able to see it. They all assumed therefore that the farang* must have imagined it and began cracking jokes about my well-known aversion to snakes. Just to make sure the snake had gone, however, I took a bamboo cane from the back of my car and cautiously poked around under the vehicle while they all laughed but they soon stopped laughing and leapt back in horror as the clearly terrified green ribbon shot out from under the front wing of the car and into a small bush growing just behind the stop-wall of the parking shade. Its camouflage colouring was so perfect that it effectively vanished in the bush and took a minute or two to be spotted again as it lay motionless in its safe retreat.

Nobody knew what kind of snake it was and it did not match with any in my little handbook except possibly a Green Tree Racer, which is listed as being harmless but if it was it must have been a very large one because it was well over a metre in length. Alternatively, it could have been a harmless Rat Snake but they are usually more brownish than green. Whatever it was, harmless or not, I never got into my car again at that parking shade without having a good look under it and under the engine bonnet first!

*****

I fell into sludge at a paper mill wastewater treatment plant.

Near the city of Nakhon Sawan two or three hours' drive to the north of Bangkok, there is a very large sugar refinery. The sugar is derived from locally grown sugar cane, which appears to be a very popular crop amongst the farmers of Thailand. After crushing and boiling to remove the sugar the waste material, known as bagasse, can be used for other purposes and at this particular place it was used to make paper pulp.

Large quantities of water are used in the manufacture of paper pulp and at the end of this complicated process, it becomes a highly polluted by-product that requires treatment before it can be disposed of, either to be reused or to be discharged into a watercourse. The company was very far-sighted and had built their own wastewater treatment plant, not only to achieve efficient water pollution control but also to recover organic material in the form of digested sludge for use as soil conditioner/fertiliser on the sugar plantations.

The wastewater treatment plant had been constructed using some second-hand equipment imported from Korea, notably the mesophilic sludge digesters, and the company was having some operational difficulty with certain items of plant. Our company had therefore been appointed to diagnose the problems with the plant and assist in optimising its performance. I was therefore asked to lead a group of four others to the plant and spend several days there trying to sort things out. The four young people were undoubtedly well qualified in their particular fields, electrical engineering, mechanical engineering and environmental engineering but their combined practical experience of wastewater treatment was extremely little so they spent the available time staring into laptop computers to find solutions to problems they did not practically understand very well.

The engineer responsible for importing the sludge digesters informed me that they did not produce very much gas and for much of the time it was difficult to

195

keep their contents at the required temperature of 30°–35°C. Since ambient temperatures are around this level for much of the time in Thailand, I found that rather difficult to comprehend and therefore decided to take a look at the digesters first. They were of all-steel, welded construction, except for the concrete bases, and did not have floating roofs. There was a great deal of surface rust on the structures and they were clearly in need of several good coats of chlorinated rubber paint or something similar. As I began to climb the roof-access ladder of the first one the smell of digester gas became quite strong and got stronger with every step nearer to the top. Once there I was rather afraid to step on the roof because there were several sizeable holes in it, holes that had simply rusted through, probably more from within than from without. There was a great deal of activity inside the digester with gas bubbles breaking the sludge surface all over. Obviously, the digester was producing plenty of gas and it was being vented to atmosphere because the roof was full of holes. A quick inspection of the other digester showed a similar situation so an urgent verbal report was necessary as well as a written report.

On talking to the company's engineer, I discovered that the structures had been erected without protective coating on the inside or the outside so they were obviously falling to pieces. No wonder there was very little gas to burn! My concern was that air would be drawn into the gas through the rust-holes and there would be, and maybe already was, a potential bomb at the top of each one. Did they have smoking/naked flame restrictions around the digesters? No? Well, they'd better get them established forthwith before the plant was launched into orbit! What about the rusting steel plates? Did they intend to close each digester down and de-rust, paint inside and out and repair with new plates where necessary? No? Well, they would soon be in desperate trouble with their sludge treatment! Amazingly the engineer did say that he would get new plates welded over the holes in the roofs as soon as possible but he hadn't thought of the possibility of setting off the potential bomb whilst welding over a leaking gas holder roof! (I immediately began to think of Frank at Brentwood Urban District Council).

"Please tell me when you plan to do it then," I told him, "and I'll make sure my people and I are a long way away from here!"

Two days later, I was inspecting the digested sludge holding tanks adjacent to the dewatering plant. Where these circular concrete tanks were built the ground was very uneven and next to one of them there was actually a substantial depression that had been filled with sludge. I suspect it had been filled regularly and allowed to dry off so that eventually the ground would be nicely evened off.

In order to get from the access stairs of one tank to the stairs on the other, it was necessary to walk in a wide arc or alternatively to walk around the wall of the second tank, effectively on the concrete base. The Thai people inspecting the plant with me decided on the latter route and therefore shuffled around the tank facing its wall and balancing with their hands against the smooth concrete. Being a much larger person I decided it would be safer to shuffle around the tank with my back to the wall and followed the others. That way I could still keep balance but could also see the soggy sludge-filled depression that started only a few inches from the tank's base. Ahead of me was one of the young lady engineers who stepped slightly too far back from the tank wall and started to overbalance. "Careful," I said as she squealed in fear and I gently pushed her back up to the tank wall. That's when SHIT happened and I lost my balance! It only happened to me but it was in full view of at least ten Thai people who were probably itching for the big farang to fall face down in the muck. This I would surely have done but not knowing how deep the sludge was I decided to step off the concrete and drop into it vertically, lest I should be unable to stand up again and be asphyxiated. In fact, the soggy mess came up to my thighs so the decision to step off the concrete was a good one but of course I could now barely move. Fortunately, however, one of the Thais did proffer a shovel which I clasped tightly as he, still chortling away just like the rest of them, tugged me out of the sludge.

Subconsciously I must have been expecting SHIT to happen in some such way because for once I had changed my good trousers for a pair of old jeans and my decent shoes for a very old pair that were ready to be thrown away. The good stuff was still in my car so after having a quick wash of my legs and feet my garb was once more suitable to meet the company's management, with whom I wasted no time in explaining their dire need for some health and safety action on the treatment works.

Eventually, our report was presented to them by our Managing Director but I never found out whether they took any notice of our recommendations and advice. There was no report of a digester going into orbit, however, and so far as I know, the company still produces paper pulp from bagasse derived from the sugar refinery so maybe, just maybe, they did.

Big snake on the screens at BMA4

At the Bangkok Municipal Administration's Number 4 Wastewater Treatment Plant I was employed as a temporary stand-in for the Project Director who had been transferred to a more important bridge construction project. The construction contractor for BMA4 was very much behind schedule and was still completing works during the twelve months operational period which was intended to be for a proving demonstration of the new treatment plant's performance and reliability. When taking over this position I was still recovering from major surgery on my left leg and needed a walking stick to get around; this was a nuisance because the offices we occupied were in a converted house about a hundred and fifty metres from the treatment plant and, furthermore, in order to reduce the ground-space requirement in the middle of the city, the treatment plant had been built as a multi-storey structure with many sets of stairs and high walkways which made it rather difficult for me to get around it quickly.

One morning during a site meeting between the Contractor's Agent, the Resident Engineer and myself, it was agreed that the inlet works, screens and grit extraction systems would be prepared for operational testing that afternoon. Having agreed the testing methodology and the time for inspections the meeting concluded and I hobbled my way back to the office to do other work but no sooner had I sat at my desk than my mobile phone rang. The caller was Paul, a Geordie friend of mine who was the Senior Electrician working for the contractor and was checking out the inlet works electrical equipment prior to the testing. In a highly excited voice, Paul said, "Quick, bring your camera! There's something at the inlet works you just have to see!"

"Can't it wait a few minutes, Paul?" I pleaded. "What's the big rush for anyway?"

"There's a big snake on the coarse screen rake and it might come up when we start the machines!" said Paul.

"Seen them before mate!" was my reply, "I'm a bit busy right now anyway."

"Not like this one, you haven't!" Paul persisted, "This one's bloody enormous and if you don't hurry up, you're going to miss the chance of a lifetime. Come on Dave be quick!"

So I grudgingly took my camera and walking stick and, rather painfully, hobbled back to the inlet works where there was a small crowd gathering. Only one or two other people had cameras with them; taking pictures with mobile phones was almost unknown at that time so my camera would be useful to record this monster invading the new plant. Just as I reached the screen chamber, somebody pressed the starter button and the creature was raised up to the ground level on the rake. Paul was right, this was indeed a bloody enormous serpent!

The snake was a large reticulated python and was indeed a most beautiful creature. Its head seemed to be relatively small, about the size of a big man's hands when bunched up palm to palm. The neck part of its body was the thickness of my forearm and gradually grew larger towards the middle so that its maximum girth was as big as my thigh muscles. The remainder of its long body tapered off to a surprisingly small tail portion, which was about the size of an average cat's tail. The snake climbed around the framework of the screens and then slithered across the top of all three. This gave a good indication of its length because each screen was three metres wide and as it crossed the middle one, I estimated approximately one metre overlapped the structure at each end, so this animal was around five metres in length. I managed to get a good photograph of it as it crossed the middle screen. Clearly, the snake was becoming agitated, probably due to the number of people standing around it and undoubtedly because of the photo flashes and this gave rise to a terrifying but subsequently rather amusing SHIT happening.

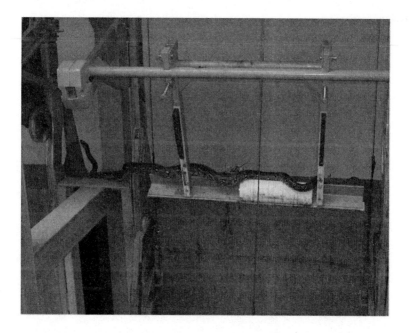

Five-metre long reticulated python crossing the three-metre-wide screen

It first went into one of the empty screenings collection bins then came out again swinging its head from side to side. It went into a second screenings bin but came out again very quickly, once again climbing over the structural framework of the machinery and for a few moments hanging there with just its head moving around, undoubtedly looking for an escape route. At this point, an exceptionally stupid individual decided to demonstrate his perceived Rambo machismo and grabbed the animal's tail, giving it a firm tug whilst looking around for admiration. I took a good photograph of the fool doing this but within a split second got the shock of my life, as did everyone else standing there. Mr Rambo, however, got the biggest shock of all as the bloody enormous serpent struck at the man's face with its mouth wide open and its fangs projecting forward. It also made a loud roar as if expelling a huge breath of air but fortunately for Rambo, its body was restricted by being curled around a part of the steel frame so the strike fell short of its mark by probably half a metre or so. It was nevertheless effective and the animal's tail was no longer held. With most of its body weight now over the open part of the screen chamber, it dropped straight down to splash heavily into the two or three inches of water at the bottom of the deep chamber with the rest of its coils rumbling off the steel rather like the python falling off the tree in the Disney cartoon film of The Jungle Book. The snake disappeared back up the new sewer pipe from whence it had arrived and was never seen again.

An idiot showing off by pulling the python's tail

The foolish Mr Rambo was a Thai person and like many of his fellow countrymen was quite dark-skinned but after the dreadful shock was now far whiter than the Europeans present. He was also reduced to a gibbering wreck for a while and had to be assisted to a chair for his recovery. A while later he was driven home, probably, as many suggested, to change his underwear. Most people had a good laugh about that part but my thoughts were with the unfortunate reticulated python. Was this magnificent creature severely injured when it fell back down the inlet chamber? I hope not but suspect that it was and possibly died in agony just because of a ridiculous show-off.

*****

Overspill from top floor of C.A.S.S. plant at BMA4

The site chosen for the construction of the Bangkok Municipal Administration's Nº 4 Wastewater Treatment Plant was very restricted for space so in order to accommodate a plant of adequate treatment capacity it was designed, like others in the city, as a multi-storey structure. On one side of a canal (or khlong as it would be called locally) is the inlet works with screens, grit separation, trash compaction etc., plus sludge treatment units and on the opposite bank is a large four-floor building containing two huge aeration/settlement tanks on each floor plus various pumps, air blowers, de-watering machinery, electrical control systems and two outfalls into the canal for the treated effluent. The two sides are joined by an access bridge across the khlong.

For various reasons, the construction completion was delayed at BMA4 so when commissioning of the plant was finally underway there were still sections that were not quite ready even for testing, let alone full operation. I was particularly gratified to become the stand-in for the Project Director because the construction company was none other than the mob that fired me in Aberdeen! Consequently, as the flow into the plant increased the final testing of several units became an almost frantic exercise and they were given no quarter by me which, fortunately, gave rise to very few major problems. Nevertheless, there were a couple of occasions when SHIT happened quite dramatically.

The treatment process used at BMA4 is a sequencing batch reactor type known as the Cyclic Activated Sludge System. Each floor has two batch reactor tanks which are sequentially filled, aerated, settled and decanted; every unit in its turn treats a similar portion of the daily incoming wastewater flow. All these batch reactors had been tested for water-tightness and left filled with water until the aeration systems, decanters, recycling pumps etc. had been fully tested, whereupon each floor in its turn was put into operation, starting with the lowest floor.

The lower floors, though open on the side next to the khlong, were shielded from the sun by the floor above but this was not the case on the top floor, which was completely open to the elements. There had been a long delay in testing the machinery on the top floor and in consequence the water held therein had become stagnant and developed a huge growth of algae and what I believe was a type of water hyacinth plant which develops long floating roots that become festooned with a biological slime. Clearly, that would need to be removed before commissioning.

Close to the rear of the building was a very fine house which was obviously quite new. It had an extensive garden that was well kept by the occupiers, sporting many beautiful flowers and flowering trees. It also had a very attractive roof of blue tiles that appeared to be lightly glazed and reflected the sunshine. Although the rear of the house backed up almost to the huge plain wall of the wastewater treatment plant it was not an obtrusive sight. The wall was tastefully painted and had blue lines around it at different floor levels. The trees around its base would have obscured most of it anyway so the house was clearly an attractive place to live.

The day came when the contractor was able and indeed obliged to test the aeration system and other machinery on the top floor. It was decided that the algae and other plant growth could be removed after the testing; it was a thoroughly stupid decision taken by somebody who had clearly not bothered to inspect it. Furthermore, it was decided that the blowers for each batch reactor should all be run-up to full power at the start of testing to ensure the aeration diffusers were all properly clear. Not only were the blowers all run together but, much worse, they were all started at the same time and in consequence the pressure in the air mains feeding the diffusers was temporarily enormous because they were all filled with the stagnant water. These air mains, constructed from glass-reinforced plastic, were around sixty centimetres in diameter and one section simply shattered over a length of several metres.

As you will have guessed, SHIT happened in the most alarming manner as a miniature tsunami formed and surged over the parapet wall, carrying with it probably a ton or two of stinking algae mixed with the slime-laden water hyacinth. The surge only affected the rear side of the tank and although there was a flood of water down the access stairs to the next level the bulk of it dropped onto the roof of the beautiful house next door, smothering the blue tiles with the stinking algae and slimy weed. It also hit a full line of washing hung out to dry and only just missed the lady that hung it there because she had stepped back into the house a few seconds earlier. Some of the lovely flowerbeds were flattened and the whole garden looked an absolute mess. It was such a shame.

Shattered G.R.P. air mains that caused a mini tsunami

The owner of the house, quite justifiably, of course, made an unholy fuss about the incident and complained directly to the Bangkok Municipal Administration. The contractor was obliged to get the whole mess cleaned up without delay and where appropriate get replacements and any repairs done as soon as possible. Furthermore, upon my insistence, the algae and slimy water hyacinth was properly removed from both the batch reactors before further testing of the blowers etc. could be carried out.

Later on when the whole plant was in operation a complaint was received from the house owner that intermittently throughout the day and night there was a very high-pitched whistling noise penetrating the outer wall of the batch reactor plant and causing a nuisance to the occupiers. The sound could be heard every few hours and it would be continuous for an hour or so each time.

With several others, I inspected the blowers and pipework on each floor as its aeration sequence came into operation and it was concluded that the noise, which was not excessively loud but nevertheless so highly pitched that it was extremely penetrating, came from one of the blowers on the third floor. It was shut down and the machine was closely inspected by the suppliers, who were certain that the fault was due to a bearing problem. Having solved the problem they restarted the machine only to find that the noise was just as intense as ever and declared that it must have its source elsewhere. Everybody disagreed with this judgement, however, because the noise most definitely seemed to emanate from within the blower housing. Everybody, that was, except one young lady engineer, Effie, who was my close assistant on this project. Effie had quietly climbed the very narrow access stairway in the pipework gallery to where her more sensitive hearing had placed the source of the sound. She invited me to climb to the same point to listen, a rather hazardous climb indeed for a large person such as myself, with a very long and unforgiving drop that was protected by only a very low handrail! Sure enough, the source of the high-pitched noise nuisance was discovered. It was inside the aluminium-encased fibreglass sound insulation at a joint in the pipeline. Once others had confirmed the source the contractor set about removing the aluminium cladding and fibreglass around the joint flanges, having first donned safety harnesses hooked securely to the handrails. What was revealed was quite remarkable. The noise, which by now was absolutely deafening, emanated from a tiny gap between the pipe flanges which allowed the escape of a trickle of air. This, in turn, caused the five-millimetre thick rubber gasket to vibrate where it overlapped the flange rims. It was possible to stop the deafening, penetrating and almost unbearable noise just by placing a finger gently on the rubber gasket to stop it vibrating. AMAZING!

No amount of bolt tightening stopped the problem at the pipeline joint but the alternative of replacing the flanges with more precise fitting ones would have been extremely difficult so it was decided to simply wrap them tightly with fibreglass tape bonded with epoxy resin. This took little more than an hour to complete and the insulation was subsequently refitted. Not another sound was heard by the occupants of the beautiful house!

A while later there was a further SHIT happening at the BMA4 plant caused by the failure of a pipeline. It took place on the lowest floor of the Sequencing

Batch Reactor plant when one of the reactors was in the decant phase and discharging treated effluent into the khlong. At the time I was standing on the top floor of the building and saw a huge brown stain appearing in the khlong. The khlong usually appeared black from above but this was largely due to the colour of the silt deposit at the bottom rather than to the colour of the water. The brown stain, rapidly getting larger and larger could only be caused by a discharge of activated sludge. I quickly determined that this was indeed the case and that the sludge was discharging from the number 1 batch reactor, though not via its decanter trough. Instead, it was discharging via the G.R.P. outfall pipe from that unit which had sheared close to where the decanter trough discharged into it. The unit had to be shut down and emptied before the broken pipe could be replaced. Clearly, the quality of the G.R.P. pipes on that site was rather suspect!

A huge stain of activated sludge in the khlong

To me, it was particularly disappointing that the khlong received such a polluting load that day because I was hitherto feeling rather pleased at being heavily involved in starting up a new treatment plant that had for many weeks been discharging very high-quality effluent into it. The khlong, like many others in Bangkok, had previously been nothing more than an open sewer, receiving wastewater and a good deal of other rubbish from virtually any imaginable source and it would only have been diluted with rainwater. The thunderous tropical rainfall in that city, however, usually washes even more filth into the khlong system but at least this one was showing very clear signs of improvement once the treatment plant was in operation.

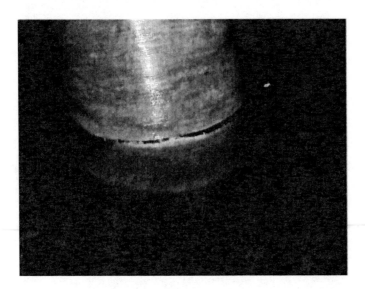

The broken G.R.P. outfall pipe that caused the pollution of the khlong

The biggest disappointment, however, came a while later when my employing company made a bid to take over the operation of BMA4 at the end of its proving period. Had we succeeded I was destined to become the General Manager of this new plant and thereby continue working in Bangkok for a few more years. Unfortunately, we were very narrowly beaten in the bidding by another company and in consequence, I no longer had a job. Sadly, I was unable to find employment with another organisation in Thailand and therefore had to move to Singapore, where I worked for an Australian company for a year or so before subsequently transferring to Townsville in Northern Queensland.

*****

People diving for junk in the khlong* at BMA4

Bangkok is full of khlongs, used both for drainage and transport in this low-lying city which was at one time regarded as The Venice of the East. More

206

recently, the number of them used for transport has been reduced dramatically so now the vast majority are simply drainage channels. The flow through these channels is carefully controlled by the use of strategically placed sluice gates to reduce the risk of flooding in certain districts during the wet season.

Until about the year 2000, virtually all the water from the city, rainwater and wastewater, finished up in the khlong systems and passed through them into the Chao Phraya River. Now, during all but very wet weather, the wastewater is mainly directed to a number of major treatment plants and the commissioning and subsequent operational management of some of these plants was my reason for being permanently employed in Bangkok in the first place. Under storm conditions, however, the sewage/rainwater mixture overflows directly to the khlong systems as before because the sewerage system is generally of the combined type and very few separated systems have been built. In consequence, some of the khlongs remain badly polluted and in some cases are still quite foul. Imagine, then, my surprise at seeing a boat being slowly punted along the khlong separating the two sides of the BMA4 Wastewater Treatment Plant, while young men were diving, yes diving, from it headfirst into the water and obviously swimming down to the bottom for a minute or so at a time. One of these characters came up with an object absolutely coated in sticky black mud and tossed it into the boat. It was difficult to see what the object was but it greatly interested a rather shapely young woman sitting at the back of the boat. To my astonishment, she stood up, peeled her rather shabby clothes off and revealed her very attractive shape indeed encased in a dark brown swimsuit (aptly coloured I thought) of a style that might have been worn by one of my grandmothers. She tucked her long hair into a plastic bag that served as a swimming cap and dived over the side of the boat, obviously to assist the young man to collect further such items from the bed of the khlong. After what seemed an age but was probably not much more than a minute, the pair re-appeared, holding a much larger filthy object between them. Clearly, this one was made of very rusty iron. She climbed nimbly into the boat to drag the object on board and I could see that she too was liberally smeared with the same sticky black mud from the bed of the khlong.

What a most upsetting SHIT happening this was, to see such an attractive young woman willingly getting smothered in filthy black muck that had surely been derived partly from decomposed excrement! I was appalled that anybody would want to do such a thing and muttered something like, "What the hell are those silly buggers doing?"

My Thai colleague, Effie, asked the boat people what they were looking for in the khlong and the reply she received was equally appalling. They were looking for anything they could subsequently sell; scrap metal, old bottles, plastic objects, pieces of wood etc., in other words, anything that had been dumped into the khlong or washed into it from the streets and markets of the city. When asked if they had found anything valuable the answer given was emphatically "No!" but doubtless they lived in hope.

I know that there are many so-called Down and Out people, even in Western countries like Britain and the United States, that willingly scavenge garbage tips, waste bins and the like to get enough for their 'fix' or their 'shot' but I had never before seen young people risking their health and possibly their lives by searching around in the very murky depths of a highly polluted, stinking khlong like that. It made me feel rather privileged to have had a good education and the subsequent opportunities to work my way into a reasonably well-paid job!

Occasionally, over the months, I worked at the BMA4 Treatment Plant, I saw the same boat and the same young men searching for junk in the khlong but the young woman was never again with them. Perhaps she had found an easier and cleaner way to earn a crust. I certainly hope so!

*****

The final stages of my career, Singapore and Australia.

Unfortunately, once we found we had been beaten in the bid to operate BMA4 it meant that I would soon be looking for alternative employment, but where would I find it? I was already into my sixties and therefore unlikely to find an employer in the United Kingdom, certainly not one of the water authorities. Private consultancy work through agencies had been getting difficult to find when I was last working in UK and that was five years earlier so I knew things would be difficult. I still felt I had a few good years of work left in me, however, so started looking around with companies in the Far East. One or two opportunities arose but they were positions far more suited to a civil engineer than a chemist with an operational background so nothing materialised. I began to despair but then a friend of mine told me there were opportunities in Australia, where they were beginning to wake up to the need to extend and modernise their incredibly poor wastewater treatment facilities. Major pollution of The Great Barrier Reef, for instance, was becoming an international issue because of World Heritage and rapid population increases in other areas had overtaken the capacity of the existing systems to cope. My friend put me in touch with an Australian employment agency and within days there were a couple of companies showing interest. One of them subsequently decided to promote one of their existing employees to the post but the other one continued to show a great deal of interest for several months. Unfortunately, it was the only interest they showed and didn't get around to making me an offer of employment until I was very firmly employed by another company at a far better salary than they could offer. I subsequently found that to be a common practice in Australia, i.e. to keep a prospective employee on a piece of string for a long time before making a decision. The Australian employment agency, however, was far more active and through them, I eventually obtained work in Singapore, albeit with an Australian company.

The job was excellent! The Singapore Government had decided to modify a section of one of its large sewage treatment works at Ulu Pandan and convert it into a Membrane Bio-Reactor demonstration unit. It was to be used for a finite period of time to make a full assessment of the M.B.R. treatment system in preparation for possible future conversion of the whole works at Ulu Pandan and maybe other major works as well. I was responsible for commissioning the new unit, optimising its performance and subsequently for producing an Operation and Maintenance Manual for it upon handing it over to the owners, i.e. the Singapore Government. Before final discharge, the first-class treated final effluent from the unit went into a huge Braithwaite storage tank, which was used as a reservoir for industrial high-quality water at a nearby factory.

Interestingly, upon first entering Ulu Pandan Water Reclamation Works as it was formally known, I had a strange feeling that I had been there before. Many aspects of the works seemed familiar, particularly the style of the main office building. Later, I read the inscription on the inauguration plaque for the works and saw the name of the design consultants. It was, to my surprise, the same company that had designed Deephams!

Throughout my stay in Singapore, there was not a single SHIT happening! The job, however, came to a conclusion and I needed to find another. It just so happened that the Company was looking for a commissioning manager with experience of M.B.R. at a works that was being upgraded in Northern Queensland. They invited me to Townsville for a few days to see if I was interested in working there and, more importantly, if I was suitable for the position. It so happened that on both counts the answer was yes and I finished up moving to Australia to work in February 2007.

My time spent at Townsville was both interesting and enjoyable. The people working there were, in the main, sociable and friendly. That part of the coastal region of Australia, roughly half-way along the Great Barrier Reef was extremely attractive and had good fishing, excellent beaches, plenty of good restaurants and many places of interest to visit. The work was satisfying and, although there were some minor problems from time to time, there was never an event that could be described as a SHIT happening. Unfortunately, the job was completed and once more a movement elsewhere was obligatory but the next move took me to an even more enjoyable place than Townsville. It was a move to Cairns, about three hundred kilometres further north.

In Townsville, I had lived in a third-floor flat which, though reasonably comfortable, was not in a particularly attractive area but in Cairns my home was a very attractive bungalow with a swimming pool, and a games room, complete with a half-size snooker table. There was also a magnificent beach no more than ten minutes' walk away. The neighbourhood was peaceful and its occupants friendly and sociable.

Workwise, the situation was not quite so attractive because I was not appointed to the position I had expected, namely the Commissioning Manager. For some inexplicable reason, this position lay within the local council's remit, so although I worked for the main contracting company, I had to answer to an extremely inexperienced character who, although he was a pleasant and polite enough person, was not prepared to take advice until his errors had already become big problems and he would then expect me to sort them out. It was a most unsatisfactory situation to be in but nevertheless, the work was completed and three treatment works were eventually upgraded as designed and the Great Barrier Reef received a bit more protection. The larger, M.B.R. treatment works actually produced probably the best-treated sewage effluent I have ever seen. It was barely distinguishable from drinking water except through fine chemical and bacteriological analysis. I would imagine, however, that the wonderful standard would not be maintained for many years because the area was developing quite rapidly.

When the work finally finished at Cairns, I was offered a job in New South Wales at a town called Tamworth. Again, I was told my position would be Commissioning Manager but it was not to be. They already had a commissioning manager who was working for the Consultant Company. He had never commissioned anything in his life and didn't know where to start! The local Council had nobody with any real idea how to operate the refurbished sewage treatment plant and therefore asked my company to provide an Operations Manager who could subsequently train the local staff to take over when construction was completed. Thanks to a change at Director-level in the company, I finished up with the rudest and most detestable boss available who told me that I could either accept that job or leave. This was a real SHIT happening! I wanted to continue working for a bit longer and was considering perhaps making an application for permanent residence in Australia so reluctantly accepted the post. It was a big mistake on my part! What I finished up with was a bunch of disinterested operatives, none of whom wanted to be trained and only two of whom would take instructions from a Pommy.* Most of them were also the most work-shy skivers I had ever come across! More senior people at the Council appeared to have an aversion to anybody that was English and were in consequence often deliberately obstructive. I put their attitude down to a genuine and justifiable inferiority complex on their part! Nevertheless, the treatment works was completed, training was given, even if it was ignored, and the works optimised. Then just before the Christmas holidays, there was a huge disagreement between the Council and my company that resulted in the contract being cancelled. Within a few weeks, I was informed that I would be made redundant. I was paid up to the end of January 2012, which was the day I returned the company car and telephone. What an ignominious end!

Subsequently, I made an application to remain in Australia whilst looking for another position and was allowed to remain there until June of that year. Unfortunately, there was little work available in my field at that time so, although there were one or two possibilities, nothing materialised and I was obliged to leave Australia and return as a sixty-nine-year-old retiree to UK.

Well, as they say all over the English-speaking world when things go bad, "SHIT HAPPENS!!"

*****

Explanation of Starred Terms

*Street raking: Larking about and getting up to mischief around the streets.

*Mixed liquor: A term used for the mixture of sewage with air-activated bacterial sludge for its treatment.

*Billy Bunter: A comic book character who was 'The Fattest Schoolboy on Earth'

*One black wellington boot and one white: Boots provided by a contractor with a black and white logo.
Every pair was a black right boot and a white left boot.

*Shove ha'penny: A game using a wooden board marked with distance lines from its starting end.
Contestants had to shove a metal disc (originally a half-penny coin) along the board with one strike of the palm of their hand. The winner would have to beat his opponent by shoving the disc exactly to each distance line in turn.

*Sparko: Unconscious.

*Official sample: A 3-litre sample of the suspect liquid collected in a single special container, later to be divided into three equal separate parts in glass bottles which were capped and sealed with a lead seal. One was to be analysed by the River Board, one was to be given to the discharger, or his representative, to be analysed if he wished and the third bottle was kept for future reference in case of any disagreement in the subsequent analyses.

*Local rags: Local district newspapers.

*Lee Catchboard: The radio call-sign for Lee Conservancy Catchment Board

*Vacci tanker: A type of self-loading farm tanker/trailer hauled and powered by a tractor.

*Luton Hoo: A famous estate near Luton, with beautiful grounds through which the River Lee runs.

*Pasveer: The name of the Dutch engineer who invented this particular oxidation ditch system.

*Kessener brushes: Rotating long, horizontal, steel brushes mounted at the surface of the liquid being treated in a tank to force air into the mixed liquor. Invented by a Dutch engineer named Kessener.

*Mannestey: The make of an automatic still for producing distilled water from a tap water supply.

*E.S.N.: Educationally Sub-Normal.

*Pick your own: A strawberry field where buyers of the fruit are able to pick their own before purchase.

*Nominated Doctor: A doctor nominated by the Council to sit in the Public Health Committee meetings to give professional guidance as necessary in matters of public health.

*E.H.R.: Eccentric Helical Rotary. The description of a type of pump comprising a screw shaft inside a rubber stator. The 'Ehrwig' was fitted with such a pump and derived its name from it.

*Mr Plod: The name of the policeman featured in the children's stories of 'Noddy' by Enid Blyton.

*Belisha beacon: A flashing yellow lamp mounted on a black and white pole indicating a pedestrian road crossing in UK. Invented by Leslie Hoare, Belisha.

*Toffee Nosed: A thoroughly stuck-up, haughty and snobbish person.

*Galabeya: The Egyptian name for a long robe worn as everyday clothing by many Islamic men.

*Upper Egypt: Southern Egypt close to Sudan.

*It Ain't Half Hot Mum: A comedy TV series about British Soldiers in Burma during World War 2.

*Farang: The Thai term for a Caucasian foreigner.

*Khlong: The Thai term for a drainage / transportation canal.

*Pommy a derisive term used by Australians when referring to Englishmen.

*****